RACHEL BELL is series producer of the BBC Bristol series *Middle Classes: Their Rise and Sprawl*, and also produced some episodes of the earlier series *Aristocracy* for BBC2. She has a degree in history from the University of Cambridge and studied as a postgraduate at the College of William and Mary in Virginia.

SIMON GUNN is reader in history at Leeds Metropolitan University. He was historical consultant to the BBC series on which this book is based, and is the author of a number of studies of the English middle classes, including the widely praised *The Public Culture of the Victorian Middle Class*.

MIDDLE CLASSES

Their Rise and Sprawl

SIMON GUNN & RACHEL BELL

PHOENIX

A PHOENIX PAPERBACK

First published in Great Britain in 2002
by Cassell & Co.
This paperback edition published in 2003
by Phoenix,
an imprint of Orion Books Ltd,
Orion House, 5 Upper St Martin's Lane,
London WC2H 9EA

A CIP catalogue record for this book
is available from the British Library.

ISBN 0 75381 721 7

Printed and bound in Great Britain by
Clays Ltd, St Ives plc

To my mother, Elizabeth Gunn

S.G.

To my parents, Rose and Colin Bell, who gave me both my class-consciousness and the wherewithal to analyse it

R.B.

CONTENTS

PREFACE

This book began as a scribble on the back of an envelope, the germ of an idea for a television series, on the train on the way to London to see the commissioner for BBC2. The year before, a small team at the BBC in Bristol had made a documentary series for BBC2 called *Aristocracy*, charting the decline of the British upper classes. That series had done well; now a couple of us from the *Aristocracy* team wanted to give the middle classes the same treatment. It seemed a long shot for a commission. While the aristocracy is a sexy subject in television terms, promising impressive houses and people with extraordinary accents, the middle classes – well, they were people just like us, lacking in glamour. But a far-sighted commissioner saw a gap in his schedule and the potential in the series, and the deal was done. It was the only bit that came easily.

What we discovered in researching the subject was that nobody seemed to have written the books we needed to guide us and that experts were few and far between. We knew we wanted to start in the mid- to late nineteenth century with the expansion of the industrial middle classes; we knew we wanted to cover housing, sex and urban life, work and education. We knew we needed to grapple with the mystery of whatever 'middle-class values' really were. But by far the majority of academic writing on the subject looked at the years before 1850 – too early for us. Then there was a vast gap until the sociologists took over in the years after the Second World War. Furthermore, however many history degrees the team had between us, none of us could really correlate what the sociologists described with our own perceptions of the way class had worked in Britain. There was nothing for it. The office was turned into a library, with a couple of people mining for seams of gold, and I embarked on a tour of academia in search of a historian who could help us fill in the gaping chasm of six fifty-minute programmes. I struck lucky early on when I met Simon Gunn, who not only seemed to know what I was talking about, but also promisingly disagreed with quite a lot of it.

Television programmes do not commonly develop theories and arguments of their own. A history series will aim to react to the arguments of others, add some practical research and interviews and illuminate a complicated subject so that it is accessible and interesting for a wide audience. The work that went into the television series *Middle Classes: Their Rise and Sprawl* went further than this because the field was so oddly uncharted. During the course of developing the series, in endless arguments and conversations and mini-seminars with Simon, those of us working on the television programmes were forced to discard many of our own preconceptions about what it had meant to be middle-class in the last hundred and fifty years. Out went the idea that the division between trade and profession was vital, out went the notion that all middle-class people yearned to become gentry, in came an understanding that many of the things that felt God-given – careers, professionalism, planning for the future – were relatively recent historical developments. Above all, in came an understanding that being middle-class was an idea rather than an income bracket and, furthermore, an idea that had changed over time.

The series in its final form was structured thematically as well as chronologically, and this is reflected in the way Simon and I have organised the book. This has allowed us to tackle the development of ideas and themes across the whole period. In television terms it allowed the team to create programmes that would stand alone, that would provide a coherent argument and narrative for the viewer who saw only one of them. In the book each of the central chapters also functions as an individual essay,

although we have cross-referenced subjects wherever appropriate. The book, like the series, is not an attempt at an exhaustive
history of the whole of middle-class experience across the period
from the early nineteenth century to the present day. Rather it
focuses on what we think are the most significant themes and
periods, and is intended for anyone who wishes to understand
something about why England is the way it is, about what has
been meant by the phrase 'middle class' across the period, and
about what it has been like to be part of the English middle class.
Reluctantly we decided that we could only really cover the
history of the English middle classes and that we could not do
justice to the slightly different forms class takes in Scotland, Wales
and Ireland.[1] This is therefore specifically a book about the
history of the English middle classes.

The television series was first shown on BBC2 in February
and March 2001. Simon and I began writing this book shortly
afterwards. While it is based quite closely on the series, it contains
far more material than we were able to use for television and in
many instances the argument has become more detailed and
complex. We have also been able to draw more extensively on
much of the original material on which the series was based and
which forms what we hope is one of the book's original contributions to the historical debate: that is, hours and hours of
interviews with more than sixty people who lived through the
times and experiences which both book and series are about. It is
to those people, who gave up their time and their own personal
histories to us, to whom we owe the greatest debt. For this reason
we would like to thank the following people very much for
taking part: Irene Bacon, Jim Barker, Molly Boomer, Sir Adam
Butler, Lady Mollie Butler, Maggie Carlow, Ellie Carr, Rashmi
Chande, Jonathan Charkham, Charles Courtauld, George Courtauld, Wilf Cross, Bernard Davies, Doris Denton, Kurshid and
Reefat Drabu and their family, James Dundas Hamilton, Mike
Emens, Tim Emens, Jack Fellowes, Rennie Fritchie, Dermot
Gleeson, Charles Gott, Corinne Grundy, Suzy Harvey, Derek and

Audrey Hickson, Peter Jenner, Eileen and Brian Kingsley, Anne Kirby, Marion Kuit, Ken Lane, Sylvia Levinson, Richard Lindley, Rob Loynes, Chris and Peta Mackenzie-Davey, Roz Macleod, Eve Mayatt, Lady Cicely Mayhew and David Mayhew, Christine Mellett, Isabel Moses, Lawrie Norcross, Jane Partington, Chai Patel, Lawrie Penny, Gordon and Michael Ralph, Julie Randall, Michael Randle, Mary and Alan Reed, James Sabben-Clare, Jonathan de Saumarez, Sabby Segall, Horace Shrubb, Mavis Skeet, Paul Stevenson, Carole Stone, Meg Stone, Dr and Mrs Sunak and their family, Dorothy Thomson, Hilary Wainwright, Martin Wainwright, Richard and Joyce Wainwright, Barbara Watts, and Angie Zelter.

A further set of people contributed enormously to the making of both series and book: historians, sociologists and writers, many of whom agreed to be interviewed about their work and found themselves also talking about their own lives and families. We would like to thank the following historians and other experts for their help and participation: Sally Alexander, Yasmin Alibhai-Brown, Joe and Olive Banks, Colin Bell, Rachel Bowlby, Peter Collinson, Rosemary Crompton, Danny Dorling, Janet Douglas, Max Farrar, Kate Flint, David Gilborn, Richard Hoggart, Anthony Howard, Chandrika Kaul, Alison Light, Tariq Modood, Bob Morris, Frank Mort, David Nicholls, Ray Pahl, Harold Perkin, Stephen Pollard, Sally Power, David Rose, Sheila Rowbotham, Iain Russell, Richard Scase, Richard Sennett, Brian Simon, Simon Szreter, Matthew Taylor, Richard Taylor, Rick Trainor, Francis Wheen and Jerry White.

Further thanks are also due to those people who have kindly allowed their personal photographs to be used to illustrate this book: Irene Bacon, Sir Adam Butler, Maggie Carlow, the Courtauld family; Michael Randle, Mary Reed and Mavis Skeet.

Television is a collaborative medium and many people helped to ask the questions and develop the arguments that find a final form in this book. Particular thanks must go to the three other producers on the series – Geoff Dunlop, Clare Hughes and

Louise Wardle. Other people whose contributions were essential include Sebastian Barfield; Peter Brownlee; Lisa Drake; Rachel Eddy, who stayed with the series well after it had turned into a book; Sarah Feltes, who brought a refreshing Canadian Marxist perspective to the whole enterprise; Julia Foot; Geoffrey Palmer; and Peter Simpson. I must add a particular vote of thanks to Sam Organ, whose idea the whole series was, and to Michael Poole, who reigned supreme over the team. Simon and I gratefully acknowledge the support of BBC Bristol and Leeds Metropolitan University in bringing the whole project to fruition.

The complicated process of developing the series into a book was hugely aided by Georgina Capel, who helped to get it off the ground; Annabel Merullo at Cassell & Co., who oversaw the complex process of production; and our editor, Neil Wenborn, who kept on asking the awkward questions that have made this a book in its own right. The book, like the series, has been a collaborative process and while Simon and I have concentrated on individual chapters, we bear responsibility together for any errors, solecisms and omissions this book may contain, for which we apologise in advance.

Rachel Bell

CHAPTER I

INTRODUCTION

Enter the middle classes

The middle classes appear an essential part of the English social landscape, as timeless and apparently unchanging as the countryside itself. The term 'middle class' is part of everyday language, understood by all. It denotes what is seen as a fundamental component of English society and of Englishness. 'England ... is the tone and temper which the ideals and determinations of the middle class have stamped upon [it]', the commentator Charles Masterman declared in 1909. 'It is the middle class which stands for England in most modern analyses.'[1] In the 1940s the novelist and critic George Orwell elaborated this idea. England, he proposed, was the 'most class-ridden country under the sun' and it was moulded in a middle-class image. The nation resembled a 'rather stuffy Victorian family, with not many black sheep in it but with all its cupboards bursting with skeletons. It has rich relatives who have to be kow-towed to and poor relatives who are horribly sat upon, and there is a deep conspiracy of silence about the source of the family income ... It has its private language and its common memories, and at the approach of an enemy it closes ranks. A family with the wrong members in control – that, perhaps, is as near as one can come to describing England in a phrase.'[2]

England is, of course, renowned for its class system, something that foreign visitors have remarked upon down the years. The middle classes themselves are frequently seen as a peculiarly English phenomenon, less given to political extremism than their counterparts in Continental countries, more status-conscious and less enterprising than their equivalents in the United States.[3] Within England key national institutions – parliament, the civil service, the bar, the universities, the public and grammar schools – tend to be viewed as 'middle-class' institutions, even if not all the people within them would define themselves as such. The identity of middle class and nation is also apparent in the oft-cited idea of 'middle England', which, the commentator Martin Jacques has suggested, is a 'metaphor for respectability, the nuclear family, heterosexuality, conservatism, whiteness, middle age and the status quo'. More positively, 'middle England' also represents the time-honoured world evoked by the former Conservative prime minister John Major when he spoke of 'the long shadows falling across the county ground', 'the invincible green suburbs' and 'the old maids bicycling to Holy Communion'.[4] However they are viewed, the middle classes appear part of the fixtures and fittings of English life; it is hard to imagine England without them.

Yet this picture of permanence and solidity is misleading. It has served among other things to idealise a particular section of society, to legitimise its influence in Britain and the world and to justify the imposition of particular values and forms of behaviour on others deemed less rational and 'civilised'. Equally important, it obscures the fact that the middle classes are a recent invention, little more than two centuries old. They have not been part of the English social landscape since time immemorial; they are, in historical terms, relative newcomers. Nor are the middle classes necessarily a permanent fixture, a formation that will endure into the future. It is the argument of this book that the middle classes began to disintegrate as a social and historical entity in the last quarter of the twentieth century and that it now makes little sense to see English society as composed of upper, middle and lower or working classes.[5] These terms have lost their meaning as the social formations to which they referred in the past have dissolved over the last thirty years or so.

This book, then, is about the rise and sprawl of the English middle classes. It is also about their curious dissolution, insofar as the term 'middle class' has become drained of its historical meanings in recent times. The focus is on England, rather than Britain, because the middle classes were largely an English phenomenon – Wales, Scotland and Ireland had their own specific social structures, shaped by religious and educational particularities.[6] As a history, it is not intended to be comprehensive. Even were this possible, it would be thwarted at present by the comparative lack of research on the middle classes in the twentieth century.[7] The book is, rather, an account of significant themes in the social history of the English middle classes in their heyday, the century between the 1870s and the 1970s. These themes include the creation of a distinct middle-class way of life in the later Victorian period; the development of middle-class suburbia between the world wars; the rise of a business plutocracy in the first half of the twentieth century, together with a culture of industrial paternalism and conspicuous consumption; the growth of middle-class radicalism and protest in the 1950s; and the relationship of the middle classes to education in the second half of the twentieth century. In the closing chapters of the book we examine the world of work and money-making, together with the changes that have overtaken the middle classes since the 1970s. The various themes are recounted using, where possible, the voices of people who witnessed the changes, as well as the views of historians and commentators. Through them it is possible to weave together a history of the English middle classes. It is not a smooth, even or continuous narrative; there are inevitably gaps and, because of its size, the subject resists easy generalisation. But it remains an important history. The middle classes have had a disproportionate influence on English society and, indeed, on much of the rest of the world during the last two hundred years. As a result, the story is an eventful, controversial and often surprising one.

Before we immerse ourselves in the substance of this history, we need to attend to two preliminary questions. Firstly, how can we define this formation called the middle classes? Secondly, how, historically, did they come into existence – what, in other words, were the origins of the middle classes?

DEFINING THE MIDDLE CLASSES

Almost everyone who has studied the middle classes has acknowledged the difficulty of defining them. One of the earliest sociological studies of the middle classes, by Roy Lewis and Angus Maude, published after the Second World War, sardonically observed that while 'it might perhaps have been held that the middle classes were composed of all those who used napkin rings', in practice 'nobody has ever found a definition of the middle classes which is short, satisfactory and watertight'. Some sociologists have questioned whether they constituted a class at all, rather than a collection of status groups lacking any common interest or 'consciousness'. Marxists, in particular, have long denied the relevance of the middle class, arguing that society is divided between those who control capital and ownership – the bourgeoisie – and the great majority – the proletariat – who are forced to work for them to earn a wage or salary. Within this dualistic schema there is no room for a social 'middle'.[8] When people are asked about their class background, on the other hand, their answers tend to centre on whether they see themselves as 'middle-class' or not. Yet they often find it hard to give clear-cut reasons for their answer. A characteristic response is that of a civil servant interviewed by Mass Observation – a research group which carried out surveys of national attitudes – in 1949: 'I definitely think of myself as middle-class. It is difficult to say why. I had a typical middle-class education. I have a middle-class job and live in a middle-class district. But none of these things would make me middle-class in themselves … I suppose it is rather a question of being born into a family and social group with particular customs, outlook and way of life.'[9]

Being 'middle-class' is evidently more than just a matter of schooling, job or where you live; it entails a whole cluster of attributes and attitudes, either inherited or acquired.

Consequently, the term 'middle class' carries different meanings according to context and these meanings frequently overlap with one another. In everyday speech 'middle class' is often used as a loose term of social description. The middle classes are associated with money, received pronunciation, detached or semi-detached homes and so on. The term can denote snobbishness and élitism, but equally decency or common sense, depending on who is speaking and in what context. 'Middle class' in the context of everyday language has strong moral connotations; it is rarely used neutrally. Often, it is deployed negatively to mean 'not upper' or – more typically – 'not working class'. Although it derives from a three-class model of English society (upper, middle, working), it also features in the two-class model of 'us' and 'them' which dominated social relations for much of the twentieth century. Here 'middle' and 'working' classes were defined in essentially hostile relationship to each other.[10]

Popular conceptions of class are distinguished from sociological definitions. Indeed, sociologists conventionally draw a sharp division between the two. They claim that popular versions of class are subjective and focus on the outward manifestations of social difference – money, accent, taste, etc. – rather than the underlying relations that produce these differences. Class analysis, in the sociological version, is objective and concerned with fundamental structural divisions, centred, for example, on the means of production or market situation. These are related to a number of economic and social criteria – occupation, income, education and so on – which can be used to build up an objective picture of the class structure of a society at any given time.[11] Within this framework the middle classes can be defined analytically in relation to fundamental divisions of ownership, wealth and power.

Both these conceptions of class have weaknesses. Popular usage is often subjective, inconsistent and more concerned to score a rhetorical or political point than accurately to reflect social differences. Sociological approaches, on the other hand, tend to exaggerate their own objectivity, failing to take into account how the perspective of the observer and the theories themselves shape and distort what they purport to be analysing. In both cases, too, there is a tendency to assume that class is a constant, always and everywhere present. Sociologists are especially prone to confusing class with social structure and to assuming that all societies are by definition organised by class – an ahistorical and Eurocentric idea. It is therefore important to take account of an historical approach to class, sensitive to how concepts such as 'middle class' came to be significant in England. An historical perspective provides us with the means to understand when and how the middle classes came into existence and their changing character over time.

How, then, can we define the middle classes, bearing in mind these various considerations? Historians have indicated that the terms 'middle classes' and 'middle class' first came into usage in England during the second half of the eighteenth century. From the outset, the historian John Seed suggests, the terms raised problems, indicating a 'grouping that fails, or refuses, to fit the dominant social divisions between upper and lower, rich and poor, land and labour'. These problems, he stresses, are not simply matters of terminology and definition; rather, 'they are rooted in the very history we are trying to understand'. Nevertheless, he goes on to provide the following definition of the middle class in the late eighteenth and early nineteenth centuries:

> Its constituent elements were distinguished from the landed aristocracy and gentry by their need to generate an income from some kind of active occupation(s). And they were distinguished from the labouring majority by their possession of property – whether mobile capital, stock in trade or professional credentials – and by their exemption from manual labour. Their economic activity thus involved the posses-

sion and management of material resources and the labour of others.[12]

This definition is concise and helpful. It indicates that from their inception the middle classes faced two ways: on the one hand, towards the landed gentry and aristocracy, the traditional rulers of England, and, on the other, towards the mass of the labouring population, soon to become known as the 'working classes'.[13] The middle classes drew their income from active engagement in manufacturing, commerce and the professions rather than from rents deriving from estates in town and country, as in the case of the landed classes. However, they also differed from the labouring classes by virtue of the ownership of wealth, property or professional qualifications, which themselves represented a form of capital. Crucially, too, they did not engage in manual labour either in the workplace or, ideally, at home. The distinction between 'mental' and 'manual' labour has remained one of the most powerful and enduring sources of class division in England. It was present, for instance, in twentieth-century industry, where clerks were conventionally identified with 'management', foremen with the 'workers'. Finally, the definition reminds us that class is not simply a matter of economic possessions or of social position, but also of power. One of the important attributes of middle-class status was the ability to wield power over others, whether immediately, in the form of employees, servants or tradespeople, or more widely, by influence exerted through institutions such as voluntary associations, political parties and parliament.

John Seed's definition of 'middle class' is intended to be historically specific; it relates to the period of the early industrial revolution. The definition changed over time in step with economic and political developments. What it meant to be 'middle-class' in the 1930s differed in certain respects from the meanings attached to the class a century earlier, even if they shared certain common features such as property-ownership and distance from manual labour. While it designates a particular place in the social order which appears sociologically static and unchanging, 'middle class(es)' is principally an historical term. It has a distinctive history from which its central meanings are drawn. It is also time-bound: the English middle classes have a beginning and – we argue in this book – an end. To start with, then, we need to understand at what point the English middle classes came into existence and how they made their entrance on the historical stage.

THE ORIGINS OF THE MIDDLE CLASSES

In his novel *Making History*, Stephen Fry wryly commented: 'As everyone knows, there is no period in history in which you can't write successfully of the newly emergent, newly confident middle class.'[14] It is certainly true that historians have been eager to see the 'rise' of the middle classes occurring at many points in the last six hundred years. The origins of the middle classes have been traced back, variously, to eighteenth-century urban society, the English revolution of the seventeenth century, the increased trade and social mobility in the Tudor period and the decline of feudalism in the late Middle Ages.[15] No major historical transition, it seems, is complete without them.

The middle classes appear to be everywhere and nowhere in English history. The case of eighteenth-century England is instructive, since it represents the chronological backdrop to what follows in the rest of this book. If we look at descriptions of eighteenth-century urban society there is much that seems familiar in class terms. Here, for instance, is the London maga-zine, the *Connoisseur*, commenting (patronisingly) on provincial fashion in 1756:

> Where the newest fashions are brought down weekly by the stage-coach, all the wives and daughters of the most topping tradesmen vie with each other every Sunday in the elegance

of their apparel. The same genteel ceremonies are practised
there as at the most fashionable churches in town. The ladies
immediately on their entrance breathe a pious ejaculation
through their fansticks and the beaux very gravely address
themselves to the haberdashers' bills glued upon the linings of
their hats.[16]

As this description implies, many of the ingredients of a 'middle
class' were apparent in the towns of eighteenth-century England.
The occupations associated with it were clearly evident – tradesmen, merchants, manufacturers, attorneys and shopkeepers.
Indeed, we know that they existed in ever-growing numbers.
Historians have variously estimated that these groups accounted
for anywhere between one-seventh and one-third of English
society in the eighteenth century and that their importance grew
steadily with the doubling of the overall population from five to
ten million people over the period.[17] No other major country in
the world at the period could rival England for the proportionate
size of these 'middling' groups. Moreover, they enjoyed sufficient
purchasing power to stimulate what has been called the first 'consumer revolution' and to engage in the genteel pleasures of
display and emulation satirised in magazines like the *Connoisseur*,
and in novels such as those of Tobias Smollett.[18] In studying mid-
eighteenth-century England we seem to be looking at a
recognisably middle-class world.

For the most part, however, historians have been reluctant to
consider the emergence of a middle class occurring before the
late eighteenth century at the earliest. They have pointed out that
the term 'middle class' itself only began to come into use in
England in the later 1700s – the first reference in the *Oxford
English Dictionary* is dated 1766. In *Letters to His Son* (1774) Lord
Chesterfield spoke (in characteristically derogatory terms) of
the 'middle class of people in this country' who were 'straining
to imitate their betters'. The well-known commentator Arthur
Young was more positive when he remarked in 1792 that

'knowledge, intelligence, information, learning and wisdom …
are all found to reside most in the middle classes of mankind'.[19]
Such examples were rare before the 1800s, however. It was much
more common in the eighteenth century for people to use the
terms 'middle ranks' or 'middling sort' to describe the groups
concerned. This language was significant. It derived from a model
of society based on a well-established idea of hierarchy. The social
order was envisaged as a finely graded hierarchy of ranks and
interests (landed, trading, legal, etc.), which existed in more or less
harmonious interrelationship. Any idea of conflict was absent
from this view of the social order. When social conflict did occur
in the eighteenth century, the tendency of those concerned was
to view it as reflecting a division between two broad groups:
'patricians', those with power and patronage, and 'plebeians',
those without. Here again there was no room for an intervening
'middle'. Nor in either case did these models correspond to class
in a modern sense: beyond the gentry and aristocracy there was
little sense of a shared outlook across different occupational
groups or of fundamental, persistent antagonism between major
social interests.[20]

So how were the 'middling sort' of the eighteenth century
transformed into the 'middle classes' of the nineteenth? The traditional view was that the middle classes were a product of the
twin processes of industrialisation and urbanisation that rapidly
overtook English society between 1780 and 1850. The industrial
revolution, it was argued, brought into being a new breed of
factory masters and manufacturers who spearheaded the formation of a new class, identified strongly with the rapidly expanding
industrial towns and cities of the Midlands and the North of
England. Birmingham, Liverpool and Manchester all metamor-
phosed from small towns to great cities of a quarter of a million
people and more between the later eighteenth and the mid-
nineteenth century.[21] However, recent research has shown this
interpretation to be at least partly misleading. There was no need
for the industrial revolution to create a new breed or class, since

the people who would make up the middle classes – manufacturers, merchants, professionals and their families – were already
numerous in the 'middling sort' of eighteenth-century England.
The industrial revolution has itself come to be seen as a mis-
nomer. Historians now suggest that industrialisation took place,
not in a sharp burst, but over a long period between the early
1700s and the late nineteenth century. Equally, the process of
rapid urbanisation was not responsible for bringing into being
the social and cultural institutions of the middle classes. The
newspaper press, libraries, assembly rooms, gentlemen's societies
and tradesmen's clubs were all established in the eighteenth
century in towns like Leeds, Birmingham and Newcastle, which
already functioned as provincial centres.[22]

There was an economic dimension to the formation of the
middle class, of course, as John Seed's earlier definition indicated.
Classical economists like David Ricardo divided society into
three groups, landowners, capitalists and labourers, which were
distinguished from each other by their sources of income – rent,
profit and wages respectively. From this it was easy for political
commentators, like Ricardo's friend James Mill, to identify these
economic interests with the three main social classes, upper,
middle and lower.[23] But economic and social definitions of class
had only limited purchase in the early nineteenth century. Of
more immediate significance in the emergence of the middle
classes as a presence and force in English society were developments in the sphere of politics, religion and morality between the
1780s and the 1840s. In particular, the middle classes were forged
out of the series of campaigns against the aristocracy, the Church
of England and the unreformed constitution that marked this
period. The French Revolution of 1789 convulsed politics in
Britain as elsewhere in Europe. It polarised public opinion
between those, like Thomas Paine, who were in favour of the
ideas of the Revolution – the extension of the vote, freedom of
conscience and assembly and so on – and their opponents, such as
Edmund Burke, the defenders of the old order. In debates of the

time the 'middle class' came to designate a middle way of moderate reform between these two extreme positions; it represented a political rather than a social 'middle', according to the historian Dror Wahrman.[24] Merchants and professional men participated in the movement to reform the constitution and extend the vote in the early nineteenth century, alongside working men and women. But the 1832 Reform Act deliberately split this alliance, giving the vote to those with property while continuing to exclude the propertyless masses. 'It is of the utmost importance to associate the middle with the higher orders of society in the love and support of the institutions and government of the country', the Whig prime minister Lord Grey declared.[25] In this sense, the 1832 Reform Act institutionalised the division between middle and working classes in England by marking out the boundary separating them. But it did not halt the continued political attack on the landed aristocracy, so important to the mobilisation of the middle classes in the first half of the nineteenth century. Under the leadership of the Lancashire manufacturers Richard Cobden and John Bright, the Anti-Corn Law League successfully campaigned for the repeal of the Corn Laws between 1838 and 1846. The Corn Laws protected British agriculture by keeping grain prices artificially high; they were therefore seen as privileging the rents of the great landowners at the expense of the profits of manufacturing industry and the needs of the urban population for cheap food. When the repeal of the Corn Laws was achieved in 1846 after eight years of campaigning, it was heralded as a middle-class triumph. Cobden urged the Conservative prime minister, Robert Peel, to recognise the political ascendancy of the middle classes: 'Do you shrink from the post of governing through the *bona fide* representatives of the middle class? ... The Reform Bill decreed it; the passing of the Corn Bill realised it.'[26]

Class was indeed everywhere in political life by the early Victorian period. '[W]hat was whispered in private in the 1780s was shouted on the platform in the 1840s', the historian Asa Briggs observed.[27] The leaders of the Whig party in particular were only too ready to sing the praises of the middle classes. 'I speak now of the middle classes', Lord Brougham declared during the passage of the Reform Bill, 'of those hundreds of thousands of respectable persons – the most numerous and by far the most wealthy order in the community … who are also the genuine depositories of sober, rational, intelligent and honest English feeling.'[28] What fuelled the class-based rhetoric of men like Cobden and Bright was the sense that an increasingly important and prosperous section of society had little or no say in the public life of the nation. Under the unreformed political system the qualification for the vote had varied from borough to borough. In many places, merchants, manufacturers and professional men had remained voteless despite their increasing wealth and prominence. Indeed, manufacturing towns of the scale of Birmingham, Leeds and Manchester had no parliamentary seat at all before 1832. Equally, local government in many towns was in the hands of non-elected bodies before the Municipal Corporations Act of 1835. The appeal to the interests of the middle classes by spokesmen and national politicians therefore played on a widespread sense of exclusion from a corrupt and unrepresentative state.

It was not only in political matters that such people felt themselves to be outsiders. Religious issues exacerbated political grievances and gave a sharp edge to the idea of the middle classes as prosperous, upright and influential yet excluded from the institutions of national life. In England's towns and cities substantial sections of the better-off did not belong to the Church of England – the state church – but were affiliated to one or other of the denominations of Protestant Nonconformity, Baptists, Congregationalists, Methodists, Unitarians and Quakers being some of the most important. In the provincial centres of Birmingham, Manchester and Leeds, Nonconformists outnumbered Anglicans among the wealthiest families.[29] But Nonconformists were legally and institutionally disadvantaged in the early nineteenth century: they were not allowed to enter parliament, to marry in their own chapels or to take a degree at Oxford or Cambridge. To add insult to injury, they were forced by law to contribute to the upkeep of Anglican churches through the payment of church rates. One by one these impediments were removed in the course of the century through measures such as the Test and Corporation Acts (1828), the Marriages Act (1836) and the abolition of compulsory church rates by Gladstone's government in 1868. But on each occasion reform occurred only after sustained public campaigns, involving prominent dissenting ministers, pressure groups such as the Liberation Society, and the Nonconformist press. The entry of the middle classes onto the political stage was accompanied by the repeated demand for 'civil and religious liberty', the Nonconformist rallying cry that echoed through the early and middle decades of the nineteenth century.[30]

What Nonconformity contributed, above all, to the middle classes was a sense of historical mission. 'The real corpus of thought uniting the middle class', wrote the political historian John Vincent, 'was a view or recollection of English history.'[31] Nonconformists saw themselves as the direct descendants of the seventeenth-century Puritans, part of a long tradition of English Protestantism to which they – not the Anglican Church – were the true heirs. Rev. John Angell James of Carr's Lane Chapel in Birmingham was one of hundreds of ministers who preached the message to their prosperous congregations: 'Nonconformists have a history rich in the records of piety, heroism and martyrdom, and which is adorned with the names of men to whom, even by the admission of their opponents, England is much indebted for the most precious of her possessions – her civil and religious liberties.'[32] The Reformation, the English Civil War and the Glorious Revolution, together with Puritan heroes like Bunyan, Milton and Cromwell, all featured largely in this history. Long-term changes such as the rise of the newspaper press, the growth of towns and industry and the spread of education were also duly emphasised. To them were added the litany of triumphs of the first half of the nineteenth century that we have already noted: the Test and Corporation Acts, parliamentary reform, repeal of the Corn Laws and so on. These, of course, were precisely the developments that historians were later to associate with the emergence of the middle classes. Through Nonconformity, in effect, the nineteenth-century middle classes fashioned their own history at the same time as they carved out a distinct political identity.

Not all sections of the propertied urban population were Nonconformist. There were Tory Anglican merchants and professional men as well as Liberal Nonconformists, this division being a frequent source of conflict in local politics.[33] But prosperous Anglicans shared certain values with their Nonconformist peers. The most significant of these derived from a common evangelicalism. The influence of the evangelical revival, spearheaded by John Wesley in the later eighteenth century, was widely felt; it encompassed not only Methodism, but also low church Anglicanism and Nonconformist denominations such as the Baptists and the Congregationalists. Evangelicalism carried with it a number of specific doctrinal beliefs, notably an emphasis on the Atonement and on personal conversion as central to Christian salvation.[34] But it also had a more general mission to reform the morals and manners of the nation. Leading Anglican evangelicals of the time included Hannah More, one of the founders of the Sunday school movement, and William Wilberforce, leader of the campaign to abolish the slave trade. Evangelicals have often been considered 'humanitarian', yet they did not support popular education and temperance simply for altruistic reasons. More and Wilberforce, like many others, were fundamentally conservative; they wished to keep the lower orders in their place and to preserve the social order. As E. P. Thompson wryly put it, in the aftermath of the French Revolution 'most men and women of property felt the necessity for putting the houses of the poor in order'.[35]

Equally important to the evangelical case for moral reform was the attack on the alleged libertinism and improvidence of the aristocracy. A defining moment in this campaign was the Queen Caroline affair of 1820–1. Caroline of Brunswick was the wife of

George IV. The couple had married in 1795, but after having a daughter they separated; it was never other than a marriage of dynastic convenience. There were rumours that Caroline had affairs and an illegitimate child, but in 1820, when George IV succeeded his father George III to the throne, she returned from the Continent to claim her rightful place as Queen. George IV was unpopular and had long been renowned for his philandering. When he attempted to divorce Caroline and instigated legal process against her for alleged adultery there was a national outcry. The trial was reported in lurid detail in the press. Both George and the government of the day were depicted as morally corrupt, while Caroline became the virtuous injured party. When the Queen was acquitted there was national rejoicing. 'All here is ecstasy', the future historian Thomas Babington Macaulay wrote from Cambridge to his evangelical father: '"Thank God the country is saved" is written on every face and echoed by every voice.'[36] Caroline was less successful in her attempt to regain her formal position as Queen and she died not long after. But the episode was widely seen as having morally purged and preserved the monarchy. It was an evangelical triumph. Evangelicals and the wider middle classes had been among the Queen's staunchest supporters throughout the affair and the evangelical ideal of domestic virtue had been successfully asserted at the highest reaches of the state and in the full glare of publicity.[37]

Evangelicalism was one of the powerful currents that fed into the political mainstream in the early nineteenth century and out of which a new middle-class identity was forged. Evangelicalism did not only affect public affairs. The attempt to reform morals and manners went to the heart of private life; it sanctified marriage, family and home. The late eighteenth-century poet William Cowper, a favourite of evangelicals, was well known for his poems celebrating domestic pleasures:

> Now stir the fire, and close the shutters fast,
> Let fall the curtains, wheel the sofa round,

And, while the bubbling and loud-hissing urn
Throws up a steaming column, and the cups,
That cheer but not inebriate, wait on each,
So let us welcome peaceful ev'ning in.[38]

Together with this picture of cosy domesticity, evangelicals urged an idealised vision of the relationship between men and women. They drew on the revival of religious fervour, initiated by John Wesley, as well as changes in household organisation, to put a new emphasis on the importance of distinct roles for men and women. A man's place was to act as breadwinner in the public world of business and affairs; a woman's place was in the home, caring for husband and children, and overseeing the daily work of servants. The growth of suburbs from the early nineteenth century – Edgbaston in Birmingham, for example, Ardwick in Manchester, Clapham in London – reinforced this division of roles. Formerly, the shop or workshop had been attached to the home and whole families, including wives and children, were involved in the business. However, the first wave of suburbanisation, starting in the early nineteenth century, separated home and workplace for the first time, if only by a short distance. In Leeds, merchant and professional families began to move to the newly built Park Square, half a mile or so from the town centre, in the 1780s. From there they moved another half mile out to the slopes of Little Woodhouse, away from the increasing factory smoke, in the early 1800s. It was only from the mid-nineteenth century that the Leeds middle classes removed to more remote suburbs like Headingley, as we shall see in Chapter Two.[39] This gradual shift of location, repeated elsewhere, had significant consequences for family and gender roles. Business became an exclusively male preserve, while women and children were confined to the domestic sphere. In the working classes, of course, both women and children continued to be part of the workforce. Conversely, among the gentry and aristocracy neither women nor men engaged directly in the productive economy, in business or the professions. A particular model of family relations and of gender roles therefore came to distinguish middle-class men and women from those of other classes.[40] In domestic arrangements, as well as in political outlook, the middle classes increasingly appeared set apart from other groups in English society.

THE MAKING OF THE MIDDLE CLASSES?

What does it mean to say that the English middle classes came into existence between the French Revolution of 1789 and the repeal of the Corn Laws in 1846? It denotes, firstly, that the term 'middle class(es)' came into usage in these years, especially from the 1820s, gradually displacing other terms, such as 'middling sort' and 'middle ranks'. Secondly, it indicates that the concept of the middle classes acquired political meaning in this period; it came to represent something recognisably new in public affairs. 'Middle class' implied support for moderate political reform within the existing constitution, rather than wholesale transformation as popular radicals hoped. It was also associated strongly with Nonconformity and the advancement of civil and religious liberty, gained by forcing concessions from church and state. In the Nonconformist version of the past, the middle classes were defined as puritan outsiders to the religious and political establishment; they represented the conscience of the nation and the driving force of 'progress'. Finally, through evangelicalism the middle classes were identified with the moral reformation of public and private life, the promotion of marriage, domesticity and distinctive roles for men and women.[41]

The entry of the middle classes onto the political stage thus involved opposition both to the aristocracy and to the labouring classes. It also implied recognition by these classes. We have seen that this was willingly granted by aristocratic politicians like Lords Brougham and Grey, who were quick to flatter the middle classes as representatives of 'public opinion'. But recognition was also forthcoming, in less sympathetic terms, from working-class leaders of the parliamentary reform and Chartist movements. Thus the radical *Poor Man's Guardian* reflected on the Reform Bill of 1832: 'By that Bill, the government of the country is essentially lodged in the hands of the middle classes; we say the middle classes, for though the aristocracy have their share of authority, it is virtually absorbed in that of the middlemen who form the great majority of the constituency.'[42] The events of 1832 confirmed to working-class radicals that the middle classes were now wholly divorced from 'the people'; they had become an independent political entity and ripe for popular denunciation.

By the 1840s, in effect, the middle classes had come to represent a distinctive political, religious and moral force in England. These dimensions were overlapping and mutually reinforcing; together they defined the middle-class presence in public life. Many of the ideas and values conventionally associated with the English middle classes go back to this period. They include, among others, a tradition of opposition to the landed aristocracy and the state; an emphasis on the overriding importance of individual conscience; and a claim to represent the moral backbone of the nation. These ideas and values were articulated by a range of spokespeople, from Hannah More and William Wilberforce to Richard Cobden and John Bright.

But if the early nineteenth century saw the 'making' of the English middle classes, it did so only in a specific and limited sense.[43] The industrial revolution did not spawn a new social class of manufacturers and entrepreneurs. As we have seen, the groups which were later to make up the middle classes were already present in English society by the mid-1700s – that is to say well before the industrial revolution is supposed to have begun. Furthermore, the middle class in the modern sociological sense of a clearly defined socio-economic grouping did not exist before the second half of the nineteenth century. When people spoke of the 'middle classes' in the 1830s and 1840s they were evoking a political and moral rather than a social entity. There was no clear or widely agreed sense of where the middle classes began and ended or what criteria, precisely, were required for membership.[44] The identification of the middle classes with a specific set of groups defined by occupation, income and status lay in the future. Similarly, the creation of a new and distinct way of living – what one could term a middle-class lifestyle – had scarcely begun before the mid-nineteenth century. It was only during the later Victorian and Edwardian periods that the middle classes were to develop these modern features and to become an established part of the English social landscape. How the middle classes began to carve out a new way of life for themselves and to establish themselves as a social presence is the subject of the next chapter.

CHAPTER 2

VICTORIAN VALUES

*Creating a middle-class culture in
the late nineteenth century*

The census of 1911 represents a watershed in the history of the English middle classes. The census had been a decennial event in Britain since 1801, but it had previously dealt with numbers to be manipulated on a geographical or occupational basis. In 1911, for the first time, the census set out to produce official information about the population on the basis of class. The purpose of this urge to categorise class was a curious one to modern sensibilities – a desire to find out which social class was the more fertile – but its significance lies in the way it chose to define class. It did so using a device straight out of the developing middle-class culture of the previous century, making the *occupation* of the male head of the household the basis of social distinction. Gone was the old aristocratic notion that social position rested upon family connections and land-ownership; in came official recognition of the idea that the type of work a man did defined him and his family.

The scheme was drawn up by the chief census officer, Dr T. C. H. Stevenson, who devised it on the basis of empirical observation rather than social science. He set up a system of five ranked grades and in Class I, at the top of his social scale, he conflated the upper and middle classes, putting large landowners together with professionals, scientists, writers, insurance officials, mine-owners and businessmen. Below them came Class II, the tradesmen – shopkeepers and publicans, actors and boarding house keepers, municipal officers and seed merchants – a lower middle class. In the following three categories came the skilled workers, the semi-skilled and the unskilled. This classification system on the basis of occupation, with the professional and business middle classes firmly at the top, remained largely unchanged until 2001. Even then the rewritten categories bear a strong resemblance to those of 1911, testimony to the way these occupational categories are felt to reflect deep-seated distinctions in English society.[1]

Occupation had become such a vital marker by 1911 because it was the nature of work which had been driving social change for the past century. Between 1881 and 1911 the number of doctors doubled, the number of government clerks trebled and there were five times as many scientists.[2] Most impressive perhaps is the increase in the number of clerical and support jobs – for every new solicitor or barrister there were two new legal clerks.[3] These occupational changes are shown at their starkest set against an increase in the male population of the country of only 50 per cent. By the turn of the century nearly a quarter of the country's working population were engaged in non-manual occupations.[4]

The increase in those doing what could be described as middle-class work was far greater than that which could have been supplied from the children of the existing middling classes; many of the men and women engaged by 1911 in white-collar work had come from working-class families. And it was not only that the numbers of those who might be called middle-class increased, but that the meaning of what it was to be middle-class was also changing. For the individuals involved it was not just a matter of having a new job title: with this change in work came the development of a new culture and a new way of life. As we have seen in Chapter One, the idea of a 'middle class' came into circulation in English society from the late eighteenth century. But it was in the late Victorian period that the middle classes really came into being in a form that we would recognise today. It is the development of a distinctively middle-class culture that this chapter will elucidate.

ENTERPRISE IN THE SUBURBS: A CASE HISTORY

English cities today are still full of streets of houses built in the late nineteenth century and lived in first by those who in 1911 would be described officially as middle-class. Take a street like Ashwood Villas, Headingley, in Leeds. It was built in the 1860s and 1870s by a speculative builder, John Wood, who paid £2,100 for the land in 1864.[5] The street still stands off Headingley Lane, a splendid row of stone-built terraced houses. Despite the traffic noise, local estate agents find the houses easy to sell to professionals with families who want to live within walking distance of the universities or hospital. One of the current inhabitants of the street is Christopher Mackenzie-Davey, a landscape gardener. He describes Ashwood Villas now as 'a lovely community but it is of one class … Terribly nice street parties, everyone does their gardens, recycles their bottles, well-spoken children.'[6] The censuses of 1881 and 1891 give the names and occupations of the people who lived there first – James Wallace, india rubber merchant; James Smallwood, solicitor's clerk; Henry Green, professor of geology – and they also tell us where the inhabitants were born. This was clearly a society physically on the move. In both census years Germans headed several households, testimony to Leeds' position at the centre of an international textile trade. Few of the households were headed by people who had been born in Leeds and over half were headed by people born outside Yorkshire.

One such was Professor William Stroud, who during the 1880s lived at 9, Ashwood Villas with his wife, baby son and servant. Stroud kept a journal recording his days there which gives the flavour of his domestic and working life. He was a physicist, an inventor, and saw himself as something of a wit. One entry records a domestic scene in 1893: 'I was seated in profound meditation in the dining-room at 9, Ashwood Villas while my wife was seated in silence on the other side of the fireplace. Suddenly I brusquely interrupted with the comment "Don't talk." My wife replied "But I wasn't talking." "No," I said, "but you looked as if you were itching to talk which no doubt was the case."[7] He failed to record his wife's retort.

William Stroud's life story provides a classic example of the mobility of the time. He was born in 1850 in Bristol, where his father was a chemist, and almost certainly spent his childhood living above his father's shop in Wine Street in the centre of the city.[8] He went to Bristol Grammar School, from there to Bristol University, and then with a scholarship to Balliol College, Oxford. At Oxford, family legend has it, he felt looked down upon by the Balliol set – the future Lord Curzon (later Viceroy of India) and his friends – for his scholarship, his shabby clothes and his provincial manners. Nonetheless, he got a double first and with a further scholarship went on to complete his studies in Germany.[9] Education at a local grammar school or academy, succeeded by a spell at one of the Continental universities, was not unusual for the sons of merchants and industrialists, as well as for aspiring scientists. Stroud, in effect, was following a well-worn path.[10]

In 1876, at the age of twenty-six, he was offered and accepted the post of Cavendish Professor of Physics at the newly founded Yorkshire College of Science and moved himself and his wife Louisa up to Leeds to begin life there. The role of professor was as much practical as theoretical. As well as lecturing to both day and evening students, Stroud spent every Monday morning making large quantities of oxygen gas, which was stored in a gasometer just below the lecture room and burnt to illuminate the evening lectures. His journal evinces the kind of heavy humour beloved of the late Victorians as well as the labours of teaching physics to the young men of Leeds:

> The evening students of electricity were as keen and eager as a professor could possibly desire – in fact it was as much as one could do to keep one lecture ahead of them by reading the latest electrical publications. The day students were a marked

contrast to the evening ones. They (as I subsequently discovered as the result of the terminal examinations) gazed at the lecturer with apparent rapture when in reality they were immersed in bovine somnolence. These day students were mainly the sons of well-to-do parents who desired merely that their offspring should have a collegiate veneer before entering their respective works to occupy a specially prepared cushy job.[11]

The day students were those whose parents could afford to keep them while they studied; the vast majority of evening students were those who had to support themselves, mainly artisans who, through education, hoped to improve their knowledge and prospects.[12]

Stroud's next-door neighbour in Ashwood Villas was another professor at the Yorkshire College – Archibald Barr, Professor of Engineering, who came originally from Glasgow and had started his working life as an apprentice boilermaker. The two spent a great deal of time together, tinkering with inventions to make their lectures more interesting. In the 1880s they patented a slide-lantern which allowed the lecturer to create his own slides to illuminate his subject. Then Barr saw a newspaper advertisement, placed by the Royal Navy, calling for a new design of range-finder that would be both portable and accurate. It was a project that would change both men's lives and, in a curious way, affect the course of military history.

For some years the two of them worked together to create such a mechanism. They spent hours on the rooftops of Ashwood Villas at night, using the moon as their focus point for infinity, struggling to get the optics both accurate and lightweight. On one occasion, while struggling with the calibration, William Stroud fell off the roof 'plump upon the providentially padded posterior at the end of the spinal column', as he put it in his journal. He spent some months recovering from the accident, but continued to mull over the range-finder problem while he recuperated. By 1892 they had succeeded in developing a reliable instrument, and the Royal Navy placed an order. Now the two professors were in business, setting up and running a small work-shop-cum-factory to manufacture all the range-finder pieces themselves. Orders for Barr & Stroud range-finders poured in from navies overseas as well as at home. By the turn of the century the Barr & Stroud range-finder was a world-leader, rivalled only by those produced by the German firm Zeiss.[13]

In 1906 Stroud left university life and Ashwood Villas to play a full-time role in the business, which was now based in Glasgow, Barr's home town. After the First World War and the naval victory at Jutland, which was partly attributed to their range-finders, both men were offered knighthoods which they declined, a recurring pattern in accounts of successful middle-class lives. The family story is that Stroud's experiences at Oxford had given him no desire ever to join the titled classes. In any case, both men had lost sons in the war and Stroud seems to have felt that in running the business he had been doing no more than his duty. When he died in 1938, some years after Barr, he left behind a firm that at its peak employed nearly six thousand men and women and was thus one of the biggest employers in Glasgow.[14] The story of Barr & Stroud is that of a classic British family firm, based on technical expertise and a skilled workforce, and the remainder of the company's history mirrors that of many others. After the Second World War and the invention of radar the firm struggled to diversify, the descendants of the two families fell out and the business was eventually sold to Pilkington, the Warrington glass firm, and subsequently to a French company. There is nothing now left of Barr & Stroud in Leeds, but the firm's name is still writ large outside its factory in Glasgow, despite the fact that there is no longer any family involvement.[15]

Stroud was representative of the development of the Victorian middle classes in several ways. Both he and Barr moved signifi-cant distances in the quest for work. Their enterprise and initiative created not only a product that was genuinely excellent, but also a business which made them money and employed thousands of workers – a productiveness which was a strong part of the self-image of the Victorian middle class. Furthermore, Stroud's move from academia to trade illustrates the fluidity of the boundary between the professional and business sectors of the middle classes in the nineteenth and early twentieth centuries. In its beginnings the firm of Barr & Stroud demonstrates the links between industry, education and prosperity that have been so formative a force for much of the English middle class. Both Barr and Stroud began their working lives as salaried employees of the Yorkshire College of Science, founded in 1874 and funded by local businessmen specifically to develop science and training for local industry.[16] They personified the Victorian ideal of the self-made man, the combination of mobility, industry and money.

HOME AND AWAY: DOMESTIC AND CIVIC LIFE

In their home lives in Ashwood Villas, too, the two men and their families reflect another corollary of industrialisation – the transformation of a city and of urban life. The map of Leeds in 1830 shows a small town, still huddled around the river Aire, surrounded by empty fields and the villas of a few of the industrial élite. Shops, houses and factories are cheek by jowl. It would have taken only half an hour to walk across it. The map of Leeds in 1900 shows a very different place. The city is now massively extended, the empty fields are filled with houses and the social divisions between areas have become explicit. The back-to-backs of the working classes fill the slopes around the grimy city centre and the river, where the factories were. The middle classes have moved out – part of a great trek outward which was to continue throughout much of the twentieth century. Headingley itself was a village in 1830 – by 1900 the fields had gone and in their place were terraced streets like Ashwood Villas and the detached houses of those who could afford them. The city had become unknowable by any single individual; one could be intimate only with a part of it. Tram and train lines now connected suburbs like Headingley, on hills surrounding the old town, to the centre where much of the work was located. In the Leeds of 1830 work and home life were tied together geographically; by the end of the century those who could afford it had detached themselves and their families from the filth and stench of industry.

In the 1870s the new inhabitants of Ashwood Villas were part of this great social movement, the move towards the suburbs. It was a process that had begun much earlier. In London, for example, it was underway as early as the 1790s, with the building of the estates in Bloomsbury by James Burton, and continued rapidly with suburban extensions into Belgravia, Pimlico, Islington, Camden and Fulham, among others.[17] The new suburban houses, set apart from the working city, offered more space for the accommodation not only of the immediate family but also of servants, visitors and resident relatives. Space and distance from the soot of the factories were not the only attractions. The sanitary enquiries of the 1840s had shown vividly how many diseases were spread by human filth and how widely mortality rates varied between areas in a city. The poor were becoming unacceptable as near neighbours.[18]

Only those with a certain income could afford to live in places like Headingley, where the cost of living would include not only the price of housing, but also the tram fares for commuting into town – the Headingley-Leeds tram service was introduced in 1871.[19] A pair of houses in Ashwood Villas were bought together for £190 in 1867 by the draper William Simpson, one for living in by his family, the other for rental.[20] At this time the vast majority of people rented, and although we do not know what the exact rent was for a house in Ashwood Villas, comparable houses in nearby Hyde Park cost between £20 and £40 a year.[21] Contemporary guides and handbooks warned that 'the rent of a house … should not exceed one-eighth of the income of its occupier'; it therefore seems likely that anyone who could afford

a house in Ashwood Villas would have had an income of at least
£200 a year.[22] In 1882 the average earnings of an entire working-
class family were reckoned at about £78 a year, putting houses
such as those in Ashwood Villas well beyond their means.[23]

Suburbanisation was about more than just living away from
the smoke and disease. More or less unconsciously it was about
creating a different way of life, one which the middle classes were
to make their own, distinct from the old jumbled co-existence. As
the historian F. M. L. Thompson puts it: 'It was only in the setting
of this kind of house, where the family could distance itself from
the outside world in its own private fortress behind its own
garden fence and privet hedge and yet could make a show of
outward appearances that was sure to be noticed by the neighbours, that the suburban lifestyle of individual domesticity and
group-monitored respectability could take hold.'[24] It is unlikely
that the new inhabitants of streets like Ashwood Villas would
have realised they were embarking on a new lifestyle of 'individual domesticity and group-monitored respectability'. What they
could not have failed to notice is how life in the suburban house
had a distinctly different rhythm from the adult lives they had
seen as children. Daily commuting enforced a different pattern
from that which William Stroud's father would have experienced
going back and forth from his chemist's shop to the family's
apartments above. Meal times shifted, with the midday dinner
moving into the evening and a lighter luncheon replacing it in
the middle of the day. The man at work in the city would eat
lunch out; the woman at home would eat it with the children in
the nursery. Neighbours in the new suburbs were often
unknown to each other and an elaborate system of social calls
developed to remedy this. Along with such formalised acquain-
tanceship came an emphasis on afternoon tea as a social occasion,
with finely cut sandwiches and cake.[25] Home life became distinctly separate, ostensibly a place of refuge rather than a place of
work – though of course there was plenty of domestic work in
the home. Shopping became an expedition, the home a place

dominated by women during the day, and work outside the home almost unthinkable for the suburban 'lady'.[26]

Like all social changes, much of this was unforeseen and unplanned. The middle classes had to respond impromptu to their new suburban existence; they had to make it up as they went along. One Leeds family, living what is now about ten minutes' drive from Headingley, has left a detailed record of their evolving lifestyle from inner-city to suburban. Dr John Heaton was the son of a Leeds bookseller. Born in 1817, he grew up above his father's shop in Briggate, in the heart of the old town. His father was evidently a prosperous man and was able to send John first to Leeds Grammar School and then eventually to University College, London, where he qualified as a medical doctor in 1843. In 1850 he married Fanny, the daughter of a Leeds stuff merchant. Their first house was in East Parade in the town centre; by 1856 they and their three children had moved into a substantial Georgian villa at 23, Clarendon Road in Little Woodhouse, for which Dr Heaton paid the princely sum of £2,500.[27] It now feels close to the city centre, but was then in a fashionable suburb. They renamed the house Claremont and set about extensively remodelling it in a contemporary style. This passion for home improvements had already become a feature of the Victorian middle-class man, as one American visitor observed in 1856: 'If he is in the middle condition he spares no expense on his house …Within it is wainscoted, carved, curtained, hung with pictures and filled with good furniture. "'Tis a passion which survives all others to deck and improve".'[28]

One of Dr Heaton's first changes was to enlarge the drawing room and install corbels in the remodelled windows, embossed with the initials of himself, his wife and their children. Then he laid Minton tiles in the front hall and put in facemasks of the four seasons over the newly created arches in the drawing room. The laying of the tiles in the front hall involved considerable labour, which he recorded in his journal:

The passage and staircase at Claremont having become very shabby and dirty, and the oil-cloth … being much worn and requiring renovation, I determined to lay down a tile floor. But before this could be done, it seemed necessary to have a better foundation than that [which] was afforded by the existing floor, the timbers of which being over the wine cellar … are very rotten. I determined therefore to take the floor out, and to place strong stone landings, seven inches thick across the passage, from wall to wall … This required the removal of all the Wine from the cellar, which was nearly full; and this was a troublesome and disagreeable job, which occupied me and Henry, the gardener, for many an evening.[29]

It is hard not to hear in this account of domestic pride and toil a precursor of Pooter, three decades later. George and Weedon Grossmith's fictional creation of the 1890s, immortalised in their perennially popular comic classic *Diary of a Nobody*, belongs to a less prosperous rung of the middle classes than Dr Heaton, but he too lives in a house which would once have had a number but now has a name (in his case 'The Laurels') and spends much of his energy on home decoration. With his troublesome boot-scraper and red enamel bath, Pooter is a wonderful satire on what by the turn of the century had become an eminently recognisable middle-class trait. The religious text which John Heaton installed above the front door – 'Thou Lord Only Makest Me Dwell in Safety' – is a more sophisticated version of Pooter's motto 'Home Sweet Home', and the Heatons' delight when the Town Council purchased a house near them as the Judges' residence ('we are very near neighbours of the Judges and hear their silver trumpets every morning during the Assizes')[30] is recognisable to anyone who remembers the pleasure Pooter took in going to the ball at the Mansion House.

But above and beyond physical changes to the house, all of them emphasising family life, Dr Heaton's journals record the elaborate pattern of their domestic affairs. There were musical soirées, theatrical entertainments and juvenile parties. Dr Heaton was happy to act as a 'sort of manager' on these occasions, even spending the day preparing some chemical experiment of explosion and combustion for the entertainment of the children. His journal records a great deal in the way of family-based entertainment: '1869 January. On Monday the 11th, I accompanied a large party of children – Marian's, ours and others ... to the Pantomime at the Theatre in Hunslet Lane.'[31] Dr Heaton seems to have been the model of the Victorian paterfamilias, involved in the minutiae of his children's lives – trips to the dentist, expeditions to the seaside – as well as in the larger questions of the education of both his sons and his daughters. For him, as for many other Victorian men of his class, marriage, fatherhood and home were a central part of existence. Dr Heaton described his wife Fanny as 'the presiding genius of cheerful regularity' and asked her to 'preach to me whenever you feel prompted to do so, that you may instil some of your goodness into me and make me somewhat like yourself'.[32] But while he may have set her up as a presiding moral force, Heaton saw the marriage between himself and Fanny as one of partnership. Both this and his emotional involvement with his children provide an excellent example of 'the climax of masculine domesticity' which historians of family life have identified in the mid- to late Victorian period.[33] Establishing a home and family and providing for them was nothing new. It had been part of the masculine task for centuries. What was new was the emphasis on domesticity. As the historian John Tosh explains, domesticity 'denotes not just a pattern of residence or a web of obligations, but a profound attachment: a state of mind as well as a physical orientation. Its defining attributes are privacy and comfort, separation from the workplace, and the merging of domestic space and family members into a single commanding concept ... home.' In Tosh's words, 'domesticity became the talisman of bourgeois culture' in Victorian England.[34]

Nonetheless, there was a yawning gap between how Heaton wished his domestic life to be and the way it was lived in practice, not least in the amount of time he actually spent at home. On the day of his daughter Helen's birth in 1851, he wrote in his journal: 'I was considerably disappointed that the baby was not a boy. The same evening I was at a meeting of the Conversation Club at which a new Society, "The Leeds Improvement Society", was constituted; and I was made Honorary Secretary.'[35] Heaton thought of his daily pattern of life as bringing him back to his family for dinner at around six o'clock, followed by an evening spent peacefully at home. In practice such quiet domesticity happened so rarely that it was matter for remark in his journal. He did not reproach himself so much for neglect of family duties as for the loss of leisure, 'desultory idleness' which came his way too rarely for his liking.[36] As he grumbled to his daughter, the now grown-up Helen, in 1873: 'I pursue my usual hackneyed routine; seeing patients; attending meetings; looking after the affairs of all the family ... and providing for their wants and keeping things going as well as I can, and generally doing a great deal for other people and for uncommonly little pay.'[37] With the increased geographical division between home and work, middle-class men spent much of their time out of the house, however important home and family were to them.

Much of what was occupying Dr Heaton's time was civic affairs. In his work he was variously physician to the Public Dispensary, the House of Recovery and the Leeds General Infirmary, as well as a lecturer and treasurer at the Medical School. As a citizen he played a notable role in the public life of Leeds. He was a founder of the Leeds Conversation Club, which often met to discuss the issues of the day in the drawing room at Claremont. He was also a keen campaigner for the creation of the Leeds College of Science. But his most conspicuous campaign was for the building of the Town Hall. On visits abroad, Heaton had been greatly impressed by the civic buildings he saw and he felt that 'if a noble municipal palace that might fairly vie with some of the best Town Halls of the Continent were to be erected in the middle of their hitherto squalid and unbeautiful town, it would become a practical admonition to the populace of the value of beauty and art, and in course of time men would learn to live up to it'.[38] Heaton and others like him looked to history for examples of what they and their city should be like and found role-models in the merchants of Venice who were the patrons of Titian and Tintoretto, the Medicis of Florence and the prosperous burghers of Ghent and Bruges.[39] The main purpose of the Leeds Improvement Society, whose founding meeting Dr Heaton had attended on the day of the birth of his daughter in 1851, was to campaign for such a civic palace in the middle of their own town.

Cautiously, the Town Council approved the scheme and by 1858 Leeds had its own Town Hall, a massive and splendid building which still stands as a monument to the pride and ambition of industrial Leeds. The huge carved panel above the main entrance depicts the town as patron of the arts as well as of science and industry. In Heaton's words, the Town Hall was to be proof that 'in the ardour of mercantile pursuits the inhabitants of Leeds have not omitted to cultivate the perception of the beautiful and a taste for the fine arts'.[40] The centrepiece of Leeds Town Hall is the public chamber – a vast concert hall seating over a thousand, with a huge organ built in London and costing over £6,000 (more than twice as much as Heaton's substantial home). The building was deliberately designed to be bigger than the equivalent one in Bradford and to rival the Guildhall in the City of London. Silhouetted against the skyline (Heaton and others had fought long and hard with the Town Council to ensure the building had a tower), it stood as a symbol of order and government and sent out a clear message to outsiders arriving by train that Leeds was a place of importance. The building was so much admired that it became the model for the town halls of Portsmouth and Bolton.[41] The mottoes on the walls of the public chamber give an idea of the kind of moral code and ambition being developed by its leading citizens. They call upon history and the Bible in order to assert a middle-class morality based on civil and religious liberty and industry in both senses of the term, as production and endeavour: Magna Carta; Trial by Jury; Honesty Is the Best Policy; Industry Triumphs over All. They proclaimed that work was the source of virtue and power, a far cry from the old aristocratic ideal of rule by right of land-ownership.

Next door to Leeds Town Hall is a slightly later display of civic pride and cultural ambition, the Leeds Art Gallery. This opened in 1888 with a public display of nearly six hundred pictures. Many were on loan (the Town Council was reluctant for decades to provide anything approaching a satisfactory purchasing budget) and the pictures represent an intriguing mixture of fine art and what would now be considered poor Victorian taste. Mrs Butler's *Roll Call* had the pride of place; opposite it hung Mr P. H. Calderon's *Aphrodite*. There were Gainsboroughs and Leightons, with an emphasis on narrative and mythical subjects. *The Times*, reporting on the opening, found the lighting as impressive as the artwork: 'The building is illuminated by about 1,000 Edison-Swan incandescent or glow-lamps of 16 candle-power each. In addition the central hall is to be lighted with six incandescent lamps of 500 candle-power.'[42] In the gallery today hangs a painting of Leeds city centre as it was when the gallery first opened: Atkinson Grimshaw's depiction of Boar Lane in 1881. It represents a romantic vision of the city at dusk, lit by electricity – an image of modern urban life as beautiful as any Tintoretto.

The Leeds Art Gallery, the words of Dr Heaton and the Town Hall tell us something important about the developing Victorian urban middle classes. In the words of R. J. Morris, historian of both Leeds and the middle classes: 'There was an enormous ambition to be a little more than people who were just making money … they wanted to be known for being something more than just mucky Leeds.'[43] Cultural aspirations were important to them. Aesthetic achievement, moral improvement and education all went together. One of the things the middle class was learning was how to look at pictures. The modern convention has become for individuals in a gallery to stand in front of a picture and be moved by it, but this was not necessarily an instinctive reaction. Reports on the early years of the Leeds Art Gallery show people gradually working out how to behave. Was a picture gallery like a circus or was it like a concert hall? Should one cheer, applaud or just gaze silently?[44] The uncertainty of how to act in an art gallery is a reminder of the newness of the culture being created by the late nineteenth-century middle classes. While many of the attitudes and details recorded by Dr Heaton in his journals clearly cast back to earlier notions of self-improvement and the importance of family life, much was being invented on the spot, as it was lived.

This is not to say that people felt completely confident in what they were creating: they certainly didn't. The novel was an art form which grew in popularity alongside the expansion of the middle classes; commuting created a whole new time in the day for men to read, while many middle-class women now had quiet leisure time at home which could be filled by novels. While much popular literature was, of course, escapist, novels concerned with family and domesticity often addressed the minutiae of life in such a way as to allow their readers to learn. A still more direct tutor was the self-help or instruction book. Samuel Smiles' bestseller *Self-help* (1859) was effectively a manual of how to achieve social mobility through industriousness, aiming to show young working-class and lower middle-class men how to use education and hard work to get on. For women, now isolated in the new suburbs, *Mrs Beeton's Book of Household Management* (1861) was an invaluable aid in negotiating the management of the household and social intercourse with the neighbours. *Household Management* sold over sixty thousand copies in its first year of publication and by 1868 had sold nearly two million.[45] Its success is testimony to the desire of a prosperous and literate public to be advised by an 'authority' on how to behave and what to do. Books like Mrs Beeton's were to play a powerful role in codifying behaviour and attitudes that were simultaneously being worked out on the ground. They were clearly aimed at the middle classes and Mrs

Beeton had no qualms about using the term: 'A noble dish is a turkey, roast or boiled. A Christmas dinner, with the middle classes of this empire, would scarcely be a Christmas dinner without its turkey; and we can hardly imagine an object of greater envy than is presented by a respectable portly paterfamilias carving, at the season devoted to good cheer and genial charity, his own fat turkey, and carving it well.'[46]

Mrs Beeton is famous now for her recipes, but early editions of the book were taken up with guidance on manners, table layout and how to manage your servants. One of the ironies of suburbanisation was that it often put the woman of the household on the raw interface of class relationships. Safe at home, away from the hurly-burly of the city centre, the woman was supposed to be secluded from confrontation and challenge. Instead, the reverse was often the case. Once the male breadwinner arrived at work he was in a relatively familiar set of power relationships. If he owned his own business he was the employer; if he worked for someone else he had familiar responsibilities upwards to his employer and downwards to those he was in charge of. His wife at home, however, was more likely to be confronted directly by social boundaries and class conflict, in the form of her relationships with and authority over domestic servants. Many of the women *Household Management* addressed would have been the first in their families to keep servants and the book displays the kind of ambivalence that such women seem often to have felt about having servants in the home. Mrs Beeton enumerates at length the qualities an ideal servant should possess – respectful reserve, modest demeanour, polite manner – in such a way that readers would understand how rarely these qualities were to be found. The chapter on servants is full of anecdotes, mostly intended to be funny, about servants pointing out their mistresses' *faux pas* in public, advising them how to play their hand at cards or reading their employers' letters. Victorian literature too is peopled by many such bumptious servants – Sam Weller in *Pickwick Papers*, Phoebe in Mary Braddon's *Lady*

Audley's Secret, Bessie in *Jane Eyre*. The underlying anxiety was about maintaining the boundary between oneself and one's servant, because so much of middle-class identity rested on not being working-class.[47]

Servants were nothing new, of course, but the proliferation of servant-keeping households was. The employment of a servant was often used as a shorthand for marking the division between the middle and working classes, as for example by Benjamin Seebohm Rowntree in his pioneering study of York in 1901.[48] Every house in the census records of Ashwood Villas in 1881 and 1891 recorded at least one live-in servant and the grander household of Dr Heaton at Claremont recorded five live-in servants in the census of 1871. These servants were not kept just from a desire to impress the neighbours; they were essential to maintain domestic comfort and routine at a time when keeping the house warm and clean took an enormous amount of physical labour. This is not to say that middle-class women did not do domestic chores – many of them did – but they generally did so while still managing servants. It was this tricky relationship – how to work alongside your servant without undermining your own authority and position – that books like *Mrs Beeton* partly set out to address. In the book itself Mrs Beeton tactfully deals with the roles of the mistress and the housekeeper in consecutive chapters, but in most middle-class households they were actually the same person. The book also includes specific instructions on how to carry out domestic tasks like polishing the silver, instructions which would be as useful if the reader was doing them herself as they would if she was instructing someone else to do them.

SUPPLY AND DEMAND: THE GROWTH OF CONSUMERISM AND MASS-RETAILING

The décor and arrangement of the late Victorian middle-class home certainly exacerbated the need for domestic help. In the clutter and display of the domestic interior conspicuous consumption was writ large. This display was fuelled by much the same economic causes that drove the expansion of the middle classes. For all the poverty and uncertainty of the time, mid- to late Victorian Britain was immensely prosperous, the most economically advanced and powerful country in the world. Middle-class incomes rose steadily over the period – that is to say, not only could more people lay claim to middle-class status, but once they did so they found themselves becoming steadily better off.[49] J. A. Banks' careful study of Victorian tax returns shows that in the twenty years after 1851, the income from salaries or annuities of most people receiving over £200 in annual income at the beginning of the period had risen by over £100 a year, well above the increase in average retail prices over the same timespan.[50] An examination of Victorian guidebooks of household economy vividly suggests that for the better-off the standard of living increased much faster than the cost of living. An article in the *Contemporary Review* of 1875 shows that some observers at least were aware of this at the time:

Owing to the increasing wealth of the wealthy, and the increasing numbers who every year step into the wealthier class, the style of living as well as the cost of accessories and comforts of which living consists, has advanced in an extraordinary ratio, and however frugal, however unostentatious, however rational we may be, however resolute to live as we think we ought, and not as others do around us, it is as we shall find, simply impossible not to be influenced by their example and to fall into their ways, unless we are content either to live in remote districts, or in an isolated fashion. The result is that we need many things which our fathers did not, and for each of these many things we must pay more. Even where prices are lower, quantities are increased. Locomotion is cheaper but each middle-class family travels far more than it did formerly. Wine and tea cost less but we habitually consume more of each.[51]

The parts of *Mrs Beeton* that are not about how to manage servants are concerned with food and entertaining, with useful tips
such as how to lay out a table for a cold supper for twenty. The
implication is that one did not just live well, one invited the
neighbours in so that they could see how well one was living. In
the circular way economies work, all this consumption created
yet more middle-class prosperity. Pictures of the interiors of the
Heatons' house make this clear. Someone made the carpet and
someone supplied it; a foundry made the stove and an ironmon-
ger sold it; a builder fitted it and an artist painted the pictures on
the walls. The individual artisan or worker who created the
product would not have been seen as middle-class, but the owner
of the business, the accountant, engineer, supplier and clerk
would all have been able to lay claim to middle-class status by the
later nineteenth century.

Above all, there was now a retail industry specifically designed
to sell to the middle classes. The department store was the
middle-class shop *par excellence* and it and the middle classes
developed alongside each other in the Victorian and Edwardian
periods. In the early nineteenth century, shops selling items likely
to appeal to a prosperous clientele had catered only for known
customers; goods were sold on account, not for cash over the
counter. Furthermore, the goods were usually kept hidden away
in drawers so that there was no way for the prospective customer
to find out the price until they had already partially committed
themselves by asking the shopkeeper to show them. The department store, as it developed in the second half of the nineteenth
century, operated in a different way. There were enticing window
displays, with the goods on show to the outside world, clearly
labelled with their price; inside the store many of the goods could
be looked at, touched and fingered, without the customer having
to address a word to a member of staff. The prices were clearly
marked – no embarrassing conversations with the shopkeeper in
order to find out whether one could afford something or not.
And while an individual could still run an account, cash was also

acceptable, so it did not matter if the customer was a stranger to the shopkeeper.

Many of the earliest department stores were in provincial cities, like Fenwicks of Newcastle and Jenners of Edinburgh. One of the first London department stores was started by a Yorkshire-man, William Whiteley, who began his career as a draper's apprentice in Wakefield. The story goes that as a young man he attended the Great Exhibition of 1851 and was so inspired by the amazing variety of things on show that he resolved to set up a shop with the same sense of flamboyant display; the difference being that everything would be for sale. By 1863 he had amassed enough capital, saved out of his wages, to open a small shop with two female assistants in London's Westbourne Grove. At the time his choice of site was ridiculed, but Whiteley was gambling on the effect on the area of the newly opened Metropolitan Line station at Queensway, and he was right. He started with the business he knew – fancy drapery – but by 1876 he had taken over fourteen shops on adjacent sites and was employing two thousand sales assistants.[52] Whiteleys was now far more than a drapers: it sold stationery, household goods, provisions and ironmongery. Soon he expanded further to include furniture, a house-building and decoration service, hairdressing, banking, florists and a menagerie. Later would come a travel agency, auctioneers and a bank. Whiteley wanted to run a store that could supply anything from 'a pin to an elephant'. He called himself the 'Universal Provider' and the name caught the public imagination.

Whiteleys was by no means the only department store, although it was one of the earliest in London. As the store expanded it attracted imitators and its senior staff were in demand: one went to manage Harrods, another founded Barkers of Kensington and a third managed the middle-class co-operative Army and Navy store. Other older establishments, like Swan and Edgar, gradually turned themselves from specialist shops into department stores. By the end of the century there were department stores in every prosperous town and suburb in the country.[53]

There were two key factors in the success of shops like White-leys. The first is that they provided a safe and pleasant space in public for the middle-class woman, who might otherwise find herself at home for much of the time. Whiteleys was easily acces-sible to the suburban housewife travelling into town by train and Underground. In the store there was almost anything she might need to purchase, without any awkward compulsion to do so, and there were also restaurants and lavatories. By the 1890s, Whiteleys had twice-daily deliveries to most suburban areas around London, so there was no need to carry home any heavy parcels. The second factor in their success is that stores like Whiteleys performed an almost *Mrs Beeton*-like function by providing models of how to dress, decorate and entertain. By the late nine-teenth century fashion was no longer the prerogative of the aristocracy; a middle-class woman could aspire to be dressed *à la mode*, and the department store showed her how – and how much it would cost. But the look of one's house was equally important. As in modern department stores, there were room settings on display and lists of what you might need to furnish a six-roomed house from scratch. It was akin to Whiteley's initial inspiration – an exhibition where one could see idealised bour-geois interiors.

In many ways the development of the department store repre-sented a radical change in retailing, so it is not surprising that such stores also aroused considerable opposition. For decades Whiteley was deeply unpopular with other local traders, who felt he was taking away their custom and undercutting their prices. This culminated in a public march down Westbourne Grove in November 1876, when the marchers carried an effigy of William Whiteley in place of a guy and burned it on a bonfire in nearby Portobello Road.[54] His store was plagued by fires – six of them in less than fifteen years – some of which were almost certainly the result of arson. In other ways, department stores generated all the problems of a consumer society. Whiteleys was at the centre of several court cases where husbands refused to pay their wives' bills, as in the Sharpe case in 1880. Mr Sharpe was Keeper of the Records at the Guildhall, earning a modest £300 a year. When his wife bought a sealskin jacket from Whiteleys, costing £12, he refused to pay. Whiteleys took him to court to recover the debt, but the judge found in Mr Sharpe's favour, saying that the jacket 'may be perfectly suitable but it cannot be called necessary and, if the husband is not generous enough nor rich enough to indulge his wife in the luxury, she must go without'. Mr Sharpe was absolved of the debt, and it was Whiteleys that went without.[55]

WHO'S WHO: STATUS, RELIGION AND THE GROWTH OF THE PROFESSIONS

The department store also provided a focus of anxiety about another characteristic concern of the late Victorian middle classes: who was, and who was not, a 'lady' or 'gentleman'. Anybody could go into a department store provided they were respectably dressed, but that was no guarantee that they would behave in a respectable fashion. The much-publicised problem of the 'lady shop-lifter' is one example of this. In one spectacular case in 1885 a woman called Mary Ann Harvey was caught hiding about her person 24½ yards of velvet, forty-two silk handker-chiefs, two pairs of gloves and some ribbons, all unpaid for. On another occasion Whiteley became aware that three girls, the daughters of an eminent barrister, were continually 'taking things away from us without paying for them'.[56] Whiteley summoned their father for a private interview and told him of his daughters' misdeeds. At first the barrister threatened Whiteley with arrest, presumably for slander, but once he had spoken to his daughters he apologised to Whiteley for his anger. The loss of honour was so great, we are told, that the barrister 'sold his house, forsook his splendid position at the bar, and left England soon after'.[57]

This concern about how to tell people apart at a time when increasing numbers could afford to dress well was reflected in many popular publications. One Birmingham journal took delight in a story about a tram passenger 'who had the

appearance of a gentleman, but soon showed himself that con-
temptible creature, a masher': mashers – dandies or ladykillers –
invariably gave themselves away by their ungentlemanly behaviour. Others printed guides to street types, drawing attention to
small differences of dress and attitude as clues to people's real
social identity.[58]

Drawing lines, distinguishing between oneself and those
below and above one, was very important to the late Victorian
middle classes, perhaps precisely because many of them felt so
uncertain about their own status. This class- or more properly
status-consciousness took many forms. Religion and religious
attendance played a key role in defining respectability in all social
classes, but most particularly in the more prosperous sections of
urban society, where regular attendance at church or chapel
remained essential until at least the 1890s.[59] Each religious
denomination had its social tone. Within Nonconformity, for
example, Unitarianism and Congregationalism tended to attract
the wealthy élite of urban society, while Methodism had a more
popular appeal. But in many towns where only a third of the
population or less attended Sunday service, religious attendance
was *de facto* a marker of respectability, if not of middle-class status
itself.[60] The presence of churches and chapels in the urban landscape signalled the continuity of an older social order, while the
massive church-building programmes of both the Church of
England and the various Nonconformist denominations in the
second half of the nineteenth century showed that these institutions had also embraced the challenge of an urban and industrial
society. Part and parcel of the development of Ashwood Villas
was the building of a Congregational church at the bottom of the
road. The Heatons too were regular churchgoers, although here
Dr Heaton differed slightly from the rest of his family in that he
was distinctly 'low church' and evangelical, and disapproved
when Fanny and Helen attended Catholic services when away
from home on holiday.[61]

In the suburbs churches and chapels acted as the centre of a whole range of activities, including missionary, philanthropic and community endeavour as well as the purely recreational. For the urban middle classes churchgoing was a social event as well as a religious rite.[62] Furthermore, as we saw in Chapter One, Nonconformity played a central role in the creation of middle-class identity. By the end of the nineteenth century almost half the churchgoing population of the country were Nonconformists and in the industrial and mining counties they were in the majority.[63] During the second half of the century Anglicanism was to regain a hold in the North, but whether Nonconformist or Anglican, religion played a direct and vital role in the lives of many middle-class families and in their sense of who they were. Its social meanings rippled outwards like concentric circles. Regular attendance at church or chapel signalled trustworthiness and belonging to the local community. In a larger context, it denoted a common Protestantism, an essential part of 'Englishness' against the perceived threat of an alien Catholicism. Still more widely, it represented Christendom, defined in opposition to the heathens both at home and abroad, the object of the 'domestic' and 'foreign missions' that Victorian and Edwardian congregations so liberally supported with their funds. Religion and class were enmeshed in a host of overt and subtle ways.

At the same time, a whole new set of institutions was created in the course of the nineteenth century which helped the middle classes define who they were: the professions. Even the idea of professionalism, with its self-governing rules and regulations, its disinterested code of ethics, its elaborate hierarchies based on qualifications and seniority, was largely a nineteenth-century invention, albeit one which took on some of the outward forms of older institutions. At the beginning of the nineteenth century there were three great liberal professions – divinity, physic and law, identified with the persons of the clergyman, the physician and the barrister or judge.[64] Advancement in these occupations came not through success in competitive examinations, as we might now expect, but through family connection, patronage and a liberal education based on the classics rather than on a specific body of expert knowledge.

It was the apothecaries who were the first to challenge the established position of the three old professions by setting up a system of registration and qualification which ensured that those who called themselves apothecaries shared a common body of knowledge and standard of behaviour.[65] The Apothecaries Act of 1815 led to the establishment of the first course of professional education to be prescribed in detail by an examining body in England. The course was noted for its relevance to the trade to be practised. The apothecaries' qualification required knowledge of Latin; certificates of attendance at lectures on anatomy and physiology, medicine and chemistry; six months' hospital attendance; and five years' apprenticeship. The associated examinations were serious attempts to test knowledge, not the answers to a few perfunctory questions at interview, which had been the norm for the old professions before this innovation.[66] As the examiners grew more confident in their system the proportion of candidates whom they failed rose from 5 per cent to 15 per cent or more. By 1834 the apothecaries' system had changed not only the way apothecaries worked but also their social standing. Other trades that had previously lurked unregulated in the shadows of the old professions, like surgeons and attorneys, adopted similar stiff systems of regulation and examination and reluctantly the physicians and barristers followed suit.[67]

Training and examinations were central to this new notion of professionalism and formed a system which could be applied to a whole range of occupations to which the concept of profession was previously alien. The route to turning a mere job into a profession was becoming clear. First one must establish a professional association to focus opinion, along with the codification of a distinct body of knowledge and an insistence upon an appropriate standard of conduct by all practitioners. Then, as soon as possible, the association should gain a royal charter. The final and essential step was to persuade parliament to pass an act conferring monopoly powers on those who had qualified – that is, those who had followed a recognised course of training and passed the relevant examinations.[68]

Turning a trade into a profession had evident economic benefits for its practitioners. Once an individual had gained the necessary qualifications he was spared competition from others without them. Furthermore, the qualifications generally guaranteed a level of competence in those who had passed. This increased the status of practitioners and allowed for a more substantial scale of fees to be introduced. By the end of the nineteenth century a whole range of other occupations had taken on the status and trappings of professions – architects, accountants, civil engineers, veterinary surgeons, surveyors, chemists and patent agents, among others.[69] Significant numbers of people had now entered the professional classes; the 1911 census records over 6,000 accountants and just under 14,000 chemists.[70]

The creation of this modern structure of the professions had a significant impact on the development of middle-class culture. The professionals were now people of considerable prestige, who through their specific access to a body of knowledge wielded power over other people's lives. Professional career structures (which were in turn to be copied by other occupations and sectors, such as the railways and the civil service) created one of the distinct cultural differences between the late Victorian middle classes and those who had come before or who were lower down the social scale. A professional career pattern created a degree of predictability about the progress of an individual's life.[71] A trainee solicitor would complete his law degree and enter a firm as an articled clerk. After a few years he would hope to pass another exam and become a qualified solicitor. With luck and hard work he would in due course become a partner and then eventually a senior partner. All this meant that he would not reach the peak of his earning capacity until he was perhaps in his forties. This was distinctly different from the expectations of even a skilled manual worker. By the time he had completed his apprenticeship and was in his early twenties, a manual worker had reached his maximum wage. This ability of young professionals to project forwards, far into the future, made planning for that future more important to them. As the historian J. A. Banks says, 'Under the Christian religion it was the future after death that was more important, but this is future in life itself and that is relatively new'.[72]

This emphasis upon the future was to form a fundamental part of middle-class culture well into the twentieth century. Deferred gratification, savings and the importance of one's children's education all stem from this notion that life can be planned on the basis of the stages in one's career. Education was central because a man's position as a professional (the professions were closed to women until well into the twentieth century) rested on his ability to pass exams. An article in the *Edinburgh Review* in 1876 emphasised the particular interest which the professional middle class had in the provision of secondary education:'Conscious that its retention of the advantages which it enjoys is still dependent on the mental activity by which they were gained ... the upper middle class seems the least likely of all to neglect its own educational concerns.'[73] 'Mental culture' grew in importance as the middle classes became more dependent on knowledge and expertise as the basis of their livelihood.

Some families also considered their daughters' education to be important. Dr Heaton was the father of six children: the three boys went to Rugby and then to Cambridge, and Heaton not only sent his daughters away to school but also campaigned for women to be able to take degrees.[74] By the 1880s there were significant numbers of girls' public schools, both day and boarding, founded to cater for the daughters of men like Dr Heaton.[75] We consider the particulars of education in more depth in Chapter Six, but the expense of educating a son until he had finished the first part of his professional training – that is until he was well into his twenties – became an increasingly significant factor in middle-class budgets towards the end of the nineteenth century. Winchester College was one of the most expensive public schools, costing £112 a year in 1892 for fees, board and tuition, but in the same year even a good day school like Bradford Grammar cost £10 a year in tuition fees.[76] Additional charges for books, stationery and extra tuition would in some cases almost double such fees. Three years at a university would cost at least £600 in total and by the end of the century it was estimated that the cost of professional training to become a solicitor or barrister was about £300 a year.[77]

Education was also considered important in families who did not aspire to a professional career for their sons. To get work as a clerk in government offices or in commercial houses a boy must be educated to the age of fifteen or sixteen, which would cost at least four guineas a year.[78] This work was considered attractive not so much for the level of remuneration (in the civil service in 1868 many clerks could only hope to be earning £150 after countless annual increases of £5 or £10 a year), but because such jobs conferred respectability.[79] 'The City is crowded with well-educated lads who are doing men's work for boy's wages', wrote one commentator. 'It is quite useless to argue with parents, and urge the propriety of sending boys to learn a trade; the idea of a lad returning from his work in the evening with dirty hands, and clad in fustian or corduroy, is quite shocking to the respectability of Peckham or Camberwell.'[80] Working with your hands, as did servants, labourers or skilled artisans, was the preserve of the working classes. In the later Victorian and Edwardian years 'mental labour' based on prolonged education became established ever more firmly as a foundation of middle-class identity.

RESPECTABILITY, SEX AND SCANDAL

By the turn of the twentieth century the demands of respectability, education and professional ambitions were having a notable effect upon middle-class family size. The idea that a man should not marry until he could keep his wife and family in comfort had become a convention by the 1860s.[81] The added costs of education meant that by the 1890s many middle-class men were not marrying until they were in their thirties. Some firms would not even allow employees to marry until they had reached a certain grade and rate of pay, and long engagements became the norm. Molly Hughes, a middle-class London woman, recalled in her memoirs the lengthy wait before her own marriage: 'The year 1896 was humming with preparations for the Queen's coming Jubilee. Arthur [her fiancé] and I too were humming a little on our own account. The Golden Jubilee [ten years earlier] had been the occasion of our first meeting, and we thought it a good idea to be married in the Diamond one.'[82]

Such prolonged courtships naturally had a limiting effect upon family size. It seems clear, though, that many couples, once they were married, continued deliberately to restrict the number of children they had. The earliest signs of the decrease in family size began in the 1870s among the families of military and naval officers, clergymen, lawyers, doctors, authors, journalists and architects. Not far behind them came civil service officers and clerks, dentists, schoolmasters, teachers, professors, lecturers and accountants.[83] Much academic debate has centred around whether these couples achieved this through 'stopping' having sex or 'spacing' – using birth control to spread out the conception of their children.[84] Certainly there were methods of birth control available, such as douching, diaphragms and rudimentary condoms. But as one historian of fertility, Simon Szreter, points out, 'The kinds of condoms that were available were not what you and I would recognise at all. They were made by the aptly named cement process of manufacture, because latex was not a process that was available until 1928 or so. There are one or two descriptions of them having to be soaked in boiling water to be made pliable before use … There is no evidence that they were available on any great scale.'[85]

Szreter and others argue that much of this restriction in family size was created by the simple policy of abstinence, referred to by the Victorians themselves as 'continence'. Evidence of abstinence is hard to come by, as evidence of people not doing something often is. What is clear is that middle-class family size shrank. By the time of the 1911 census (which, as we have seen, was specifically designed to look at fertility rates against occupation) middle-class couples tended to have only two or three children against a norm in the 1850s of five or six. By the 1930s this limiting of family size was to become part of the culture of the respectable working classes as well. But in the 1890s and 1900s, when the shrinking birth rate became apparent, it led to fears of the middle classes being engulfed by a much more fertile working class and added fuel to the growing turn-of-the-century eugenics movement.

The difficulty of recruiting soldiers for the Boer War in 1899–1902, because of the high rejection rates of young working-class men due to physical defects like flat feet and inadequate physique, caused public alarm. The government appointed a Committee of Inquiry into Physical Deterioration. Among the arguments and explanations the Committee heard were those based on a pessimistic social Darwinism, which proposed that the nation's biological stock was declining. One such eugenicist was a man called Karl Pearson. In his Huxley lecture of 1903 Pearson claimed: 'The mentally better stock in the nation is not reproducing itself at the same rate as it did of old. The less able and the less energetic are more fertile than the better stocks. The only remedy, if one be possible at all, is to alter the relative fertility of the good and the bad stocks in the community ... Intelligence can be trained, but no training or education can create it, you must breed it.'[86] It was a strange argument, not least because so many of those in the middle classes had risen relatively recently from the so-called poorer stock, but it was taken seriously. Pearson and his allies argued that the middle classes should be given handouts to encourage them to breed more profligately and that sterilisation should be considered to prevent those deemed to be of low intelligence breeding at all.[87]

However, most discussion of middle-class sexuality at the time revolved around the different standards of behaviour applied to men and women. Contemporary accounts like Walter's *My Secret Life* and Frank Harris' *My Life and Loves* give vivid if exaggerated pictures of the sexual activities of the middle-class man, exploits often involving prostitutes and servants, but almost always women of a lower social class.[88] It is a pattern which can be found also in the lives of those who did not seek such self-publicity. The department store owner William Whiteley, for instance, was married with four children, but he also kept a mistress, a woman called Louisa Turner, whom he met when she worked in the toy department of his store. Louisa and her sister Emily would spend weekends in Brighton in the company of William Whiteley and his friend George Rayner, a financier in the City. Whiteley rented a house for Louisa in Kilburn and on occasion George and Emily would visit. Both women had children by these relationships – Louisa a boy called Cecil Whiteley, and Emily two boys and a girl, all of whom took the surname Rayner. When Whiteley's wife found out she threatened divorce, but in the end settled for separation and a substantial annual allowance. The biggest argument the estranged Whiteleys had was over who should have control of their children's education.[89]

Whiteley's complicated sexual life was eventually to have dramatic repercussions, but for several decades he was able openly to maintain a mistress and a wife. Middle-class women led much more restricted sexual lives and stories of wives being infected with venereal diseases picked up by their husbands outside the home were rife. The public rhetoric was increasingly of self-control and continence for both sexes. By the turn of the century the evident double standard of sexual morality was becoming a matter of public debate. It was a major issue for the early feminist movement, which argued not that women should have sexual freedom, but that men should exercise sexual restraint. Such restraint was presented as a moral duty: 'Society has condoned incontinence in men, but has visited incontinence in women with severe condemnation ... Not only must impurity and absolute wrong-doing be checked but the lesson of self-control and self-reverence must be taught to all children alike.'[90] Self-control, self-restraint: these were the moral refrains of the late Victorian middle classes, even if they did not apply them to the decoration of their houses or, in all cases, to themselves. It was a morality that sensibly reflected what was needed to maintain social position. Respectability was vital, not superficial. Without respectability you could not get credit, your son might not get the right sort of career opening and your daughter might not be able to marry into a well-to-do family. As R. J. Morris puts it, 'respectability was as real as a bank balance or a credit rating is today'.[91]

Yet respectability was precarious and easily damaged. While Whiteley was able to carry on with his life after the scandal of his near divorce, neither of his two daughters ever married and his wife lived quietly outside London. Disasters like sexual scandals, unemployment, illegitimacy or failed investments only befell a minority of families, but many felt a genuine anxiety that they might be affected. There was much else to fear that could spell disaster for an individual and a family. Mortality rates were still high, even among the middle classes, and untimely death was a real possibility. Dr Heaton's second-eldest daughter, May, died aged twenty-six shortly after childbirth and her husband wrote a harrowing account of her death:

> The last thing she took was some water from Helen's finger. Once – some time before this – she asked where her mother was, and in her ramblings she seemed to be planning an excursion. The hour was very painful. Dr Heaton could not bear to look on and sat huddled up in a chair with his back to her, coming forward only at intervals to feel her pulse. I held her hand to the end, but she did not feel it or anything else. Her breathing was very laboured, then it got slower and slower and about twelve minutes to six she gave what we thought was her

last gasp. I sprung from her side but she gave one more heavy
sigh and then all was over. Her father closed her eyes.[92]

In his journal Dr Heaton recorded his own sufferings after May's
death: 'My heart ached with actual physical, as well as mental,
pain and I felt too truly that happiness would no more be mine,
but that I should go sorrowing all my days.'[93]

May's death was a tragedy, but it did not threaten the position
of her family. The death of the father of a family would have had
much wider ramifications, since most of the financial props of
twentieth-century middle-class life, like life insurance and
pension funds, were in their infancy. As a group the middle
classes were powerful, but it is not surprising that as individuals
they often felt vulnerable and insecure in the Victorian and
Edwardian eras.[94] These fears were a staple of Victorian fiction,
especially the fear of what might happen if you lost your money.
The novelist Anthony Trollope wrote particularly vividly about
people investing their savings in dubious South American railway
schemes, only to find out later that their money existed merely
on paper. Another common plot was what happened to a family
if the father died without providing properly for his widow or
children – George Gissing's *The Odd Women* (1893) tells the story
of three respectable but penniless sisters hurled out into the cut-
throat world of contemporary London, a place where it was not
easy to make a living as a single woman. More sensational fiction
often revolved around the revelation of dark secrets in a person's
past – whose child they were or, worse still, whose child they
had had.

For the most part these stories were confined to fiction, significant to the historian because of the fears they display rather than
the actual experiences they reflect. On occasion, however, real
lives also took a melodramatic turn and were seized on by the
popular press. William Whiteley's own life culminated in just such
an incident and became a long-running story in the newspapers
of the time. Well into his seventies Whiteley had continued to run

the great department store which bore his name. On 24 January 1907 he was at work as usual in his office on the top floor of the building when a young man came to see him using the name of a solicitor known to Whiteley to gain entry. One witness later described the man as 'gentlemanly' and looking like 'a managing clerk or something of that sort'.[95] The man had been in with him for about twenty minutes when Whiteley came out of his office and asked his secretary to call the police. But almost immediately the man followed him out and produced a revolver. He shot Whiteley twice in the head and then turned the gun on himself. When the police arrived they found William Whiteley dead and his assailant seriously injured. The man had a note in his pocket: 'To Whom It May Concern. Mr Whiteley is my father, and has brought upon himself and me a double fatality by reason of his own refusal to a request perfectly reasonable. R.I.P.'[96] Over the following days it emerged that the assailant – now recovering in hospital although he had lost the sight of one eye – was called Horace Rayner. He was the son of Emily Turner, sister to White-ley's mistress Louisa, and his official father was George Rayner, Whiteley's old friend and companion on the trips to Brighton. There was no hard evidence to suggest that he was Whiteley's son rather than George Rayner's, and anyone who might have been able to provide an answer was now dead. The question of Horace Rayner's paternity was never resolved.

The story of the murder filled the newspapers and gripped the public, and there was an astonishing amount of sympathy for Horace Rayner. He was married to a respectable girl and they had two small children and another on the way. For some years he had worked for British businesses in Russia (a job it seemed likely that George Rayner had obtained for him), but on return to England he had been unable to find other work. The papers were full of accounts of how he had made 'desperate but unsuccessful attempts to obtain an appointment', how his wife and children had had to return home to her aunts in the country, how he had been forced to pawn everything he owned and even so had scarcely been able to afford to eat.[97]

It took some months to nurse Rayner back to health. Once he was well enough he was tried for murder at the Old Bailey. The trial lasted only a day and at the end of it the judge put on his black cap and sentenced Horace Rayner to death. There was a public outcry. Something about the case – perhaps Rayner's struggle to remain respectable, or his months spent recovering in hospital so that he might be sentenced to death, or his suffering due to the stigma of illegitimacy – had caught the public imagination. Over a million people signed a petition asking for leniency and as a result, the death sentence was commuted. Instead, Horace Rayner was sentenced to twenty years' hard labour.[98]

William Whiteley's funeral was a lavish affair. Thirty thousand people lined the streets of Bayswater to see the cortège pass, heaped in wreaths which epitomised the elaborate taste of the time – floral harps and Maltese crosses, an anchor from the fish department and a broken column from the store's buyers and managers. He left an estate valued at around £1.5 million and in his will bequeathed one million of it to set up Whiteley Village, a model community eventually built near Weybridge, 'to be used and occupied as homes for aged poor persons'. He also left Louisa Turner and her son an annuity of £150.[99] Whiteley Village is still a charity and provides a home for around four hundred elderly people. His department store has had a more chequered history. It was sold to Selfridges in the 1920s, was closed altogether in the 1970s, and is now a shopping mall and cinema, still going under the name of Whiteleys but with no family connection. The years of Whiteley's life, 1832–1907, had encompassed an extraordinary growth of the British middle classes, precisely the people whom his store served with its twice-daily deliveries to the London suburbs. During this time the notion of 'middle-classness' had developed into a complicated assortment of cultural ideas, social codes and ways of behaving. In the decades after William Whiteley's death the idea of middle-classness was to change further and envelop still wider sections of the population in the new suburbs. It is this subsequent expansion which we will examine in the next chapter.

CHAPTER 3

BUILDING MIDDLE ENGLAND

Suburbia between the wars

On a summer evening in 1935 Irene Bacon and her fiancé rode their tandem bicycle into Hall Green, a newly built suburb of exclusive private housing near Birmingham. They were visiting his parents for the first time and both the place and the occasion were still fresh in Irene's mind sixty-five years later: 'It was absolutely grand to come to Hall Green. We came on this particular night on a tandem, came into the road ... dirty old shorts and hair all blown about. I would have loved a wash and brush up before I came but I didn't get the chance, so I don't know what they thought of me when they saw me. It was lovely, it really was.' The visit was obviously a success. Irene and her fiancé were married and, like many young couples of the period, moved into the house at Hall Green with his parents. She never moved again. Irene Bacon's early memories of Hall Green are vivid partly because the house and the area contrasted so strongly with the back-to-back house in Bearwood, Birmingham, where she was brought up without electricity, bathroom or inside lavatory. Hall Green seemed another world: 'When I saw the house I just looked at it and I thought "oh I love the place". I didn't dream that this would ever belong to me.' The move to the suburbs implied a social as well as a physical transition: 'It was moving out, moving out of the old ways and everything that entailed and moving into new quarters, a new life.'[1] Irene's was a journey from an older city-based environment to a new, middle-class suburban way of life that was repeated by millions of men and women between the two world wars. More than any other development, the ubiquitous spread of suburbia symbolised the growth and transformation of the middle classes in the first half of the twentieth century.

Between the death of Queen Victoria in 1901 and the outbreak of the Second World War in 1939 the social composition and public perception of the middle classes underwent radical change. Whereas in the Victorian period the middle classes were associated with the figures of the industrialist, the banker and the 'lady', by the inter-war years they were more likely to be identified with the office worker and the 'housewife'. The typical middle-class man was no longer seen to be an employer but a salaried employee, the typical middle-class woman no longer defined as the manager of household and servants but as a domestic worker herself. During the first decades of the twentieth century the middle classes became synonymous with the suburbs, a distinct spatial location between countryside and city. In the early 1900s journalists labelled the middle classes the 'suburbans', and the title stuck.[2] Henceforward it was common for the use of the term 'middle classes' to be prefixed by the word 'suburban', the two increasingly being viewed as indivisible.

There was, of course, nothing new about the suburbs. From the late eighteenth century the wealthiest inhabitants of London and the provincial towns found themselves mansions in the surrounding countryside and the term 'suburb' was in common use by the early 1800s. From the 1820s the families of larger employers and professionals began to move out of town centres to terraces and villas a short walk or carriage drive away, like Ardwick in Manchester, Little Woodhouse in Leeds, Everton and West Derby in Liverpool. As these enclaves began to be overtaken by the rapid process of urban growth, so the families moved further afield. As we saw in Chapter Two, during the second half of the nineteenth century the most prosperous sections of the middle classes established substantial suburban communities like Headingley in Leeds, Bowdon near Manchester, and Edgbaston in Birmingham, often at some distance from the city proper. By the early 1900s whole suburban towns had begun to be developed, like Letchworth, the first 'garden city'. According to its inspirer, Ebenezer Howard, the garden city ideal would bring together town and country in a 'joyous union', from which would 'spring a new life, a new civilisation'.[3] Even so, between the two world wars suburbanisation accelerated at an unprecedented rate, faster than anyone had dreamed possible, incorporating wider and wider sections of the middle classes. In 1934 fifteen hundred new houses were built every week by private contractors in Greater London, while in 1936 the nation's total housing stock grew by 3.3 per cent, the highest rate for a single year ever recorded. Altogether some four million houses were built in Britain between 1918 and 1939, three-quarters by private firms.[4] As the middle classes swelled in numbers, so towns and cities began to sprawl out further and further into the surrounding countryside. Between the wars the middle classes as a whole were suburbanised.

The expansion of the middle classes in the first half of the twentieth century was based on the growth of the occupational groups associated with 'mental' as distinct from 'manual' labour. It has been estimated that non-manual occupations expanded from 20 per cent of the working population in 1921 to 30 per cent in 1951.[5] Moreover, significant changes occurred in their composition.

One feature was the extraordinary increase in the number of white-collar workers such as clerks and teachers. The number of clerical workers, for instance, grew from 887,000 in 1911 to 2,404,000 in 1951, or from 5 per cent to 11 per cent of the workforce. Women were an important part of this occupational expansion, especially in domains such as office work. A further significant change was the decline in the numbers of self-employed professionals and employers, such as lawyers and industrialists, and the simultaneous rise in the numbers of salaried professionals, managers and administrators. Growth was most marked among engineers and technicians, reflecting the shift from older sectors like textiles and coal to newer, science-based industries such as light engineering and pharmaceuticals, often based on sites on the urban fringe.[6] As a result, during the inter-war years the middle classes came to be defined in two ways that were new: as a salariat, a class of salaried employees; and as suburban house-owners, or owner-occupiers.

Rejection of a suburban background was *de rigueur* for artists and writers of the 1950s like John Osborne, who described the London suburb of Stoneleigh, where he was brought up, as a 'Byzantium of pre-war mediocrity'.[7] But those who moved out to the new suburbs between the wars, often from flats or cramped houses in the city, saw matters very differently. Mavis Skeet, whose parents, like those of John Osborne, moved to Stoneleigh in the 1930s from a flat in Putney in south-west London, recalled her mother's delight with the house and garden: 'She was so pleased to be here. The whole sense of having a house of your own, of having a piece of land of your own, was something that you were going to cling onto.'[8] The space, the greenery and the sense of freedom that the new suburbs offered created a lasting impression on those who made the move. This sense of pleasure at the new surroundings was frequently mixed with pride at having achieved a place in suburbia. 'We were so proud', Irene Bacon recalled of her husband's family house at Hall Green. 'We were very proud of this little road, and we still are because it's still a bit unique.'[9] As Irene Bacon's case indicated, moving out from the city was clearly equated with moving up in the world. According to Wilf Cross, whose parents moved to a private housing estate in Oxford, the suburbs represented a 'new world': 'we were all taking a step into something which was a little better than we were accustomed to'.[10] Outsiders might sneer, but in the inter-war years large swathes of the middle classes entered for the first time into a love affair with the suburbs which, for many, has lasted to this day.

BUILDING THE SUBURBS

The race to the suburbs was both cause and consequence of the sustained housing boom that occurred between 1919 and 1939, set in motion by successive housing acts through which central government encouraged house-building. Local councils and private builders were both exhorted to take an active part in the drive to increase the nation's housing stock. The growth of privately owned suburban housing was also encouraged by a number of other factors. Firstly, rent controls, introduced during the First World War, were extended in the post-war period, making building for rent unprofitable. For the first time the majority of houses built in Britain were for private sale and ownership, not for rent. Secondly, cheap mortgages were available, encouraged by government through the Housing Acts of 1923 and 1925 which enabled local councils to lend to housebuyers. By the 1930s this role was taken over by building societies such as the Halifax and the Woolwich, their coffers swelled from the capital market following the Wall Street Crash of 1929 – financial investors saw building societies as a safer haven for their funds than the stock market. Mortgage rates of 6.5 per cent in 1924 had been reduced to 4.5 per cent by 1935, while the annual loans of the building societies nationally increased from £32 million in 1923 to £140 million in 1936.[11] In no period during the twentieth century were the terms of house purchase so favourable. An analysis across time shows that the percentage of a male secondary schoolteacher's annual salary required to pay the mortgage on the same three-bedroom London house was a mere 8 per cent in 1936 compared to a massive 43 per cent in 1990.[12]

House prices in the outer suburbs did not generally rise between the 1920s and the 1930s, if anything, they tended to fall. In the Surrey and Middlesex suburbs of London, a two- to three-bedroom 'semi' could be had for £700, while outside the London area the same house might be as little as £450. The deposit was normally small, as low as 10 per cent of the purchase price, while the monthly repayment was £5 10s on an £800 house in 1928, less than 25 per cent of a bank clerk's average monthly salary and 10 per cent of that of a dentist.[13] Most of those within the 'middle-class' income range – what the novelist George Orwell termed the 'five-to-ten-pound-a-weekers' – could therefore afford to buy a place in the suburbs. They included many of the least well-paid sections of the salariat – elementary teachers, senior clerks and technicians, even some 'superior' shop assistants.[14]

It needs emphasising just how unprecedented this development was at the period. In 1914 only 10 per cent of the national housing stock was owner-occupied; renting was by far the most common form of residential accommodation among all social classes before the First World War. By 1939, however, the proportion of owner-occupiers had risen to 31 per cent. This rise was almost wholly accounted for by the expansion of middle-class house ownership. According to recent research, manual workers actually owned a smaller proportion of owner-occupied houses in 1939 than they had done in 1915, despite the private housing boom that had occurred.[15] It is no surprise, therefore, that the ownership of a detached or semi-detached house in the suburbs was identified so strongly with the middle classes, since statistically there was a clear correspondence between the two. As the historian Ross McKibbin has emphasised, the expansion of interwar suburbia was not the product of large-scale upward social mobility from the working class. Evidence indicates that the majority of those who bought houses for the first time in the 1920s and 1930s made their living in professional, small business and white-collar occupations; buying a house, especially in the remoter suburbs, was simply beyond the means of most manual workers.[16] The spread of the suburbs and owner-occupation in these years widened the gap between the salary earner and the wage earner. House ownership became for the first time a defining feature of the middle classes, distinguishing them from the mass of workers who occupied rented (and increasingly council-owned) accommodation.

The Stoneleigh estate, some seventeen miles south west of central London, provides a good example of suburban development between the wars, displaying many of the characteristics of other similar private housing estates across the country. The area south west of London was one of the prime sites for house-building in the 1920s, due in large measure to improvements in transport facilities. The railway line from Wimbledon was electrified in 1925 and the extension of the London Underground to Morden was completed in 1926. Stoneleigh lay just beyond, close to the country village of Ewell. Attempts had been made to develop Stoneleigh as a suburban estate before the First World War, but they met with little success. In the 1920s it was still a rural community, a small village with a handful of shops, surrounded by open fields. It was only with the building of Stoneleigh railway station after 1930 that the whole area of 350 acres underwent development as a large-scale private housing estate. When it came, the transformation was dramatic. According to Gordon Ralph, whose family had been blacksmiths at Ewell forge for three generations, 'in five years, six years perhaps it was completely changed. You could walk through Ewell right across what is now Stoneleigh into Worcester Park across the fields. Then suddenly [it was] finished, sold to the builders and developed, hundreds of houses.'[17]

As many as twenty building firms were involved in developing different parts of the Stoneleigh estate during the 1930s. The majority of the houses on the two main estates, Stoneleigh Hill and Stoneleigh Park, sold for between £725 and £1,350, houses on the former, to the west of the railway line, being considered slightly superior. Mavis Skeet remembered 'right back when I was small people saying "Oh that [Stoneleigh Park] side of the railway is the half-crown side". I think people on the [Stoneleigh

Hill] side felt that they were just a little bit better than we were, the houses were a bit bigger, their jobs were a bit different.'[18] Builders used advertising to appeal directly to the social sensibilities of potential clients with a mixture of flattery and snobbishness. 'Novean Homes' on Stoneleigh Hill were offered to 'families of good breeding'. The brochure of the building firm Gleeson's advertised their homes as 'superior class country houses' and highlighted their proximity to Nonsuch Park, site of 'Henry VIII's Renaissance palace' (which, sadly, had long since been pulled down). In the Gleeson's section of Stoneleigh, called, predictably, the Nonsuch Park Estate, there were six types of houses based on number of bedrooms, all priced at the upper end of the market. Dermot Gleeson, who grew up on the estate built by his uncle's firm, considered that the degree of variation between house types was a critical factor in establishing the social tone of an estate; the more uniform the houses, the less socially distinguished the area was likely to be. But proximity to the railway and central London was even more important in determining the success of the estate as a whole. As Dermot Gleeson pointed out, 'if you look at the marketing literature [of the 1930s], more pages are devoted to railway timetables and the cost of season tickets than anything else – it was absolutely crucial'.[19] Despite its rural pretensions, Stoneleigh was designed from the outset as a commuting community and revolved around the train times. Mary Reed recalls how 'the whole street came alive to catch the 8.12 to London Bridge. My father joined our neighbours as they walked across the common land to the station, which was quite pleasantly situated in the countryside.'[20]

Almost all the recollections of the people who came to live on the Stoneleigh estate in the 1930s linked them with office work in London – in 1911 over half of all jobs in London and the South East were in the service sector and the proportion rose steadily thereafter.[21] Descriptions of the newcomers might be occupationally vague, but they were firmly identified as middle-class. In Ewell, Gordon Ralph saw them as a 'middle-class sort of people –

office workers and all this sort of thing'. Eve Mayatt, who grew up in Stoneleigh, had friends whose 'fathers were accountants and those sort of people lived in the same houses. But I don't think there were many people who were builders and labourers and electricians, I think they were engineers or civil servants.'[22] The newcomers generally shared a small business or salaried status, but they came from diverse occupations and different parts of the country. Few if any had experience of an estate like Stoneleigh, precisely because it represented a new way of living. Dermot Gleeson observed that while everyone on Nonsuch Park Estate 'belonged broadly speaking to the same financial category, they came from very diverse social, professional and geographical backgrounds indeed and nobody was quite clear what the rules of social engagement were'.[23] Many of them would have been new not only to the suburb but also to the region; over a million people migrated to the London area from all over Britain for employment reasons between 1921 and 1937.[24] Consequently, the rules of suburbia had to be worked out on the ground by the individuals and social groups concerned.

These included older rural communities in the immediate vicinity of the new estates. The wealthy established inhabitants of Ewell viewed Stoneleigh with alarm. Those in the big houses who were able to move away did so; some were bought out by building firms, the houses pulled down and the land built over. Poorer people, who earned their livelihood in Ewell, found it harder to leave and had to adapt accordingly. The decline in agriculture and rural activities meant that the village blacksmith, Gordon Ralph, could no longer survive merely from shoeing horses. Instead, he turned to making gates and other types of ironwork for the new houses and gardens on the Stoneleigh estate. The advent of Stoneleigh irrevocably changed the older social order of Ewell, with its 'squire', in the form of the banker Lord Glyn, its big houses and the local workforce of tradespeople and servants dependent upon them. For suburban Stoneleigh was not tied to the big houses, nor to the locality as such, since its workers earned their livings elsewhere. It represented an irruption of the 'middle' in a rural social world that had previously revolved around a traditional binary conception of 'upper' and 'lower', rich and poor.[25]

Those who came to Stoneleigh in the 1930s, on the other hand, seem to have only good memories of making the move. The modern character of the houses made a lasting impression. Mary Reed's family moved from West Norwood to Stoneleigh as a result of her father's success as a tea salesman and later director of Twinings. The house had running hot water, which was new to them, and 'all modern conveniences': 'I can remember when the telephone came. That was a great thrill when we got plugged in.' Others recalled their first instinct as being to go round the house switching on the electric lights and turning on the water taps, captivated by the newness of it all.[26] Eve Mayatt's first impressions were of greenery and space, of the 'delightful surroundings, the tree-lined road [which] even when it was made up was done sympathetically so the trees weren't destroyed, and fields opposite. It was quite an experience for a London suburb.' All these features spelled freedom and independence after years of cramped housing and interfering landlords, advantages that were especially appreciated by women. 'I think it was my mother who really loved being here', recalled Mavis Skeet. 'She just enjoyed the whole sort of freedom of it, the garden, not having to drag a large double pram up a flight of stairs every day, the fact that there was hot running water, that you had an upstairs and a downstairs that were your own and nobody around to say that you can't do this and you can't do that.'[27] Stoneleigh, of course, was not unique. In towns and cities across the country families were discovering the delights of suburbia in newly laid-out estates on the fringes of the countryside, like Hall Green in Birmingham, Ruislip, west of London, and Levenshulme in Manchester. If this was not exactly virgin territory, the inter-war suburbans were pioneers of a kind. They were carving out a new social place and a new way of life to go with it.

MODERNITY AND RESPECTABILITY

In many ways the outer suburbs of the inter-war period were the domestic equivalents of the new industries of that time – light engineering, pharmaceuticals, food manufacturing – epitomised by firms such as Hoover, Boots and Heinz. Both tended to be located on frontier zones between city and country, to be situated in estates (industrial or residential) and to be linked to the centre by new arterial roads and railway lines. Both were also taken to represent modernity, to be identified, not always positively, with novelty, consumerism, Americanisation and femininity. It was the pioneering aspects of suburbia that struck many contemporaries; the dominant mock-Tudor and mock-Jacobean styles of architecture were not generally seen at the time as reflecting a deep-seated nostalgia for the past.[28] As Irene Bacon remarked of her in-laws' house at Hall Green: 'Everything was absolutely brand new – that was the point.' Not only were the houses new; so too were the social relationships and the life that had to be made. The parents of Eve Mayatt moved to Stoneleigh 'when the houses were built and other people had arrived at the same time. So they were all sort of newcomers, and then they set out to carve their little niche in life.'[29]

Suburban life in the 1920s and 1930s differed in important respects from middle-class life before the First World War. In the Victorian and Edwardian periods the presence of a living-in servant was an automatic corollary of middle-class status. Any family with a serious claim to be middle-class (and others besides) had at least one domestic servant and often more. In the aftermath of the First World War, however, this convention changed with the advent of the so-called 'servant problem'. The post-war edition of *Mrs Beeton's Household Management*, still a middle-class bible, warned that 'good servants are hard to get, harder still, perhaps, to keep and even the wealthiest people prefer houses of manageable dimensions, with labour-saving fittings and appliances'.[30] As a consequence, servant-keeping ceased to be a badge of middle-class status. This did not mean that domestic service itself disappeared. It continued to be a feature of wealthier middle- and upper-class households; the 1931 census reported that approximately 500,000 households in Britain, some 5 per cent of the total, had one or more servants living in. Most suburban households also seem to have employed some outside help in the form of a cleaner or gardener. But the newer suburbs became notable for their relative lack of living-in servants. What distinguished the newcomers in Stoneleigh from the 'big houses' of the established middle class in Ewell was not only that the Stoneleigh houses were smaller and more modern, but also that the occupants did their own housework. This was not purely a matter of choice; fewer and fewer young women were prepared to exchange the relatively good wages and independence associated with jobs in the new factories for a life in domestic service. Even for better-off families it was becoming increasingly difficult to find a live-in servant. As a result, many middle-class women became for the first time, in the design historian Deborah Ryan's phrase, 'workers in the home rather than managers of it'. [31]

The modernity of the suburban home was strongly associated with the figure of the 'housewife', a new social type of the 1920s. Like married women in the Victorian middle classes, the suburban housewife was not expected to engage in paid work outside the home. Despite the Sex Disqualification (Removal) Act of 1919, which eliminated the legal restrictions on women entering the professions, a *de facto* 'marriage bar' was maintained in many areas in which middle-class women worked, like schoolteaching and the civil service. Lady Troutbridge lamented in 1926 that 'years of blind adherence to what most of us now consider was false tradition have robbed women of their proper development in business and professional life, and in many cases woman is regarded as mentally inferior to man for the simple reason that she is a woman'. [32] In the official view, women in the new suburbs were primarily home-makers, concerned with looking after husband and children, with shopping, cleaning and cooking. One consequence of this was that women were targeted as consumers in a more vigorous and systematic way than had previously occurred, through newspapers, magazines like *Woman's Own* and advertising. Firms marketing new consumer durables sought to appeal to women directly through advertisements in which labour-saving devices for the home, such as vacuum cleaners and washing machines, were identified with a new domestic science. The suburban woman was thus linked to 'modern' forms of technology and know-how; instead of simply a wife, she was constructed as a professional in the home, a 'housewife'. Newspapers like the *Daily Mail* and the *Daily Express* saw women in the suburbs as an important market to tap and devised the idea of a 'women's page' to do so, dispensing tips on etiquette and homemaking. The *Mail* in particular projected itself as the housewife's champion, campaigning on housing issues between the wars and in 1908 establishing the Ideal Home Exhibition, at which the newest techniques and gadgets for the home were annually displayed. By consistently emphasising the figure of the housewife and her presumed consumerist and social aspirations, the *Daily Mail* skilfully sought to promote a conservative femininity and to associate it with a specifically suburban ideal of modernity.[33]

The suburban home was identified with a further feature of 'modern' living, the 'companionate' marriage.[34] The model of the Victorian and Edwardian family had emphasised the separateness of parental roles, the father representing patriarchal authority within the home, the mother concerned primarily with the management of servants and, less directly, with the upbringing of the children. In some cases this model of marriage seems to have persisted into the inter-war years. Suzy Harvey, brought up in the suburb of Summertown, north Oxford, saw her parents' relationship as very different from later marital ideals. Parental roles were 'distinctive': 'my father was the power, and my mother was quite subservient ... Equal was a word that I don't think was part of that society.'[35] But her parents' experience was not necessarily typical of all. Others brought up on suburban estates between the wars remember their parents as having different roles to play as breadwinner and home-keeper, but also as having a more equal and companionable relationship than their grandparents' generation. Both of Mary Reed's parents were active in church-based associations, Sunday school and Boys Brigade, and took a strong interest in theatre locally. Their own relationship was of prime importance. Mary's mother would take a rest in the afternoon and change her clothes so as to be fresh for her husband's homecoming, and they would always socialise together.[36] Above all, married couples in the suburbs shared an enjoyment of, and pride in, home and garden. At weekends, Mary Reed's parents 'were fully involved with making as much of life in their new home as they were able to. A lot of that time was spent in the garden where they would be landscaping.' For Mavis Skeet's parents the suburban home was a symbol of their achievements together, which they clung to in the face of economic adversity: 'Financially they were struggling really when they moved here, but they felt it was worth it because it was something they had done for themselves, they had got through the Depression and … this was their life and they weren't going to let it go.'[37] The idea of the modern companionate marriage, combining partnership and emotional equality within a framework of marked gender differences, took root powerfully in the inter-war suburbs.

At the same time, the importance of affirming respectability made for strong social boundaries and codes. There was little spontaneous friendliness or 'dropping in' on neighbours in ways common among people in other places and classes. Having been brought up in a circle of Irish doctors, dentists and priests, the Gleeson family found their neighbours at Stoneleigh withdrawn and unsociable: 'There were many families on the estate who were extremely reserved, perfectly courteous, perfectly civil, but not in the business of inviting their neighbours in even for a cup of tea.'[38] Etiquette, manners and appearance were crucial to demonstrating respectability in public; they were a 'badge you wore', as Mr Hickson, a retired engineer, put it. Language, accent and clothing could confirm or betray credentials and status: 'There were some people who would talk about lounges, toilets and serviettes and there were others who would talk about drawing rooms, lavatories and napkins.' In Hall Green, Birmingham, Mrs Hickson recalled her grandmother emphasising the difference between 'those who put their gloves on in the house before they leave and those who put them on going down the road – they were not so careful with their dressing, not so particular, a bit more slovenly with their attire'. Respectability lay in the detail and in the opinion of others, especially neighbours. 'What people thought of you was very important then, you didn't just go along and do your own thing. Your position in society was very important to you and so what people thought of you was all-important. You had to be beyond reproach.'[39]

Respectability implied moral rectitude; in the suburbs moral codes permeated all aspects of behaviour. Frugality and temperance were valued not just in themselves but also as indicators of the uprightness of individuals and families. Mary Reed's mother made a virtue of spending the family money carefully when shopping, and as Methodists and teetotallers both her parents profoundly disapproved of the improvident habits of those who frequented the local pub: 'My mother and father lived at the end of the road where a pub was on the corner and in 1924, when money was very hard to get, they would see working-class people spending all their money on liquor and coming home with nothing to give to their family. I really was brought up with a def inite fear of alcohol.' The historian J. F. C. Harrison grew up in the suburbs of inter-war Leicester. His parents had a terrible fear of debt, but equally characteristically, given the consumerist aspirations of the period, his mother had one extravagance, for unsuitable shoes that she would buy and never wear, and which would live at the bottom of her wardrobe.[40] Strong rules also governed what could and could not be discussed. Conversation in suburban households was hedged about with subjects that were not to be mentioned: politics, religion, money, class, intimacy and, above all, sex. In Summertown, Suzy Harvey recalled, 'we had these two dear ladies who lived next door, and looking back on it I am sure that they were a gay couple who lived together, and yet it would never ever have been approached at all, certainly in my household. A lot of subjects were taboo in those days.'[41]

Sexuality, or rather its denial, lay at the heart of respectability. For middle-class women, whose sexuality was especially regulated, one of the conundrums of the period was how to be able to express sexual desire without compromising the standards of respectable behaviour. Middle-class codes of respectability differentiated them from the working classes, where attitudes towards sex were assumed to be more relaxed and 'natural', and from the aristocracy, who were deemed morally decadent and irresponsible. These themes featured prominently in the bestseller *Rebecca* by Daphne du Maurier, published in 1938. It tells the story of a young middle-class girl who marries into the aristocratic de Winter family. At first she flounders, lacking the self-confidence and poise to handle her new surroundings. She is assailed by the image of Rebecca, the first Mrs de Winter, who is now dead, but who comes back to haunt her successor. Rebecca represents the corrupt sensuality of the aristocracy and its disdain for the opinions of others. Rebecca 'did what she liked', 'lived as she liked' and 'cared for nothing and no-one'. The middle-class girl is also confronted by sexual associations of a different kind, as the critic Alison Light observed. She is propositioned by Rebecca's cousin, Jack Favell: 'when this "awful bounder" gives the heroine the once-over, she ... comments "I felt like a barmaid" (as though a barmaid thinks of nothing but sex)'.[42] The heroine, however, manages to chart a way between the Scylla of Rebecca and the Charybdis of the barmaid. Her triumph is the triumph of middle-class decency over aristocratic libertinism. The book's success no doubt owed much to the allure of Rebecca herself as a symbol of sexual daring and of the fantasy of being able to act without fear of the consequences. But the ultimate victory of the values of suburban femininity and respectability was equally important in explaining the book's appeal to a middle-class audience. *Rebecca* articulated the problems of sexuality and respectability for middle-class women, while providing a resolution that vindicated conventional bourgeois morality.

Suburban society was often viewed as monotonous, conformist and narrow-minded and there was undoubtedly some truth in the accusations. Suzy Harvey's memories of Summertown were dominated by the image of her father's rose garden, symbolising the stiffness and regimentation of the suburban world of her childhood.[43] At the same time, there were good reasons for the insistence on respectability and its codes. Fear of bankruptcy and social disgrace haunted the Victorian middle classes, as we saw in Chapter Two, and economic instability was a persistent feature of the inter-war years, feeding a sense of insecurity. In the aftermath of the First World War the newspapers were full of stories of the 'new poor', of well-to-do families who had fallen on hard times caused by inflation and the effects of post-war economic dislocation. Thereafter the fear of unemployment and the horror of debt never entirely receded, even among those with middle-class occupations relatively insulated from the worst effects of the Depression of the 1930s. For Irene Bacon in Hall Green, economic insecurity between the wars shaped the outlook of her generation. They grew up with an instinctive aversion to spending and an exaggerated concern about appearing prodigal, lifelong traits which they put down to the anxieties that the Depression brought in its train. According to Eve Mayatt at Stoneleigh, 'the only real fear' her parents had 'was that for some reason or other my father might lose his job, because that of course would wreck their whole financial planning and their orderly way of life which was how they wanted to live'.[44] The dangers might have been more apparent than real for the majority of the middle classes, but they were sufficiently powerful to sustain habits of frugality and abstinence and an abhorrence of risk-taking of any kind.

Equally important in explaining the cult of respectability was the novel character of estate life itself and the social rules that had to be established. As Dermot Gleeson pointed out of Stoneleigh, 'Given the great uncertainty about the rules I think people found it easier just to keep to themselves. It was a new estate. There were no bonds deriving from shared schooldays and of course people who worked didn't see each other during the day.'[45] What applied to Stoneleigh was also true of similar estates elsewhere. The elaborate, formal codes of behaviour found in the suburbs between the wars related to their new and untried character as communities. Modernity and respectability were not contradictory facets of suburbia; they were vital elements in the construction of a new type of community with its own social rules and way of life.

CONSTRUCTING COMMUNITY

In *Howards End* (1910) the novelist E. M. Forster spoke of the 'red rust' spreading out from London into the countryside of Surrey and Hampshire. He articulated a fear of the destruction of older rural communities as the encroaching suburbs overtook them. This fear is a repeated motif in literary descriptions of England between the wars and it has shaped much subsequent thinking about the effects of urban growth. It is certainly the case that suburban development disrupted village life and the rural social order – we have already seen something of this in the effects that the building of Stoneleigh had on the village of Ewell and its various classes of inhabitants. Yet it is important to keep in mind that while suburban development destroyed older communities, it also created new ones. This is not an easy idea to accommodate, since the suburbs are generally associated with privacy and isolation rather than with collective life. Even its staunch defender J. M. Richards termed suburbia 'a psalm to individualism', while for many critics the terms 'suburban' and 'community' appeared to be an outright contradiction in terms.[46] But a community and a distinctive way of life were carved out in the suburbs in the

1920s and 1930s – this was an important dimension of their pioneering role. Home was the starting-point for suburban living, and its focal point, but life did not end at the garden gate. In the 1930s, notably, a social infrastructure of associations and facilities was created with extraordinary zeal and rapidity.

In the suburban world home and family occupied a central place. It is clear that for most adults the bulk of their leisure time was spent within the domestic and familial context. Reading was an important activity, especially for women. Eve Mayatt's mother, a former English teacher, was a 'voracious reader' of Shakespeare, Jane Austen and Thomas Hardy, as well as of contemporary writers such as Daphne du Maurier, and she had definite views about literature: 'She did not enjoy the sort of sugary romance of a certain well-known series [Mills and Boon]. She liked a book which could be discussed afterwards, it wasn't just read and put away.'[47] Other activities, such as listening to the radio and gardening, were more likely to be engaged in by both partners. Dermot Gleeson remembered people at Stoneleigh spending most of the weekend in the garden. Eve Mayatt's parents both 'loved the garden'; 'he loved gardening anyway and she liked to have the garden for the children to run in [and to] pick apples off the tree'.[48] For the family as a whole, and children especially, the high spot of the year was the annual seaside holiday. Eve Mayatt remembered it as a 'magical fortnight', usually spent at south coast resorts such as Bournemouth and Swanage. As a child Mavis Skeet looked forward to the two-week holiday at Clacton, which brought not only entertainment in the form of repertory shows, but also a new set of clothes for the year. Holidays abroad were still the preserve of the upper middle classes and the seriously wealthy: 'It would not have entered my parents' heads to go abroad for a holiday, they were very content with having a fortnight at the sea.'[49] But the spread of motoring offered increased opportunities for day-trips into the country, while the car developed as an important middle-class symbol of status and freedom. In Irene Bacon's family four cars filled with relatives would regu-

larly drive out for picnics and games of cricket on the banks of
the Avon or the Severn rivers: 'it was quite a party'.[50]

Despite the importance of home and family, though, social life
was not restricted to them. In the new suburbs associational life
had to be built from scratch; there were no pre-existing institutions to fall back on. Considerable efforts, therefore, went into
building community institutions beyond the home. The most
important of these, in terms of frequency of use, were the local
shops, the 'shopping parade', which became a feature of inter-war
suburban estates and a further sign of their modernity. A parade of
shops, known as the Broadway, was part of the development of
Stoneleigh from the outset, laid out by builders in 1933. By 1938 it
contained over thirty shops, including dentists, hairdressers,
grocers, a branch of Woolworths, an hotel and a cinema. Most
importantly, it also had a tea room which 'quickly became
Stoneleigh's first social centre. Here were held the fortnightly
whist drives organised by the Residents Association; here, amid tea
and buns, the Stoneleigh and Ewell Motor Club held its first
meeting in March 1935.'[51] Mavis Skeet recalled the numerous
shops on the Broadway in more personal terms: 'Madame Ada's
the hairdressers, Sunny's the bookshop, the dress-shop next door,
greengrocers, butchers, baker, Job's dairy, another hairdressers.'
Since women tended to shop daily, the parade became a natural
focus for sociability: 'Because it was a routine, people used to go
out the same time of the day and so they met up with the same
people, and that was another way of building on your friendships.'
Being known by name to the local shopkeepers and tradesmen
was important to feeling 'part of the place', part of a continuous
community. With its dress shops and hairdressers, the parade also
lent glamour to the suburb – having your hair waved or hands
manicured became part of a new (if sometimes arduous) idea of
feminine luxury: 'You sat in the chair and if you were going to
have your hair waved there were all these various wires … and if
by any chance you were having a perm as well you were there for
four hours at least with all these wires stuck on your head.'[52]

There were also more formal associations to which men and women belonged. Some, like the Rotary Club and the Townswomen's Guild, were sex-segregated, but the majority were enjoyed by both sexes. The local tennis club was one such venue, accessible to the new suburbans but still sufficiently expensive and exclusive to deter the working class. Amateur dramatics and opera were both very popular, enabling adults to make friends while engaging in activities which could be defined as culturally improving – by the inter-war period Nonconformist and low church opposition to the theatre had dissolved. Staunch members of the local Methodist chapel, Mary Reed's parents were also active in the amateur dramatics society in Stoneleigh. For them such activity was a welcome and desired part of their newfound situation: 'It was cultural, and they hadn't really had culture before. They had a bit more space in their lives. I think that people who had moved from just being poor had this opportunity to read and be involved with a group activity they hadn't been [involved with] before. They were able to think, "what could we do that gave us pleasure and moved us out into something artistic?"'[53] Weekly visits to the cinema were also common, especially among women: in Stoneleigh, the carefully named Rembrandt cinema, opened in 1938 with a first-floor café and a rose-pink auditorium, sought to encourage women to combine shopping with a cinema visit in a luxurious and respectable environment. As the cultural historian Paul Oliver perceptively observed, certain films could offer suburbanites a glamorized mirror-image of themselves: 'The westerns depicting migrants, settlers, newly established townships, heroes who arrived with no details of their past, all together forming a community, bonded by the railroad or linked by the express stages, reflected, if only dimly, suburban audiences' own situation.'[54] The new suburbs were, in their own way, frontier towns, and their inhabitants pioneers.

The pace at which the associational life of such suburbs grew was vigorous. The Stoneleigh Residents Association, founded in

1933, had a membership of 600 in 1936 and 1400 by 1939. A whole gamut of activities and organisations was set up under its auspices: whist drives, dances, cricket club, motoring club, cycling club, an orchestra and choral society. According to the historian Ross McKibbin, in the small Oxfordshire town of Banbury there were over a hundred formal associations, 'nearly all of them ... dominated by the middle classes'. Between the wars, no less than in the Victorian period, one of the characteristics that distinguished the suburban middle classes from other social groups was 'their obvious propensity to join clubs and organisations by way of formal membership and direct subscription'.[55]

If institutions like church and chapel, and social activities like coffee mornings and tea parties, are added to this conspectus, it is clear that the suburb was not the isolated, private place that critics such as the writer George Orwell or the architect Clough Williams-Ellis described.[56] Social relationships may have been formal and reserved, but in new estates the institutions of community life grew up with alacrity. Looking back, Eve Mayatt described Stoneleigh as 'claustrophobic' and 'dreary', but didn't consider that her mother was lonely or bored: 'I don't think she probably had time to feel isolated, her days were extremely busy. Perhaps as the children began to leave home she might have felt more isolated but I think by that time she had joined things like women's institutions, the Townswomen's Guild and so on.'[57]

The suburban ideal was, indeed, extraordinarily powerful between the wars, helping to refashion the image of Englishness itself. For many contemporary critics, suburbia epitomised the decline from an heroic age of Empire and adventure before the First World War to a post-war world that was altogether narrower, more provincial and commonplace. It was a viewpoint given literary expression by Virginia Woolf, describing lives of drab gentility in her short story *The New Dress*:

> They petered out respectably in seaside resorts; every watering place had one of her aunts even now asleep in some lodging

with the front windows not quite facing the sea. That was so like them – they had to squint at things always. And she was doing the same, she was just like her aunts. For all her dreams of living in India, married to some hero like Sir Henry Lawrence, some empire builder (still the sight of a native turban filled her with romance), she had failed utterly. She had married Hubert, with his safe, permanent underling's job in the Law Courts, and they managed tolerably in a smallish house, without proper maids.

Yet such disparaging views seem to have been those of a minority. There was also a less jaundiced way of viewing suburbia, in which an aggressive, imperialist version of Englishness gave way in the aftermath of the First World War to a more peaceable and domesticated national self-image. After 1918, Alison Light suggests, a 'new kind of Englishness' was articulated, 'giving us a private and retiring people, pipe-smoking "little men" with their quietly competent partners, a nation of gardeners and house-wives'.[58] Bloomsbury might sneer, but an idealised vision of suburbia came to occupy a place close to the heart of national identity during the inter-war years. The suburban middle classes moved from the wings to centre-stage in the public imagination; they came to stand for 'middle England', the hard-working, home-owning and respectable backbone of the nation.

CLASS AND THE POLITICS OF SUBURBIA

The idea of 'middle England' is a reminder that politics and class itself were never far from the surface of suburban life, however taboo they might be as topics of conversation. Suburbia was riddled with the consciousness of class, one manifestation being the petty (and sometimes gross) snobbery for which the suburbs were renowned. Suzy Harvey remembers her father, an optician, as being 'very conscious of his class', a man who clung to the outward signs of status and respectability.[59] But consciousness of class went beyond mere snobbishness. It took on a sharp political edge in the visceral hostility directed towards manual workers and their institutions, especially trade unions, which recent historians of the inter-war years have seen as a defining feature of social relations at the period. Anti-working class feeling was an essential ingredient of what it meant to be middle-class in the 1920s and 1930s.

These sentiments were manifested in actions as well as attitudes. At Summertown, north Oxford, in 1934 the private residents of a suburban estate paid to have walls constructed to cut them off from the Cutteslowe council estate, recently built on adjacent land. Ostensibly, the walls were intended to reduce traffic in the private estate. But other factors clearly entered into the decision to put them up. The company that built the private estate objected to the city council relocating supposed 'slum families' from central Oxford to Cutteslowe. More generally, the inhabitants of Summertown had no wish to be associated with those whom they regarded, explicitly or implicitly, as their social inferiors. Doris Denton, who moved to Cutteslowe in 1935, vividly remembers the intensity of feeling: 'They treated us like dirt because they thought we was scruffy and rough. They was it, they fancied themselves. The people who lived over there [on the private estate] thought the wall was put up to separate the good people from the bad. They put spikes and glass on the top, shows how bitter they was.'[60] During the years that followed, the walls were twice knocked down and rebuilt, and though Oxford City Council fought a long legal campaign to have them removed, they were only dismantled for good in 1959.[61] When the walls came down for the final time, people on the council estate celebrated what was perceived as a form of liberation: 'We all queued up and cheered, we had flags and waved, we had a party in the streets. It was lovely.' But on both estates the memory of the walls lingered. Twenty-five years on, in 1984, the episode was re-enacted in a school play at Cutteslowe. From the Summertown side Suzy Harvey saw the walls as emblematic of a continuing divide: 'Even though it's not there in the physical [sense], …there is an underlying feeling of a problem that people don't want to discuss or bring to the surface. I still think there is a wall between the thirties estate and the council estate. I think it has a lot to do with class.'[62]

Cutteslowe was not the only place where such barriers were erected. At Bromley in Kent a similar high wall was built in 1926 by residents of a private housing estate to cut themselves off from a newly built London County Council estate. These were merely instances of a more general social antagonism that pervaded public life between the wars. The middle classes saw themselves as assailed by threats on all sides. The Russian Revolution of 1917 encouraged fears of a similar revolution in Britain, exacerbated by the advent of the first Labour government in 1924 and a series of lengthy labour disputes which culminated in the General Strike of 1926, the first and only general strike in British history. The ten-day strike mobilised the middle classes on the side of government and order in an unprecedented manner. Business-men and clerks left their jobs in offices to drive lorries and buses, to maintain essential services and to keep the country running at what was perceived to be a moment of national emergency. Fears of the trade union movement and of manual workers generally ran high. For many professionals in suburban communities like Ewell, getting to work as usual was a matter of duty, despite the lack of trains and the hostility of the strikers. According to the historian Ross McKibbin 'the 1920s experienced more severe class conflict than at any other time in modern British history'.[63] Moreover, the fears did not melt away after 1926 but coloured the inter-war period as a whole. The General Strike was followed by concerns about political extremism, focused on the activities of the Communist party, the British Union of Fascists, the hunger marches and the rise of Hitler in Germany. Still more fundamen-tally, there were persistent anxieties about the survival of capitalism as an economic system. A short-lived boom after the First World War was followed by a series of severe and protracted slumps, the worst occurring between 1931 and 1934. No government appeared capable of managing the economy and for a time there were real fears (and, for some, hopes) that Marx's prediction of the collapse of capitalism would be borne out by events.

In this heightened atmosphere it was unsurprising that middle-class identity should hinge so strongly on opposition to manual workers and trade unions. Episodes such as the General Strike were stark and highly public examples of open class hostility. But in general, short outbursts of class antagonism alternated with longer periods of low-level animosity, characterised by a studied mutual disregard. Peter Collison, who carried out surveys on social attitudes at Cutteslowe for Oxford City Council in the 1950s, found that outside times of high feeling 'people were indifferent to each other', a view supported by Doris Denton's assertion that 'we kept to ourselves, you know, never bothered, just kept to ourselves'.[64] In these circumstances the sense of social difference easily hardened into a form of unofficial apartheid. At Hall Green in the suburbs of Birmingham Mr Hickson, whose wife's grandmother's views on the etiquette of dressing we quoted earlier, recalled the strong boundaries that inhibited social mixing between middle classes and workers: 'There was a distinct difference. For instance, at work you would have staff and works, and the staff would be middle-class, the works were certainly working-class ... They [the middle class] wouldn't mix with the working class and they wouldn't share the same interests and hobbies and the same sporting pursuits, and they wouldn't relax in the same way.'[65] This sense of class distinction extended into the intimate details of life, including matters of social habit and hygiene. With some sense of shame, Suzy Harvey recollected being shocked as a child going to the flat of a friend, aged nine or ten: 'It smelled, it was awful and I had this image in my mind thinking this child is poor, this child is not from the same class as me. I can't remember what my mother said to me, but there's an image of me thinking ... I didn't like that, I didn't like the smells.'[66] Being 'middle-class' was understood as related not only to wealth, occupation and social status, but also – and perhaps more fundamentally – to a specific and habituated set of responses, of disgust, restraint and embarrassment.

If the relationship to manual workers loomed large in the social landscape of the middle classes between the wars, there was also the relationship to the landed class, the aristocracy and gentry, to be negotiated. For the majority of the suburban middle classes this relationship was lived out exclusively in the realm of the imagination. Relations were not with the 'upper classes' as people so much as with the monarchy or 'the rich' in symbolic form, represented in pageantry, in the celebrity columns of the newspapers, in romantic fiction or, more tangibly perhaps, in the figures who opened a local fête or charitable event. In 1939 E. M. Forster remarked that the middle class 'slaughtered the aristo-cracy and has been haunted ever since by the ghost of its victim'.[67] The aspirations of the suburban 'middles' have often been considered by commentators and historians to derive from those above them in the social pecking order, in a 'trickle-down' effect, but matters were not so simple.[68] In practice, any tradi-tional deference middle-class men and women might have shown to the upper classes was by the inter-war period far from automatic and unqualified. Aristocrats like Lord Roseberry, who lived in Epsom, had no direct relationship with the upper middle-class families at nearby Ewell, let alone the new suburban inhabitants of Stoneleigh. The main impression is one of distance and separateness; upper and middle classes occupied different social worlds. In public, middle-class opinion was often less respectful, taking the form of hostility to the aristocracy and the rich as profiteers from the First World War, a criticism that lin-gered on well into the 1920s in journalism and popular literature. Moreover, as the example of du Maurier's *Rebecca* showed, middle-class attitudes to the aristocracy often combined admira-tion of inherited prestige and 'breeding' with a moral critique of irresponsibility and decadence. The relationship of the middle classes to the landed class was at best ambivalent, reflecting the decline of aristocratic wealth and power before and after the First World War.[69]

As the fortunes of the landed aristocracy waned, so those of the middle classes waxed, coming to occupy a central place in British political life during the inter-war period. After 1918 the framework of politics changed significantly. In 1918 the vote was extended to all adult males and to women over thirty; in 1928 women gained the vote on the same basis as men. For the first time, therefore, Britain had a genuine mass democracy. Additionally, the Liberal party went into precipitous decline after 1918 and was replaced by the Labour party as the main opposition to Conservatism. The electoral system was now organised on strongly class lines. Yet middle-class allegiance to the Conservative party was by no means assured in the early 1920s. The middle-class vote had traditionally been split between Liberals and Conservatives. Moreover, the decline of aristocratic influence hit the Conservatives hardest, as the traditional party of the landed order. It became essential, therefore, for Tory politicians to win the middle classes for Conservatism if the nation was to be preserved from the threat of Labour in government, a prospect that appalled many traditionalists.

This aim, in turn, required the reworking of Conservatism to enable the party to appeal to those establishing themselves in the ranks of the suburban middle classes. The key figure in this transformation was Stanley Baldwin, leader of the party from 1923 and prime minister in successive Conservative and Conservative-dominated governments in the 1920s and 1930s. Baldwin's achievement was to transform the Conservatives from the party of the landed élite to the party of the suburban man and woman. Several strategies were used to create and cement this new identity. Firstly, the Conservatives actively promoted home-ownership from 1923 through a series of measures to stimulate private house-building and provide tax relief for housebuyers. Conservatives viewed the creation of a class of suburban home-owners as providing a propertied bulwark against the possibility of socialist revolution. Secondly, and by extension, the idea of a property-owning democracy provided a clear, class-based source of demarcation from the Labour party, which favoured the construction of council-owned property for rent. Owner-occupation thus became not only a marker of middle-class status, but also a dividing-line between Conservatives and Labour. Thirdly, the Conservative party, together with newspapers such as the *Daily Mail*, sought to project the suburban middle classes as synonymous with 'public opinion' and the 'national interest', against the Labour party and the trade unions, which were depicted as representing selfish sectional interests. After the General Strike, in particular, the Conservatives were able to play on suburban hostility to organised labour, capable at any moment of 'holding the country to ransom'.[70]

All these rhetorical devices aimed to isolate Labour and to project the Conservatives as the party of the nation. In his speeches Baldwin summoned up an England in which the suburbs united town and countryside and the middle classes were portrayed as home-lovers and gardeners: 'Nothing can be more touching than to see how the working man and woman after generations in the towns will have their tiny bit of garden if they can, will go to gardens if they can, to look at something they have never seen as children, but which their ancestors knew and loved. The love of these things is innate and inherent in our people.'[71] Under Baldwin, Conservatism came to take on a new tone. It was less haughty and imperialist, more reassuring and focused on the domestic virtues associated with 'middle England'. Baldwin wooed the suburbs for Conservatism by flatteringly representing them as a new arcadia; his reward was that the Tory party dominated government and parliament for seventeen of the twenty years between the wars.

Nevertheless, not all sections of the middle classes embraced the suburbs. Those who moved to new estates at the period and were brought up in places like Hall Green, Stoneleigh and Summertown generally looked on them with affection. They represented space, modernity and freedom. A house in the suburbs was easily the largest single purchase that a middle-class family was likely to make and its principal form of saving. Small wonder, then, that so much energy went into maintaining appearances and that so much hostility was directed at those groups, such as organised labour, which were seen as potentially threatening this investment. But to many in the established upper middle classes, in the literary intelligentsia and on the political left, suburbia was anathema. In the novel *Coming up for Air* (1939) by the Eton-educated writer and socialist George Orwell, the central character, George Bowling, describes it in vitriolic terms:

> When you've time to look about you and when you happen to be in the right mood, it's a thing that makes you laugh inside to walk down these streets in the inner outer suburbs and to think of the lives that go on there. Because after all what *is* a road like Ellesmere Road? Just a prison with cells all in a row. A line of semi-detached torture chambers where the poor little five-to-ten-pound-a-weekers quake and shiver, every one of them with the boss twisting his tail and his wife riding him like a nightmare and his kids sucking his blood like leeches.

Orwell's image is striking for the violence of its language and its misogyny, but it also reflected a specific set of political concerns. He considered that suburban home-ownership was a swindle – 'building societies are probably the cleverest racket of modern times'. The Conservative idea of a property-owning democracy was likewise merely a confidence trick to persuade people that they had a stake in capitalism instead of being exploited by it, and that they had an interest in preserving the country from socialist revolution. More than this, writers like Orwell depicted the suburban middle classes as wracked by fear and hostility towards the working class; the suburbs were the home of snobbery and class hatred. In this last respect, interviews with working-class neighbours of the new suburban home-owners suggest that Orwell was not wholly wrong. At Oxford, a council estate resident, Jack Fellowes, saw the residents of the Summertown private estate as characterised by 'sheer snobbery': 'they feared that a lot of homeless families were coming to Cutteslowe. I think they thought they [the families] were deprived, and that they were not up to the standard of what [the private residents] wished.' The oral historian Jerry White concurs: 'Council tenants who moved to the suburbs often describe themselves as feeling as though they lived in a leper colony. That's how they describe the way they were treated by their middle-class neighbours. One has to think that rarely, if ever, have class distinctions been so spiteful and so wide.'[72]

The powerful and conflicting emotions which middle-class suburbia aroused in contemporaries reached their height in the 1920s and 1930s. In 1937 the poet John Betjeman issued his famous declaration, 'Come, friendly bombs, and fall on Slough / It isn't fit for humans now'. Three years later his poetic fantasy became reality in the Blitz.[73] It was not only the cities that attracted the bombs, but also the suburbs. In many ways the Second World War marks the natural end of a particular phase in the history of the suburbs and of the middle classes. After 1945 the election of a Labour government ushered in a new era of collectivist democracy, epitomised by the construction of the welfare state, supplanting the individualist democracy of the inter-war years, with its priorities of low taxation and strictly limited state intervention. On the whole, the chief beneficiaries of the post-war redistribution of wealth were working-class, not middle-class, families. Furthermore, the building from the late 1940s of 'new towns' like Harlow and Stevenage to house people from the city slums meant that the suburbs were no longer identified exclusively with the middle classes. Ownership of a suburban home became a realistic aspiration of the better-off sections of the working class as well.

In the middle classes, too, times were changing. By the 1950s rebellion was in the air among middle-class youth, as we shall see in Chapter Five. For 'angry young men' like John Osborne (and for many young women), the suburbs were not so much a place to get into as somewhere to get out of. They no longer represented, in any sense, a pioneering form of modern living. 'Semi-detached suburban' became a synonym for a way of life that was deadening, dated and provincial. If the obsession with class reached its height in England during the inter-war years, so the period also saw the middle-class infatuation with the suburbs at its peak. Never again would class be quite so powerful a force in English social and political life, nor would suburbia hold quite such allure. From the 1950s onwards the relationship of the middle classes with the suburbs came to resemble not so much a love affair as a marriage of convenience – necessary, institutional, but no longer passionate.

CHAPTER 4

SOCIAL LEADERS AND PUBLIC PERSONS

Rise and fall of the upper middle class

A group of middle-aged men and their wives pose for a photograph on a lawn in the summer of 1935. The setting is private and domestic, but the group is formally arranged, the most senior figures seated, the others gathered stiffly around. At the centre of the picture is the prime minister, Stanley Baldwin, head of the all-party 'National' government. Behind him is the Tory grandee Lord de la Warr, with the rising young politician R. A. ('Rab') Butler. Samuel Courtauld, chairman of the great industrial company of the same name and Butler's father-in-law, stands alongside the celebrated conductor Malcolm Sargent, whose concerts he sponsors. Power, influence and money come together in an English garden.

The photograph is more than just a group snapshot. It is an image of the powerbrokers of British society, frozen at a particular historical moment between the world wars. The story behind the photograph is the subject of this chapter. It is about the growth of a new 'upper middle class', supplanting the landed aristocracy as the single most powerful force in British society in the early twentieth century. The upper middle class was differentiated from the lower middle class by scale of income, inherited wealth and extent of education, but above all by its access to positions of power and the authority it was able to exert in (and sometimes beyond) English society. Its members were 'social leaders and public persons', a phrase coined in the late nineteenth century to describe the melding of the urban wealthy with the landed gentry in county government.[1] The term 'upper middle class' itself first came into usage in England in the 1870s. By the early 1900s we find it in the novels of writers like George Gissing and John Galsworthy, author of that testament to Edwardian upper middle-class life, *The Forsyte Saga*.[2] The unmistakable features of the group were vividly captured at this time by another novelist, Arnold Bennett: 'Their assured, curt voices, their proud carriages, the clothes, the similarity of their manners, all show that they belong to a caste and that caste has been successful in the struggle for life. It is called the middle class, but it ought to be called the upper class, for nearly everything is below it.'[3]

The new upper middle class of the early twentieth century was composed of different social elements. It brought together old gentry families, such as the de la Warrs, who had traditionally governed the country, with a new political class from urban and industrial backgrounds. Stanley Baldwin was emblematic of such men, the product of a Black Country iron-founding dynasty who became prime minister in 1923 and remained a dominant figure in politics until his resignation from government in 1937.[4] The political class was closely linked by marriage and financial interests to business, to dynasties like the Courtaulds who ran the major firms in the new corporate economy. Big businessmen and politicians in turn mixed in London's 'high society' with leading figures in the arts, like Malcolm Sargent and the playwright Noël Coward. In the upper middle class politics, business and culture were conjoined in a complex web of interrelationship. Yet the ascendancy of the upper middle class as 'social leaders and public persons' was to be relatively brief. After the Second World War the group began to disintegrate under the effects of economic competition, rising taxation and the challenge to a traditional order of authority represented by the post-war politics of Labour.

The story of the rise and fall of the upper middle class can be exemplified in the history of a family, the Courtaulds, whose giant firm was a significant feature in the industrial landscape of

Britain for most of the twentieth century. Of course, no single family can be expected to embody all the changes affecting a social group over a long historical period. But the Courtauld family illustrates to an unusual degree the characteristics of upper middle-class England between 1920 and 1960: the possession of wealth allied to a certain inherent puritanism, the power of position linked to an ethic of *noblesse oblige*. Despite being the equivalent of multimillionaires at today's values, the Courtaulds never ceased to think of themselves as essentially middle-class. As George Courtauld, one of the last family members to work in the firm, put it: 'My family have always been middle-class. "Middle-class" is slightly disparaging in a way because anything middle sounds mediocre and dour, but I must say we're not aristocrats, though some of the female members of the family married into the aristocracy, and we're not working-class, though I resent the term "working-class" because it suggests that other people don't work … So we're basically a middle-class family who have always managed to have the right touch.'[5] In the history of the Courtauld family we can see reflected the major social changes that affected the powerful in twentieth-century England. Their story tells us much about the changing fortunes of the upper middle class as a whole, about wealth, leadership and the values and modes of behaviour associated with them.

COURTAULDS AND THE GROWTH OF
THE CORPORATE ECONOMY

Like many of the manufacturing dynasties of Britain's industrial revolution, the economic capital of the Courtauld family was built up over generations; there was no sudden 'rags to riches' transformation in their fortunes. They came to England as Huguenots from seventeenth-century France, fleeing religious persecution but already with a place in trade. George Courtauld recounted the family story: 'We came over as reasonably well-off ship-owners, mariners, from the Ile d'Oléron. We had a hundred years of being very successful silversmiths and then we went into textiles and generally did very well in that. We seem to have had the golden touch.' By the nineteenth century the Courtaulds had established themselves as a major force in the textile industry, the lead sector of Britain's industrialisation, with mills in a number of Essex towns: 'Basically, Courtaulds had made its money by mourning crape, which was the black crape with silk which everybody wore. We had pretty much the monopoly and luckily for us Queen Victoria's husband [Albert] died which meant she went into black for forty years or so. This meant Britain went into black which meant the empire went into black – a third of the world was wearing black and every time there was a funeral the coffin was draped in it, the horses were, the door knobs, and it was all made locally in Halstead, Braintree and Bocking.'[6]

By the late Victorian period Samuel Courtauld and Co. was the largest manufacturer of silk crape in the world and still a private family firm. In the first two decades of the twentieth century, however, the firm was to undergo a series of dramatic changes. In 1904 Samuel Courtauld and Co. followed the example of many of the larger firms in textiles and engineering and became a public company with shareholders and a board of directors. It needed to do so in order to raise the capital to start up a new line of production in viscose spinning, a process of artificial silk manufacture for which Courtaulds had bought the English rights. A year later, the firm opened a major new works at Coventry, producing viscose yarn by chemical processes. With this step, Courtaulds became a major chemicals as well as textile manufacturer. In 1911 the first branch in the United States, the American Viscose Company (AVC), was opened in Pennsylvania. The result was meteoric expansion: between 1908 and 1920 company profits increased almost twentyfold to over £2 million per annum. In the words of its historian, 'the sound but unexciting Essex silk business with its decaying crape trade had become easily the largest silk producer in the world'.[7]

But even this success was dwarfed by the astonishing

expansion of the 'man-made' fibre, rayon, between the wars. As a term 'rayon' came into use in the mid-1920s; it designated all synthetic yarns made from a cellulose base, including what had previously been called 'artificial silk'.[8] According to Courtaulds' most recent historian, it was the source of 'one of the greatest industrial booms in recent history' and in Britain it was synonymous with Courtaulds.[9] The rise of rayon was in large measure attributable to changes in women's fashion from the early 1920s, notably the trend to shorter skirts. In 1919 the hem of women's skirts was six inches above the ground; in 1920 it went to twelve inches, in 1925 to eighteen inches. By 1927 the hemline had reached knee-height, where it remained. Consequently, stockings came more and more into vogue and by 1922 silk or rayon replaced the traditional black cotton variety.[10] Rayon stockings were a third of the price of silk and, though still expensive, this brought them within the range of the majority of women, not just the well-off. Rayon was used to produce a whole new and affordable range of women's clothes, including underwear such as 'cami-knickers'. As a magazine proclaimed in 1936, 'silk stockings and dainty underwear are no longer the privilege of the wealthy'.[11] These were lines in which Courtaulds were market leaders; as George Courtauld bluntly put it, the firm was identified with 'frocks and knickers'. The effects on the firm of the move into rayon production were, again, dramatic. Between 1921 and 1940 the company's production of rayon increased fourteenfold so that by the latter date the firm produced 70 per cent of total UK output, while the numbers it employed in Britain rose from 3,000 to over 18,000.[12] Moreover, Courtaulds owned or had a stake in textile, chemical and rayon firms in a whole range of overseas countries, including the United States, Canada, France, Germany, Italy and India. As a result, between 1910 and 1939 the company was transformed into a new type of enterprise, a multinational, multipurpose industrial giant.

Courtaulds was not the only firm to undergo this kind of transformation in the first third of the twentieth century. The

1920s and 1930s saw the emergence of a series of large-scale
industrial combines, such as Unilever, Imperial Chemical Industries (ICI) and Imperial Tobacco, which increasingly dominated
the British and imperial economy. The rise of the large corporation, which Courtaulds exemplified, was part of a number of
fundamental changes identified with the creation of a 'corporate
economy'. These changes included the decline of family-based
ownership and control of businesses, an increase in average firm
size and the introduction of more bureaucratic forms of
company organisation and management.[13] The growth of the
corporate economy had long-term consequences for the composition and outlook of the middle classes. In the first place it
occurred simultaneously with the decline of the wealth and
power of the landed aristocracy. During and after the First World
War rising taxation of the super-rich and the dwindling prof-
itability of agriculture resulted in the sale and break-up of many
of the old landed estates; the golden age of the British aristocracy
was over.[14] The wealth and political influence of the peerage was
still considerable, but it was no longer exceptional. Brewers and
food retailers, together with cotton, steel and chemical magnates,
joined landowners in the ranks of the very rich, and peers were
forced to sit alongside lawyers and businessmen in parliament,
government and Cabinet. All the leaders of the Conservative
party between the wars, Andrew Bonar Law, Stanley Baldwin and
Neville Chamberlain, were the heirs of industrial dynasties.[15]
Aristocracy was overtaken by plutocracy and wealth succeeded
birth as the organising principle of power in Britain, though in
practice the two remained closely related. After 1918 land ceased
to be the sole or even necessarily the main source of income for
what had long been called the 'landed' nobility and gentry.
Instead, those peers who were able to do so hastened to find
themselves directorships on the boards of insurance companies,
banks and industrial firms. By 1923, it has been estimated, 272
peers held directorships in over 700 public companies.[16]

   The decline of landed power was one important by-product

of the growth of the corporate economy. But the main change
was in the character of business itself. For most of the nineteenth
century the basic unit of economic activity was the family firm.
Ownership and control, as well as the day-to-day running of the
business, remained in the hands of the male members of the
extended employer family – uncles, cousins and brothers-in-law
as well as fathers and sons. From the 1880s, however, amalgama-
tion and, above all, the spread of the limited liability company
began to loosen the hold of the employer family on the individual firm.[17] Family influence diminished as power was transferred
to shareholders, increasingly in the form of institutions, such as
banks and insurance companies, rather than private individuals.
Family control was replaced by a more impersonal board of
directors, the most important of whom now tended to be professional managers. This occurred earliest and fastest in the most
advanced sectors of the economy, such as textiles and engineering, and among the largest firms. In the 1920s the management of
new giant corporations like Unilever and Morris Motors passed
from family hands into those of career managers.[18]

All these trends were apparent in the development of Courtaulds. In 1904, as we have seen, Samuel Courtauld and Co. was
converted from a private to a public limited company. Outwardly, there appeared to be little immediate change. Half the
new stocks and shares were offered to the public for the first time,
but the board of directors remained the same, with family
members, Samuel Augustine and George Courtauld, alongside
other industrialists such as the Nettlefolds, members of a Birmingham engineering dynasty. Change there was, however: as in
other enterprises, 'going public' reduced the ownership and
control of the family significantly over time. By 1913 the Courtauld family owned only 32.5 per cent of the company's
holdings, the rest being divided between the other directors and,
to a smaller extent, public shareholders.[19] After the inter-war
years the balance of power tilted further away from the family
and the board. The current George Courtauld perceptively

observed: 'As time went by the family lost its influence and when ICI tried to take us over in 1962 the family by then only owned 4.5 per cent of the shares, the Church of England and the Pru[dential] 10 per cent each. They were the big shareholders. So I was brought up as a child to think Courtaulds was a family business, but it wasn't.'[20] Family control over management of the firm was simultaneously weakened. Two non-family members, Henry Greenwood Tetley and Thomas Latham, were made managing directors of the new company in 1904 and took charge of the most dynamic branch of Courtaulds production, viscose, which was responsible for the meteoric growth of the company during the first two decades of the twentieth century. They represented early types of the professional manager, the non-owning, salaried, career businessman. Tetley had been brought into Courtaulds in 1893 from Lister and Co., a leading Bradford textile firm, to oversee the development of new lines of production; Latham joined a year later as head salesman. Tetley and Latham provided the firm with strategic direction, entrepreneurship and financial acumen after 1904. By contrast, the Courtauld family members were sidelined. George Courtauld III and his son, Samuel Augustine, had opposed the public flotation of the company and thereafter Samuel Augustine confined himself to managing the decaying crape branch in Essex. Between 1921 and 1946 his cousin, Samuel Courtauld IV, was to act as chairman of the company, presiding over its most spectacular phase of growth, but he was the last member of the family to hold this role. In the first half of the twentieth century the history of Courtaulds reflected the decline of the family firm and the rise of the modern corporate enterprise, with its diverse business interests, board of directors, professional managers and institutional backers.

The upper middle class that took shape in the first half of the twentieth century was shaped by the rise of the corporate economy. The complexity, diversity and interconnection which marked the new 'impersonal capitalism' had their corollary in the growing mobility of the well-off, the openness of 'high society' to new forms of wealth and the blurring of divisions between business, professions and government.[21] Corporate capitalism might be more impersonal than the older family-based variety, but it generated massive fortunes for the individuals and families who directed it. Between the wars the Courtaulds enjoyed wealth on a hitherto unimagined scale. Mollie Montgomerie, later Lady Butler, who married Samuel Augustine's son August in the 1930s, saw the Courtaulds as 'people to whom money was no object'. David Murdoch, curator of the Courtauld Institute, established by Samuel in 1931, concurred: 'They lived well, the directors of major companies in those days, company style was lavish.'[22] Not all sections of the upper middle class, to be sure, could attain such heights of affluence. Professional groups such as higher civil servants, senior army officers and lawyers, who might consider themselves on a social par with bankers or industrialists, earned only a fraction of their income and typically left modest amounts at death.[23] Characterised by significant disparities of income and capital, the upper middle class remained small; one study published in 1949 estimated that it comprised no more than 6 per cent of the population.[24] Nevertheless, all the social and occupational groups included within the ambit of the upper middle class considered themselves firmly marked off from those below them in the social order. In the words of Lady Butler, 'before the [second] war there was a much bigger divide between the so-called gents and the lower classes'.[25] Between the wars the upper middle class enjoyed a golden age, based on substantial wealth and income, the power of command and a remarkably cohesive set of assumptions about status, duty and social behaviour.

THE CALL TO DUTY

One characteristic shared by men and women of the upper middle class was power over others. This power was exerted in many different forms. It included power exercised by politicians over the electorate, colonial governors and administrators over native populations, higher civil servants over their departments and employers over their workforce, often extending to many thousands of women and men. At a more routine level power also meant command of servants of all kinds: domestic servants, butlers, grooms, gardeners, as well as local tradespeople who were frequently treated as an extension of the servant class. There were continuous complaints of a shortage of servants in the inter-war years, as we saw in Chapter Three, but the 'problem' hardly affected the upper middle class, many of whom continued to live in the grand manner. Vivian Buckley enjoyed the hospitality of the rich in Britain and the United States in the 1920s and 1930s and recorded their lives in photographs. While working in the City of London he was often invited to weekend country house parties. 'Occasionally I stayed in very grand houses with at least thirty guests and almost as many servants', he recalled. 'Once when I was getting out of my small car the butler greeted me with the words, "Will your manservant be coming later?"' On learning that he would not, the butler responded, 'In that case, George the third footman will have to look after you'.[26] This power of command encouraged a high degree of authoritarian-ism and subordination in the relationship between employers and employed. In the Victorian period the Courtauld mills in Essex were dominated by the patriarchal figure of Samuel III, who automatically dismissed young women when they became preg-nant and likewise fired any mill worker who dared to strike. Relations between employer and workforce were conducted in a strict framework of paternalism and deference. In return for employment, housing and welfare, factory employers like the Courtaulds demanded unquestioning obedience from their workers, which they often received to a remarkable degree.[27] George Courtauld vividly recollected the war memorials he saw as a young man in the woollen and worsted mills in Yorkshire, 'when the son of the mill owner had marched out and all the weavers, spinners, dyers and combers had marched out after him into the trenches and the whole lot had been wiped out at once.

Horrific, but they all went out drums beating, colours flying and singing patriotic songs.'[28]

There were, however, less harsh sides to the exercise of power and other ways in which authority was legitimised. Many in the upper middle class subscribed to the ethic of *noblesse oblige*, the idea that wealth and status carried a responsibility to act morally and to demonstrate care towards those under their authority. With privilege – so ran the upper middle-class ideal – went duty, personal self-discipline and public service. Such ideas may originally have been identified with the aristocracy, but by the early twentieth century they were as likely to be found in the factory or charitable institution as on the landed estate. The concept of *noblesse oblige* can appear complacent, self-serving and hypocritical; it upheld even as it softened the realities of social inequality. But as an idealised code it informed much of upper middle-class behaviour in business, as well as in government, the professions and philanthropy.

An important foundation of this ideal lay in the concept of discipline, and specifically self-discipline, early instilled through school and family. The public schools for boys and girls specialised in this aspect of upbringing.[29] Despite his family's strong connections to Cambridge and academic life, Sir Adam Butler, the son of Rab Butler and grandson of Samuel Courtauld IV, considered the primary attributes of public school to have been the inculcation of the skills of leadership and self-control, not the stimulation of intellectual or creative abilities. Lady Mayhew, wife of the Labour politician Sir Christopher Mayhew, similarly recalled the overarching emphasis on service and self-sacrifice in her education at Cheltenham Ladies' College in the 1930s:

> As far as Cheltenham went, the thing that was dinned into us … was the ideal of service. And always it was very spiritual. On Dorothea Beale's memorial, which you still see there, [it says] 'do not think of this life as discontinuous with the eternal'. This was a very strong ethos when I was there, the

ethos that if you were fortunate enough to be there and have this sort of education, it was up to you to use those gifts for the good of other people.[30]

Moral discipline as part of an ideal of *noblesse oblige* was emphasised if anything even more strongly in the family context, to be impressed upon the young by parents and the old. Charlie Courtauld, a successful journalist of a younger generation, broke with family tradition in many respects, but the moral element remained from his upbringing:

> I can't overemphasise the extent to which family gives you a moral code. There are several occasions I can remember when my father took me aside and told me his belief that bigotry was the worst attitude of mind to have. Because it's very easy if you go to the sort of privileged school I went to, to be arrogant, to be élitist, to be snobbish … Family do tend to give you sorts of rules and tell you that it's not only disgusting and unfair to be élitist, it's actually not the done thing.[31]

Childhood in the upper middle class tended to be a spartan affair, whatever the wealth and luxury of the surroundings. Sir Adam Butler describes his upbringing as strongly marked by the idea of personal discipline instilled by his mother, Sydney Courtauld, which he attributed to her family's Protestant inheritance: 'She was very independent in her thinking and that stems, I think, from that particular stream. The family had to decide whether they were going to stay as Protestant and leave their country [France] which most of them did, and that brings about a certain inner discipline that, I suspect, stayed with the family and has stayed with us.'[32] A streak of puritanism ran through the upper middle class, contrasting with the opulent material circumstances of many such families in the 1920s and 1930s. The Courtaulds were certainly fabulously rich, but they too had strong puritan leanings. According to his wife, August Courtauld cared little for either food or comfort: 'his idea of heaven was to be in a small boat at sea, which is not comfortable'. He could also be very severe: 'The first time I put on lipstick after we married he said "I could divorce you". I was so naïve I didn't realise that it wasn't grounds for divorce.'[33] The personal austerity of Samuel Courtauld IV as chairman of the company between the wars was legendary. He railed at consumerism and 'Americanisation' and denounced advertising as a 'weapon of industrial warfare', 'sheer economic waste for the community'.[34] Such puritanism was not confined to families like the Courtaulds with a background in nineteenth-century Protestant dissent. As late as the 1970s, the Scottish journalist Neal Ascherson could remark on the 'impressive dilapidation' of the English upper middle class, the 'common spectacle of relative austerity in the midst of unrealised wealth'.[35]

The code of *noblesse oblige*, however, required that personal virtue should not be confined to the family and the private sphere but set to work for the public good. A public service ethos was embedded in the family tradition of an important section of the upper middle class, notably those with a reforming instinct. The Empire and, in particular, experience in the Indian civil service was the background of many of the individuals who were instrumental in the major social reforms of the first half of the twentieth century: R. H. Tawney and William Beveridge, the architects of the welfare state, for example, and Rab Butler, who reshaped the system of secondary education. Butler himself claimed that the 'great ambition of my life was to be Viceroy of India'.[36] His son, Sir Adam Butler, saw public service as part of the family inheritance: 'The Butlers were academics, schoolmasters and then very much serving – public servants I suppose is the right word. Particularly in my great-grandfather's generation, two of them were very senior in the Indian civil service – that would be very much in line with the family tradition.' The entry of Rab Butler into politics in the 1920s followed naturally from his father's upbringing within this tradition, according to Sir Adam; politics was 'in the family blood' and meant being 'in the service of others first of all'.[37] The upper middle-class ideal of politics as a form of public service transcended party divisions. Sir Christopher Mayhew came from a well-to-do middle-class family and was educated at a public school, Haileybury. He joined the Labour party in the 1930s, stood for a Norfolk seat at the 1945 election and was made parliamentary under-secretary to the foreign minister, Ernest Bevin, in the post-war Labour administration. He was later knighted for his services to the state. According to his wife, commitment to justice was Mayhew's driving instinct: 'He was not personally ambitious. This was entirely true, it was not the most important thing. If he felt that things were unjust or unfair, to fight for them, that's what drove him.'[38] While such men were 'educated to rule', in Lady Mayhew's phrase, their behaviour was strongly shaped by an ethos of public duty. Jonathan Charkham, employed in the Public Appointments Unit during the 1970s to enlist the 'great and the good' on government bodies, felt this sense of duty to be all-pervasive in his childhood: 'You didn't need a definition of duty, it was surrounding you.'[39]

For both women and men philanthropy was a natural extension of *noblesse oblige*. Lady Mayhew remembers her husband's mother as 'extremely active in the poorer districts of North Kensington. She ran a girls' club there; this again was part of the ethical approach of the family.' Her husband's father, a highly successful accountant, likewise worked with the Red Cross in the First World War and was knighted for his contribution to it.[40] Conventionally, philanthropic activity was carried out through numerous small-scale activities: clubs and societies, garden fêtes, home-visiting and the like. But on occasions public bequests could be spectacular. According to the social historian Harold Perkin, through their charitable trusts the industrialists Lord Nuffield and Andrew Carnegie, the expatriate Scot, gave more to British universities between the wars than the British government.[41] Equally, as chairman of Courtaulds in the 1920s and 1930s Samuel IV gave £50,000 to the Tate Gallery and his own personal collection of Impressionist paintings, his house in Portman Square and a further £70,000 to found the Courtauld Institute of Art in London.[42] On his engagement to Samuel's daughter Sydney in 1925, Rab Butler recalled seeing for the first time the celebrated works of art hung on the walls of Portman Square: 'Sam Courtauld took Sydney and me aside and said "I hope you will both understand if I give this house and its contents to the nation"', a proposal with which they 'fully agreed'.[43] Art was yoked to the public good. In the words of Sir Adam Butler, it was 'something which raises you above yourself and Samuel was determined to ensure that these paintings were on show, given effectively to the nation'.[44]

These ideals were as much part of the world of big business as they were of the liberal professions and government. At Courtaulds public duty was balanced with private profit and industrial relations were conducted within an ethical framework. The chairman, Samuel Courtauld, pronounced in 1930: 'Courtaulds ... have always stood for conciliation, agreement and ordered growth.' At the annual meetings of shareholders, according to George Courtauld, Samuel would take the opportunity to 'lecture those who had bothered to come and listen on the ideals and ethics of industry and then give them rather a small amount of money and send them off happy'. During the Second World War he became well-known for the remark that 'employers should seriously consider the quality of the person who left the factory gate in the evening, meaning they had a responsibility towards that person, that quality should be every bit as good as the product itself'.[45] There were, of course, limits to this benevolence. Like other large firms, Courtaulds suffered their share of strikes between the wars and refused to recognise trade unions in the company's rayon plants till the later 1930s. Significantly, the attempt by Samuel to appoint a trade union representative on the board in 1942 was successfully vetoed by the directors. Nevertheless, a strong vein of paternalistic concern ran through company policy towards its expanding workforce. In the midst of the slump in the early 1930s Courtaulds kept its textile workforce employed at mills in Halifax and elsewhere, despite the financial losses incurred. Welfare provision was stepped up and after Samuel's death in 1947 Gatcombe Park, his country house, was transformed into a convalescent home for the company's workforce. By the 1940s Courtaulds could claim to be in the vanguard of the welfare paternalism pioneered before and after the First World War by large companies like Rowntrees, Cadburys and Boots.[46]

It is easy to idealise paternalism and public service, to see them as a reflection of purely personal and moral qualities rather than as products of particular kinds of social and economic relationships. But for all that it was rooted in humanitarian empathy, *noblesse oblige* was also a product of power; it was a luxury that only the rich and secure could afford. Fine gestures were not an option for small businessmen in the 1920s and 1930s, struggling to keep going in the midst of the most severe international recession of the twentieth century, let alone for workers whose wages had been cut and who feared for their jobs. The ethic of duty and public service with which the upper middle class was identified was predicated on a fundamental inequality of power. Gestures of concern, however well-meaning, were always *de haut en bas* and inevitably served to reinforce a relationship of paternalism and deference, authority and dependence. They confirmed the power of the upper middle class at the very moment they proclaimed its disinterested generosity.

STYLES OF LEADERSHIP

The characteristics of social leadership and personal integrity found their embodiment in the archetypal figures of the 'lady' and the 'gentleman'. As ideal types the lady and the gentleman were essentially the product of the Victorian era, but the charisma attached to them in English society reached its peak between the wars. In part, this reflected the respect accorded to seniority at the period, as the historian Raphael Samuel observed: 'Age was not only more powerful than youth, it was also, in some sort, more glamorous. The matinée idol was, by modern standards, middle-aged, a man with grown-up children (like Gerald du Maurier) ... Likewise the idealised English lady, represented on stage by the middle-aged Gladys Cooper, was a mature beauty.' It was in the 1920s and 1930s that the term 'old boy' became a favoured form of address among middle-class, and especially upper middle-class, men.[47] 'Lady' and 'gentleman' were appellations that all sections of the middle classes respected and admired. According to Lady Mayhew, they signified 'civilised, educated people'. Much sought after, they were nevertheless conferred by others, not by the individuals concerned, as George Courtauld pointed out: 'It would be very conceited to call oneself a gentleman and also slightly pompous. It would be nice to be called a gentleman, but certainly one wouldn't call oneself one. But one hopes that one is a gentleman.'[48]

One of the more important functions of these social identities was to help integrate the various groups that comprised the upper middle class, with backgrounds in land, finance, industry and the professions. The purpose of the public schools, like Roedean and Benenden for girls or Eton and Harrow for boys, was precisely to create 'ladies' and 'gentlemen' who could take on leadership roles in the household, on the estate, in the company or in government and administration. Accounts written before and immediately after the Second World War emphasised how the public schools promoted a 'certain freemasonry' of the rich and powerful. For social rather than educational reasons, so it was argued, such schools had 'an implicit lien on most of the key points in our national life'.[49] By the inter-war period, as with *noblesse oblige*, the insignia of gentility had little to do with older aristocratic ideals of birth or title. Rugby-educated, high-minded and with a commanding presence, Samuel Courtauld could be considered the epitome of the gentleman, but he declined a peerage in 1937 and never sought a life of aristocratic ease. Other developments reinforced the dominance of the lady and the gentleman as ideal types and accelerated the process of social integration among the upper middles. One of the more important was the spread of 'received pronunciation' as an accent that distinguished them from the lower middle and the working classes, who generally continued to speak with regional accents and to use dialect phrases. The historian Ross McKibbin has noted how even before the First World War what became known as Received Standard English was synonymous with upper middle-class usage. Pronunciation followed phonetic spelling (whereas, traditionally, aristocratic pronunciation was idiosyncratic as in 'huntin' and shootin" and the use of terms such as 'ain't'); likewise with vocabulary, 'in areas of contention upper middle-class usage became polite usage'.[50] 'Received pronunciation' (or RP) became the accent of authority between the wars, of the public schools, Oxford and Cambridge universities, the army, the law and the British Broadcasting Corporation, which adopted RP from its establishment in 1926. Crucially, RP was an accent that could be easily appropriated by those who entered the upper middle class rather than were born into it. Lady Mayhew was brought up by aunts who were teachers in Sheffield in the 1920s, won a scholarship to Cheltenham Ladies' College and eventually worked in the Foreign Office. In the course of this social journey she lost her Yorkshire accent and acquired a new way of speaking: 'If I try to talk Sheffield where I grew up, that would be artificial. Because it's just imperceptibly and unconsciously gone. Maybe the Foreign Office had something to do with it, I don't know.'[51] Like the public schools, received pronunciation both reflected the formation of a national upper middle class after 1920 and helped to cement it as a group. 'The "educated" English accent is today one of those intangible links which bind the upper middle classes together', a sociological study of the 1940s breezily affirmed; 'many a too-eager social climber has been summed up (and perhaps dismissed) with the cryptic comment: "N.O.C.D." (Not Our Class, Dear).'[52]

The upper middle class was therefore the creation of certain unifying processes, of common education, accent and norms of behaviour. But there were also a variety of ways of demonstrating social leadership and of enacting the roles of the lady and the gentleman. During the 1920s and 1930s the Courtaulds exemplified certain of these ways of behaving within a single family. Particular individuals and branches of the family embodied, often strikingly, different upper middle-class styles of leadership.

'High society' was represented by Stephen Courtauld and his wife Ginny, who were known as one of the most glamorous couples in inter-war London. Stephen was Samuel's brother, but was not involved in the family firm. Ginny was reputed to be a descendant of Vlad the Impaler, 'part Hungarian, part Romanian and Italian'.[53] Stephen and Ginny were renowned for the extravagant parties they gave at their house in Grosvenor Square, with celebrated guests from the composer Stravinsky to the socialite and diarist 'Chips' Channon. Lady Butler recalled Ginny as a society hostess with awe: 'she was marvellous at mixing people'.[54] But the main project undertaken by Stephen and Ginny Courtauld was the restoration of a tumbledown mansion, Eltham Palace in south London. Drawing on the enormous wealth generated by the family firm, they transformed a medieval ruin into a model of 1930s taste, lavishly furnished in the most up-to-date art deco manner. Both partners contributed to the design of the Palace – 'it was fifty-fifty between Ginny's extravagance and Stephen's rather Spartan simplicity' – and it became a social centre for the Courtauld clan as well as for London 'society' in the 1930s. Picnics, swimming and dinner parties were all part of the grand style encouraged by Ginny, whose skill as a hostess was matched only by her reputation for unconventional behaviour. 'She was very vivacious and very eccentric – in those days if you were very rich you could be as eccentric as you wanted', commented George Courtauld. 'I remember there was a banquet given in her honour and she called for a finger bowl. The call went down all the line of footmen, "finger bowl for Lady Courtauld, finger bowl for Lady Courtauld". Finally a finger bowl arrived for Lady Courtauld and she whipped out her teeth, rinsed them in the finger bowl and jammed her teeth back in.'[55]

The society lifestyle led by Stephen and Ginny Courtauld, with its taste for the modern and the extravagant, was one way of expressing one's social status as part of the upper middle class between the wars. The flaunting of wealth was acceptable so long as it was done with taste; the flouting of conventions was admissible so long as it was merely a flamboyant gesture, not a challenge to the accepted order of things. Stephen's brother Samuel adopted a rather different way of displaying his gentlemanly status, his role as a social leader and public person. Samuel's chairmanship of Courtaulds and his position in the world of business gave him great wealth and personal authority, as well as a high public profile. Like Stephen and Ginny, Samuel and his wife Elizabeth sought social recognition, but they were more interested in culture than in high society. As David Murdoch, curator of the Courtauld Institute, comments, 'When they bought the house in Portman Square, they were obviously wanting to establish themselves in London society. But it is surely interesting that the branch of London society that they wanted to establish themselves in was not Westminster politics, was not great aristocratic events, it was actually the outgrowth of the Cambridge Unitarian tradition as represented in London in the Bloomsbury group.'[56] For Samuel, gentlemanliness and social leadership were not a matter simply of the accumulation of wealth, but of the acquisition of culture in its various guises. In the 1920s this involved the building up of the Courtauld collection of Impressionist art. Sir Adam Butler recalls the great significance of art in Samuel's life:

He had this tremendous love of art, of paintings, and he talked about that being the biggest influence in his life. Now that for a successful industrialist is a remarkable thing to say. So he collected this wonderful set of paintings, Impressionists and many others, over a comparatively short period of his life. But it was

his collection, he would open the crates and he would hang
the paintings on the walls. That was a real joy to him.[57]

For her part, Elizabeth – 'a formidable Irishwoman' known to
family and friends as Lil – became a leading patron of music,
an active supporter of the Royal Opera House, Covent Garden,
and founder of the Courtauld-Sargent concerts in London in
1929.[58]

In fact, 1929 was to be a turning-point in the lives of both
Elizabeth and Samuel Courtauld. The Wall Street Crash of that
year put financial pressure on the firm, and during a holiday in
Canada Elizabeth was diagnosed with the cancer from which
she was to die in 1931. Elizabeth's death seems to have set off a
protracted crisis in Samuel. He gave the house in Portman
Square and a substantial part of his art collection to found the
Courtauld Institute. He continued to direct the firm with no less
vigour than before, but he virtually ceased collecting and began
instead to engage in creative activity himself.[59] Through a protracted process of self-reflection, according to David Murdoch,
Samuel Courtauld began to free himself from 'the depth of a
repressed upper middle-class psychology' and to emerge as
'much more self-expressive, a person who sits down and writes
poems, a person who writes long essays and autobiographical
fragments in a painful effort to explain the things that are inside
himself'.[60] Culture came to denote not only the impulse to
collect beautiful works and objects, but also, following Victorian
example, a means to self-knowledge and spirituality. In this
regard, the path that Samuel came to pursue was the path of the
cultivated Christian gentleman for whom social leadership is
complemented by the personal search for beauty, self-
knowledge and spiritual truth – the quest for self-perfection, in
Matthew Arnold's formulation.[61]

Another version of the gentlemanly ideal was the adventurer
or explorer, exemplified in the Courtauld family by Samuel's and
Stephen's cousin, August. Given the popularity of tales of Empire

and derring-do in the first half of the twentieth century, such a figure had a strong appeal, especially for boys. George Courtauld recalled: 'All the other family were in rather boring things like Courtaulds or farming and my ideal was the explorer. My cousin August was my ideal ... I admired him enormously – he was a very nice, gentle gentleman.'[62] August was famous for the heroic resolution he displayed on the 1930 British expedition to the Arctic, when, in appalling weather conditions, he volunteered to remain on the Greenland ice cap while other members of the expedition returned to base camp to replenish supplies and equipment. As events turned out, August remained alone in the tent for five months, entombed in snow and with his meagre rations rapidly diminishing. His wife, Mollie, recounted the story: 'On 5 May 1931 his primus [stove] gave its last gasp. Within an hour he heard an extraordinary noise outside and it was the rescue party who had found the station. But do you know, during that time ... he never once thought that he would not be rescued. He was perfectly certain that God doesn't mean me to leave my bones on the ice cap – the most amazing faith.'[63] August's calmness and courage in the face of appalling adversity captured the public imagination. Like Scott of the Antarctic, Sir Ernest Shackleton and, later, Sir Edmund Hillary, he came to exemplify the unassuming heroism of the gentleman explorer.

This spirit of adventure was carried over into the early stages of the Second World War, when the Courtauld firm and family played a central part in the establishment of the Special Operations Executive, a secret organisation designed to undertake espionage and sabotage behind enemy lines in Europe.[64] Members of the family, including August and George Courtauld senior, became active in the organisation. Stephen and Ginny made Eltham Palace a centre for intelligence operations and many of those who were employed at Courtaulds' head office in London were transferred to work at the headquarters of the SOE in Baker Street. George Courtauld junior indicates that their involvement was, initially at least, inspired by the romance of the gentleman adventurer: 'My father said really we were all brought up on Bulldog Drummond and John Buchan and we thought of ourselves as a gang of amateurs, but we were all pretty naïve.'[65] 'Gentlemen behaving in an ungentlemanly manner' – so ran one description of the SOE and its activities. It accurately captures the imaginative hold of an ideal of gentlemanly adventure and heroism on the English upper middle class during the first half of the twentieth century.

Stephen and Ginny, Samuel and August Courtauld represent different ways in which the figures of the 'lady' and the 'gentleman' were personified in the upper middle class and the different styles in which social leadership was enacted. Such ways of behaving were not always charming or beneficent; they could easily descend into snobbishness and pomposity. At Courtaulds, Samuel was succeeded as chairman in 1946 by John Hanbury-Williams, who, in the words of the firm's historian, was 'a snob, liked titles, married a Byzantine Princess, and relished Court appointments', while remaining proudly ignorant of the technical and personnel requirements of the company over which he presided. As chairman Hanbury-Williams insisted on being referred to as 'governor' of Courtaulds, echoing the role of governor of the Bank of England, the most prestigious institution in the British business firmament. Yet even under Samuel's chairmanship in the 1930s, the company's board of directors was divided between 'gentlemen', public school and Oxbridge educated, who dominated decision-making, and 'players', those who had risen through the company ranks on technical and managerial merit, but who nevertheless generally occupied a subordinate position on the board.[66] Snobbery was not the only vice of the gentlemanly order. Alongside it there ran a deep strain of misogyny, epitomised by the bar that precluded married women from working in business and the professions and the frequently expressed distaste for the 'brisk voice of feminine authority'.[67] The power of the upper middle class was embedded in codes of exclusion that could seem brutal and arbitrary to those who had to suffer them.

Yet perhaps the most enduring impression of the upper middle class between the wars is that of the largely unquestioned assumption of leadership and authority. Such people saw themselves (and were seen by many outside their class) as born to rule not merely Britain itself, but the great tracts of the world that made up the British Empire at its height – within the Courtauld clan, Rab Butler's father and uncle were both governors of provinces in India.[68] As the historian Rick Trainor has put it, the English upper middle class 'were confident in themselves and in their own social group. They also had great confidence in the institutions of the country. They were worried, obviously, by economic downturns, but there was still an assumption by most people that these were temporary interruptions to Britain's very strong world economic and political position. After all, this is a country where in the mid-nineteenth century it was taken as a matter of course that it was the most powerful economic and political power in the world – and these people were raised with those assumptions.'[69] But in the aftermath of the Second World War these verities no longer appeared self-evident. Neither the power of a nation, nor that of a class, could be so confidently assumed. Between the later 1940s and the 1960s the power and distinctive ethos of the British upper middle class began to crumble.

POST-1945: DECLINE AND FALL

There were few who foresaw this fall from grace when the war ended in May 1945. 'Society' events soon resumed their normal course despite the climate of 'austerity' and the upper middle class was often described in post-war surveys as continuing to exert disproportionate social influence, locally and nationally.[70] But changes were afoot whose effects on the rich and powerful were felt during as well as after the war. According to David

Mayhew, the war itself was 'a big mixer', which had greatly contributed to the socialist views of his father, Sir Christopher Mayhew:

> He wrote how before the war he felt this acute consciousness of having nothing in common with the youngsters that his mother would work with in North Kensington. But then the experiences of the war, serving in the British Expeditionary Force and his involvement with the Labour party and so on, went quite a long way to break down some of those divisions, not to make everybody the same obviously, but to make him feel more at ease with people of a very different background.

For the sociologist Colin Bell, no single event in the twentieth century did more to transform Britain's class structure than the Second World War.[71] The most potent symbol of these changes was the surprise victory of the Labour party over Churchill's Conservatives in the 1945 election. For men and women of the upper middle class the consequences of the new, more meritocratic social and political order were soon felt. The creation of the welfare state, characterised by the National Health Service and social security for all, meant that the scope for philanthropy and public benefaction of the pre-war variety was greatly reduced. Servant-holding, once an emblem of middle-class status, also declined as the long-feared 'servant problem' became reality: the proportion of families with one or more household servants fell from almost 5 per cent in 1931 to 1 per cent by 1951. Most critically of all, taxation began to bite more sharply into earned and unearned wealth. The rate of income tax for those on annual incomes of between £700 and £2000, described in contemporary surveys as 'upper middle-class', rose from 9.3 per cent in 1938 to 22.7 per cent in 1947. Still more stringently, the 'supertax' on the very rich increased from 6d (2½ p) in the pound in 1909 to 9s 6d (47½ p) in 1945.[72] The material foundations of the way of life of the inter-war upper middle class, associated with mansions, servants and conspicuous consumption, were rapidly eroded under the post-war Labour government.

On the political and economic stage, too, the British upper middle class was faced with a series of challenges to its leadership after 1945. The pre-war generation had been brought up to believe unquestioningly in Britain's world role as an economic and imperial power. Among an older generation of colonialists Empire might continue to be regarded as Britain's 'grand destiny', but the reality of post-war imperial politics was of steady, inglorious retreat. One after another, British colonies gained independence: India in 1947, Burma in 1948, Sudan in 1956, Nigeria in 1960, Jamaica, Trinidad and Tobago in 1962, Kenya in 1963, and so on. By the late 1960s the British Empire was to all intents and purposes dead as a political reality, even if it was to enjoy an extensive afterlife in the national imagination.

At the same time, it became increasingly difficult to sustain the pretence of economic power. Though the British economy recovered after 1945 and became sufficiently buoyant to underpin the 'affluence' which replaced 'austerity' in the 1950s, productivity and growth rates were sluggish by international standards. British manufacturing, in particular, lagged behind that of the most dynamic post-war economies, the United States, Germany and Japan.[73] The organisation of business continued to change, too, in favour of increased corporate concentration, the replacement of owner-employers by professional managers and growing investment in manufacturing by outside institutions such as insurance companies and building societies. All these shifts raised a question. What was the role of the old upper middle class, once the social, imperial and economic institutions over which it had presided had either dissolved or changed out of recognition? In 1950s Britain the upper middle class with its ideals of duty, service and automatic leadership appeared increasingly anachronistic. Richard Hoggart, the cultural critic, tells a personal story that is suggestive of the passing of the old order. Hoggart, from a working-class, grammar school background in

Leeds, encountered the foreign editor of the *Financial Times*, Andrew Shonfield, at the doors of the BBC in London:

> We were in partner artillery regiments in Italy, side by side, and I got to know him then. I was going to the BBC – it was about 1958, I suppose – and he was coming out. He had the most perfect Balliol accent, you could have put it down with your bread and butter it was so beautiful. He had just done a broadcast on Ireland and he said, 'Ah well, there we are, our lot are going down, your lot are going up with your northern accents'. And in a way he was right.[74]

The changes were reflected in the post-war economic fortunes of Courtaulds. There were signs of things to come as early as 1941, when the firm was forced to relinquish its American subsidiary, AVC, as part of the Lend-Lease agreement between the British and United States governments, designed to support Britain's war effort. At a single stroke, Courtaulds lost its most valuable asset, estimated at $100 million, and Britain its largest piece of industrial property in the USA. After the war had ended, the company never recovered the dynamism or levels of profitability of the previous forty years. Sam Courtauld retired as chairman in 1946 and died a year later. As we have seen, he was replaced by John Hanbury-Williams, whose chairmanship 'verged on the disastrous' according to the firm's historian.[75] By the early 1950s it was clear that the boom in rayon had passed. The company faced increasing competition in foreign markets and the machinery, particularly in its British plants, was now antiquated – in 1945 it was found that 43 per cent of machines in the firm's mills dated from the first two decades of the twentieth century or earlier.[76] From the late 1950s Courtaulds began to diversify, buying up companies, some of which were in related areas of production, like Gossards the bra-makers, while others were in lines such as paint and packaging in which the firm had no previous track-record. Courtaulds remained an industrial giant, but it was an increasingly unwieldy and even ailing giant. It was not wholly surprising, therefore, when in 1962 a bid was launched by ICI to take over Courtaulds. The take-over bid – the largest in British industrial history up to that point – was effectively repulsed by Courtaulds. But the company increasingly appeared to be living on its past, a state of affairs captured in a lampoon of the meaningless pomp and circumstance of the board of directors at this time, written by George Courtauld senior:

The Directors of the Gadarene Manufacturing Company Limited are discovered seated around an oval table. In appearance they are a distinguished body of men, well fed, well groomed, some even smoking cigars. Having assembled, they complain bitterly to each other in low voices about everything. Enter the Chairman. The Board staggers to its feet and for ten minutes stands in profound silence with bowed heads to mark its deep sense of appreciation of the fact that The Monarch has graciously bestowed the Order of the BE on the Chairman Himself. Sir Galahad is a strikingly handsome man, representative of all that was best in [the] England of yesteryear.[77]

From the 1960s Courtaulds entered its final phase, marked by a lengthy decline. As the twentieth century closed, the Courtauld name disappeared into industrial history – it was sold along with the remains of the old textile business to an overseas conglomerate in May 2000. For George Courtauld junior its passing was a cause for both sadness and anger: 'Suddenly we were taken over by a Dutch company, vanished, the biggest textile firm in the world seemed to have gone in a puff of smoke … It needn't have happened, but people were getting complacent, they lacked drive and initiative.'[78]

The Courtauld family's capacity to play the role of social leaders and public persons also diminished in the post-war period. No Courtauld replaced Samuel as chairman of the company after

1946. While members of the family continued to hold places on the board, the leading players were academic scientists, like the Cambridge physicist A. H. Wilson, managing director in the 1950s, and Lord Kearton, a career manager, chairman of Courtaulds and later of British National Oil. In the post-war period the ties between the Courtauld family and the company were increasingly vestigial, a matter of business history rather than of corporate reality. Equally, as we have seen, the extension of the welfare state from the 1940s meant that there were fewer opportunities for the wealthy in general to engage in community leadership and in acts of conspicuous philanthropy. George Courtauld recalls the effects of this shift on his own relatives: 'They saw there was a change, perhaps from the patronising individual doling out of money to things which they liked doing, like building hospitals, having art galleries, to the state doing it instead. I don't think they liked it because it was much more fun being in control of your destiny and maybe even other people's destinies.'[79] Gatcombe Park, the Courtaulds' country house turned convalescent home for employees, was closed down and subsequently sold to the Queen as a home for Princess Anne and Mark Phillips. The old paternalism was in retreat.

In other ways, too, the family began to distance itself from the lifestyles of the 1920s and 1930s. Ginny and Stephen left Eltham Palace following the war, never to return. Instead, they headed for Scotland and then abandoned Britain altogether, settling in Rhodesia. Here on the margins of Empire it was still possible to maintain an ethos of *noblesse oblige*, to mix wealth with leadership and largesse. 'When they went to live in Rhodesia they were enormously good to the native population', Mollie Butler recalled. 'Stephen built a hospital, he built an art gallery, there was a farm where the Africans could learn to farm so that they could look after themselves. They were very fond of the Africans and in those days the Africans were very fond of the whites.'[80] Meanwhile, August, the explorer, died of a degenerative illness in 1959. His widow, Mollie, married Rab Butler, the Conservative politician, whose own wife, Sydney Courtauld, had also recently died. The Courtauld connection lived on in a new partnership that brought great personal happiness.[81] Yet even in the case of the Butlers, marriage was followed soon after by withdrawal from the public limelight. In 1963 Rab Butler was expected to win the party leadership election after the resignation of the Conservative leader and prime minister, Harold Macmillan. Much to the surprise of the press and political opinion, he was defeated by Sir Alec Douglas-Home, an aristocratic outsider. Thereafter, Butler retired from government and re-established family connections with the academic world as Master of Trinity College, Cambridge. In these different ways the Courtauld dynasty drifted out of public life, out of the worlds of big business, politics and high society, in the two decades after 1945. A younger generation of the family confirmed the break with tradition. The journalist Charlie Courtauld was candid about his rejection of class expectations: 'I think there is quite a mental break with the past in my generation. I didn't go to Oxbridge, I didn't join the army, I didn't join the church ... The types of career that were open to upper middle-class boys fifty years ago didn't interest me.' Nor did the gentlemanly ideal of his forebears hold much appeal:

> The connotations, the baggage that 'gentlemen' brings with it tend to be of someone nice ... but beyond niceness they have quite a narrow field of vision, they tend to be very set in their ways, they tend to be very narrow-minded ... There was a belief that what they were doing was either because of something that they had been told by previous generations or something that they had to do to fulfil certain criteria – the way they dressed, the way they speak has all been determined centuries ago. That is something with which I don't particularly feel sympathy.[82]

During the post-war decades, the influence of the upper middle class, epitomised by families like the Courtaulds, visibly waned.

There was no leadership role for them in a society that was becoming more determinedly meritocratic, post-imperial and consumer-driven. Change, of course, was more evident in some quarters than in others. The upper middle class lingered on in the boardrooms of City merchant banks, as well as in the higher reaches of government. Even so, it no longer appeared to manifest the old confident assurance of power and some were quick to extrapolate to the middle class as a whole. 'Are the middle classes doomed?', the socialist Raymond Postgate hopefully enquired in 1949. In certain respects, the valediction was premature.[83] The 1950s and 1960s were to see the revival of middle-class protest on a scale not seen since the early nineteenth century, as we shall see in the next chapter. Moreover, the Conservative party slogan 'you've never had it so good', first aired by the prime minister Harold Macmillan, was importantly a token of the revival of political and consumer confidence among large sections of the middle classes as 'affluence' replaced 'austerity' in the mid- and later 1950s. But resurgence characterised the experience of some sections of the middle classes, not all. For the upper middle class the heyday of wealth and leadership had passed, even if the threads of power were to unravel only slowly during the second half of the twentieth century.

CHAPTER 5

TROUBLEMAKERS

The tradition of protest

One of the stereotyped characters of post-war England is the middle-class liberal with a small 'l', wracked with guilt about having had it easy and keen to assuage his or her conscience. Such characters, captured by cartoonist Posy Simmons in her weekly strip for the *Guardian* over many years, are associated with protest marches, petitions and vegetarianism. They are the sort of people who in the 1980s were described as 'right on' and in the 1990s as 'politically correct'. The notion of middle-class radicalism has often aroused a peculiar antagonism, both from within the middle classes themselves and from outside. This is neatly illustrated by the graffiti scrawled over the title page of one university library's copy of Frank Parkin's book, *Middle-class Radicalism*, published in 1968. Where one reader first wrote 'thank God I'm upper class', another added 'God won't save you when the revolution comes!' and a third accused the title itself of being an oxymoron.[1]

In this chapter we will show that middle-class protest is neither a recent phenomenon nor a passing fad. It has had a long history and an important role in shaping the cultural and political identity of the middle classes. In particular, we will look at the protestors of the 1950s and 1960s in their historical context; at what was familiar about the attitudes of those involved in the various protest movements, and at what was new. At different times over the last two centuries, protest and radicalism have been an essential part of the history of the middle classes. This chapter is about that history.

RADICALS AND DISSENTERS

It would be absurd to claim that the history of protest movements in England is pre-eminently a middle-class history, but it would be equally foolish to deny how deeply rooted radicalism has been in some sections of the English middle class. There are some self-evident explanations for a connection between the two – wealth and financial security allow people to spend time on non-economic pursuits, education and authority give them the confidence to speak out. But the connection between radicalism and particular sections of the middle classes goes far deeper than this, deriving partly from the struggle of the middle classes for power and position and partly from deeply held religious and moral convictions.

We discussed in Chapter One the vital role played by campaigns for political and economic reform and religious freedom in creating a distinctive 'middle-class' identity in England during the first half of the nineteenth century. Many of the traditions of middle-class radicalism derive from this early fight for political recognition and influence. While twentieth-century middle-class protestors often appeared to act from a position of relative security and power, their predecessors in the first part of the nineteenth century were political outsiders in a country still largely run by a territorial aristocracy. In 1821, for instance, Manchester had a population of 32,000, none of whom had the franchise, not even the city's most prosperous merchants and industrialists. That was the year in which a Manchester textile merchant called John Edward Taylor, with some wealthy radical friends, launched a newspaper, the *Manchester Guardian*, to act as a mouthpiece for political reform.[2] The 1832 Reform Act went some way towards satisfying their demands, effectively enfranchising the male middle classes as a group, and Taylor among others retreated from the campaigning fray. The *Guardian* newspaper, however, continued to act as a focus for northern, middle-class radicalism, as it still does in a less geographically specific way today.

The word 'radical' – from the Latin for root – had been used in the seventeenth-century to describe those who wanted root and branch reform of the political system. By the early nineteenth century it was being used as a term of abuse for anyone who demanded what was then seen as extreme change. However, it was taken up by radicals themselves as a term of approval for anyone who wanted change in a broader sense. Another word, 'dissent', is often found in association with radicalism; this, conversely, underwent a narrowing of meaning. From standing for all forms of disagreement, the opposite to consent, dissent came specifically to stand for those who did not agree with the teachings of the established church – the Church of England. In practice, from the seventeenth century on, radicals and dissenters were often the same people and it is worth unpicking why this should be so in order to understand the moral tradition that was being created.[3]

As we saw in Chapter One, in the early nineteenth century there were still serious obstacles in the way of anyone who was not a member of the Church of England. Until the Test and Corporation Acts of 1828, holders of public office had to receive Anglican communion and to reject the Catholic doctrine of transubstantiation, thus preventing non-Anglicans of any kind from becoming members of parliament. Even then, the same barrier still prevented anyone who was not a member of the established church from taking a degree at Oxford or Cambridge until 1856 or from teaching there before Gladstone abolished the University Religious Tests in 1871. It was natural, therefore, that dissenters of all kinds should play an active role in campaigns for religious freedom and for disestablishment of the Church of England – that is, the complete separation of church and state.

However, it was not only campaigns for religious reform that attracted dissenters, or Nonconformists as they were increasingly called in the nineteenth century. They were also frequently to the fore in political movements that sought to promote the interests of industry and manufacturing. The most famous example was the Anti-Corn Law League of the 1840s, the first great middle-class protest movement. A campaign to promote the interests of free trade and industry against the economic protection enjoyed by agriculture and the landed classes, the League used mass meetings, pamphlets and even primitive public-opinion polls to fight for repeal of the protectionist Corn Laws. Its leadership was both radical and dissenting: although Richard Cobden was an Anglican, John Bright was a Quaker. As we saw in Chapter One, the arguments and language of the leaders of the Anti-Corn Law League were distinctly anti-aristocratic. John Bright famously described the Empire, with its protectionist economic laws, as a gigantic system of outdoor relief – state charity – for the aristocracy. Through the promotion of free trade, privilege was to be attacked. This was a class-based programme, directed against the aristocracy and with a clear selling-point to the working classes (cheap bread in the case of the Anti-Corn Law League). Working-class support was necessary, as it had been in the campaign for political reform, because, as Cobden argued, 'we need something in our rear to frighten the aristocracy'.[4]

Nonconformity was more than just another issue on which a large section of the middle classes had to fight their corner: it was a fundamental source of their social identity and of their commitment to public activity, whether political or philanthropic. Naturally, Nonconformist denominations had a variety of beliefs and appealed to different social groups. Sects based on apocalyptic visions of an imminent future in which a Saviour would arise to promote the meek and mild tended to attract a popular audience precisely because they reflected the struggles and aspirations of the poor and powerless. Other forms of religious dissent, like Quakerism, Unitarianism and Congregationalism, emphasised religion as a way of attaining a state of grace or individual redemption. It was these kinds of Nonconformity, with their emphasis on the individual, that were more likely to be found among the middle classes. As we saw in Chapter One, Victorian middle-class Nonconformists liked to envisage themselves as in a direct line of descent from the seventeenth-century Puritans. They were united as a group by a powerful sense of their own place in a long tradition in English history, with its panoply of heroes like John Bunyan, John Milton and the parliamentarian Oliver Cromwell. For the Anti-Corn Law leader John Bright, Milton was 'the greatest man who ever lived'.[5] This historical tradition reinforced their sense of mission and righteousness. Issues like church rates, disestablishment and educational reform, which were naturally sources of grievance to non-Anglicans forced to support financially a church of which they were not members, were charged with moral intensity for radical dissenters. One such was Sir Richard Tangye, a Birmingham manufacturer and inventor of the hydraulic press. The descendant of generations of dissenters, he saw politics in terms of a historical tradition derived from the English Civil War, not in terms of immediate material issues such as the needs of industry. For Tangye, Cromwell was the man who made civil and religious liberty possible and the established church was the institution that had forcibly carried off a flitch of bacon one winter when Tangye's grocer father had refused to pay the church rate.[6]

As we have seen, the middle classes defined themselves partly by their opposition to the land-owning aristocracy. An implicit aim of middle-class radicals was to spread their own developing system of moral values. Self-help, temperance, *laissez-faire*, education, individualism: these were ways of thinking that distinguished the middle classes from the old aristocracy and were reflected in the causes which their radical element chose to promote.[7] The campaigns for temperance, girls' education, legal and prison reform, for changes in sexual morality and so on, were frequently driven by moral conviction – the celebrated 'Nonconformist conscience' – as the language used by middle-class radicals across a whole range of issues indicates. Nineteenth-century radical movements were not monolithic. Not everyone who supported religious freedom would also promote free trade or be interested in the anti-slavery movement or the abolition of capital punishment; nor were all radicals Nonconformists. But the circles were overlapping and a sense of a moral mission or crusade is clearly identifiable as a common thread or impulse, as it continued to be long after the battles against religious discrimination and political disability had been won.

GREAT CRUSADES AND MORAL MISSIONS

The passion for reform felt by individual Victorian radicals is exemplified by Josephine Butler. Butler was at the forefront of the late nineteenth-century movement to reform the way prostitutes were treated by the legal system and the state. Just before she got married, her fiancé George Butler, who was to support her work unfailingly, wrote to her: 'I have a longing to be of use.' This matched her feelings exactly.[8] The language Josephine used to describe her drive to change the system was fervent: she talked about feeling a cry from the soul, a cry to holy war.[9] She called her account of the history of the movement *Personal Reminiscences of a Great Crusade*. While Butler was not strictly a Nonconformist – of Huguenot descent, she went to church to support her husband, who was a Church of England minister – her moral education was as much about social conditions as about the scriptures. On Sundays her father read the Bible aloud to Josephine and her siblings, but he also insisted that they read the parliamentary Blue Books which described in exhaustive detail the social conditions of Victorian England. As an adult Butler drew no line between her personal life and her campaigns: she took destitute prostitutes into her own home and led the campaign against the Contagious Diseases Acts, knowing how much it would damage her reputation and that of her husband and sons. The Acts were intended to lessen the likelihood of prostitutes' clients acquiring venereal disease by forcing prostitutes to have regular, often brutal, medical examinations. Women who were suspected of being prostitutes could be arrested and forcibly examined, and imprisoned if they resisted. Butler describes her motivating emotion for her campaign against the Acts as an all-consuming anger: 'Nothing so wears me out body and soul as anger ... and this thing fills me with such anger, and even hatred, that I fear to face it. The thought of this atrocity kills charity and hinders my prayers.'[10] The Contagious Diseases Acts were finally repealed in 1885 after two decades of a campaign which had begun with polite letters and pamphlets but had developed to include mass meetings to rally popular support against them.

By the end of the nineteenth century a pattern of middle-class protest had formed. The methods were non-violent and rested heavily on the written word: petitions, placards and pamphleteering, often combined with marches. Some radicals were also prepared to court imprisonment – as the militant suffragette campaign gathered momentum in the decade before the First World War, 240 suffragettes were imprisoned in 1912 alone for acts of arson (generally setting fire to post-boxes) and calling false fire-alarms.[11] The campaigns revolved around passionately felt single issues, but embodied a number of common themes: individual freedom set against the perceived power of the state; a desire to empower the disenfranchised; and a concern with the sort of social or cultural issues which were not generally dealt with in formal politics.[12] There was an overlap between some of these single-issue campaigns and the politics of the Liberal party, but while individual members of parliament were often targeted for persuasion, the campaigns of conviction were largely conducted outside party politics.

A glance through the pages of the *Manchester Guardian* (from 1871 under the celebrated editorship of the Unitarian C. P. Scott) shows the wide range of subjects with which the more radical wing of the middle classes concerned themselves at the turn of the twentieth century: abolition of capital punishment, feminism, Zionism, pacifism and municipal socialism, among others. But by 1900 this radical wing rarely included the leading businessmen and industrialists who had been so involved in movements like the Anti-Corn Law League sixty years earlier. Over the decades, many of the interests of the industrialists and the aristocracy had blended. Both were capitalists after all, and just as peers took to investing in the railways and developing mines on their land, so many industrialists were happy to buy large country houses and for their children to marry into landed families. Despite Bright's railings, imperialism had also become a general good on which businessmen and aristocrats could agree, with its promise of cheap raw materials, overseas markets and administrative perks.

By 1900 the industrialists who had retained their radicalism were more than likely to be those who continued to hold religious convictions other than Anglicanism, like the Quaker Rowntree family. Joseph Rowntree, the founder of the family confectionery firm, had carried out two major surveys into poverty in Britain in the 1860s. As the business became more successful, he went on to establish three trusts to support research and philanthropy across a range of social concerns.[13] His second son, Benjamin Seebohm Rowntree, had become a director of the company in 1897, but spent much of his time studying diet, housing and social conditions, publishing influential works such as *Poverty: A Study of Town Life* (1901). He was, as the social reformer Beatrice Webb put it, 'more a philanthropist than a capitalist'.[14] But this close connection between business and radicalism was becoming a rarity.

By 1900 intellectual circles were generally distinct from business ones and the intellectuals were far more likely than businessmen to be radicals. It is a distinction portrayed by E. M. Forster in *Howards End* (1910) in the opposition between the intellectual liberals Margaret and Helen Schlegel and the conservative businessman Henry Wilcox, who 'says the most horrid things about women's suffrage so nicely'.[15] Radicals, social reformers and philanthropists had been staple characters in English novels since at least as early as Dickens' *Bleak House* (1853), where Mrs Jellyby is described with affectionate satire as 'a lady of very remarkable strength of character who devotes herself entirely to the public. She has devoted herself to an extensive variety of public subjects, at various times, and is at present (until something else attracts her) devoted to the subject of Africa.'[16] Novels of the 1880s and 1890s had great fun at the expense of earnest radicals, with their enthusiasm for 'rational dress' and other such fads. So the feminist Cicely Hamilton was able to begin her novel *William – an Englishman*, set in the years before the First World War, with the statement 'William Tully was a little over three and twenty when he emerged from the chrysalis stage of his clerkdom and became a Social Reformer' in the confident knowledge that her readers would know exactly what sort of person she was describing.[17] E. M. Forster's treatment of social reformers is in fact unusual in its lack of comic tone; the desire to poke fun at well-meaning, high-minded liberals is a long tradition of which Posy Simmons and *Private Eye* are among the better known modern representatives.

However, the middle-class radicals of the early twentieth century were not a group apart. There is an evident relationship between the importance accorded to individual conscience by the reformers and the code of duty and social responsibility often found in upper middle-class families like the Courtaulds and others described in Chapter Four. R. A. Butler was a descendant of Josephine Butler and was proud of the connection, becoming vice-president of the Association for Moral and Social Hygiene which she had founded because, he asserted, 'I had great admiration for [her] saintly and courageous career'.[18] As we saw, the Courtauld family were originally Huguenots, with a history of religious persecution, and they had in the nineteenth century been leading advocates of the abolition of church rates and the disestablishment of the Church of England.[19] The notion of individual conscience, of standing up for what one believes in, was a powerful strain through middle-class culture generally. The difference between Rab Butler, a reforming Conservative politician, and the more direct political descendants of Josephine

Butler is one of political ideology and pragmatism, perhaps best expressed in the title of Rab Butler's autobiography, *The Art of the Possible* – an attitude to politics which the fervent Josephine Butler would scarcely have countenanced.

TWENTIETH-CENTURY DISSENT AND THE ALDERMASTON MARCHERS

The campaigning tradition did not disappear in the decades between the world wars, although it was perhaps less conspicuous than at other times. Both the Liberal party and the Nonconformist denominations suffered a substantial fall in support after 1918, but this did not eclipse middle-class protest. The League against Cruel Sports was set up in the 1920s by Henry Williamson, author of *Tarka the Otter*. The cause of the Spanish Civil War and support for republican Spain, the activism of radical figures like the writer Naomi Mitchison and her brother, the evangelist for science J. B. S. Haldane, and the endeavours of Victor Gollancz and the Left Book Club, all have a historical relationship with the campaigns of the late nineteenth century. They represented emotionally charged causes and a radicalism that resisted subsumption into conventional party politics.

One family whose history shows the continuity of this concern with individual conscience is the Wainwrights from Leeds. Richard Wainwright was the son of a Methodist minister who had spent his life working in the slums of Leeds. Richard was a conscientious objector in the Second World War and after the war became Liberal MP for the Colne Valley in the industrial heartland of West Yorkshire. His wife Joy played an active part in her husband's political life and their children had a conscience-driven, liberal upbringing. Richard's son Martin is now the *Guardian*'s northern editor and remembers the institutional icons of his 1940s childhood vividly: 'When I was a boy it was like the Holy Trinity really. You had the Liberal party as the political instrument, you had the Rowntree Trust as the kind of treasury, which provided chocolate money for good, and you had the

As timeless as the English countryside. Tea at the Women's Institute remains an enduring symbol of what it is to be 'middle-class' at a time when the term has been drained of its specific historical meanings.

Self-made men: Archibald Barr and William Stroud (on the right). Barr and Stroud's enterprise epitomised the entrepreneurial strain in Victorian middle-class life.

'Wainscoted, carved, curtained, hung with pictures and filled with good furniture': Dr Heaton's house at Claremont embodies the Victorian middle-class passion for home improvements.

Boar Lane, 1881, Leeds, John Atkinson Grimshaw's depiction of Leeds city centre.

Precarious respect-
ability: William
Whiteley with his
four children, but
signally not his
wife, about 1885.

Above: Life in the new suburbs revolved around railway timetables. Commuters board a London-bound train at Worcester Park station in 1936.

Right: Not just a wife but a 'housewife': between the wars, middle-class women became for the first time workers in the home rather than managers of it.

Left: Mary Reed, dressed up in her father's travelling bowler and walking stick, remembered how the whole street came alive every morning to catch the 8.12 train to London Bridge.

Metro-land: in the years between the wars, the middle classes became synonymous with the new suburbs and, for the first time, with home-ownership.

METRO-LAND

PRICE TWO-PENCE

Detailed plans such as these by architect Herbert Welch showed prospective purchasers what they could expect from their new homes. There is no accommodation for a servant, but the kitchen and dining room are still separated.

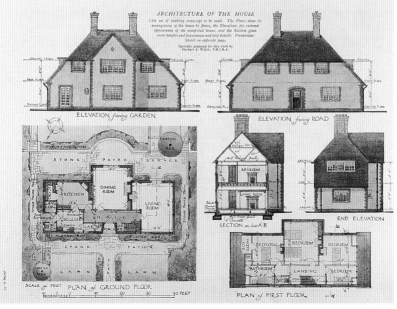

ARCHITECTURE OF THE HOUSE

This set of working drawings is to scale. The Plans show the arrangement of the house by floors, the Elevations the external appearance of the completed house, and the Section gives room-heights and foundation and roof details. Perspective Sketch in opposite page.

Specially prepared for this work by Herbert A. Welch, F.R.I.B.A.

ELEVATION facing GARDEN

ELEVATION facing ROAD

PLAN of GROUND FLOOR

SCALE of FEET

SECTION on Line A B

END ELEVATION

PLAN of FIRST FLOOR

For the average middle-class family, the high spot of the year was the fortnight's holiday by the sea. Expanding car ownership also opened up the countryside for day-trips and picnic parties.

Cycling clubs were a conspicuous feature of the thriving associational life of the suburbs.

Constructing class barriers: in north Oxford the private residents of Summertown paid to have walls erected to separate them from the newly built council estate in 1934.

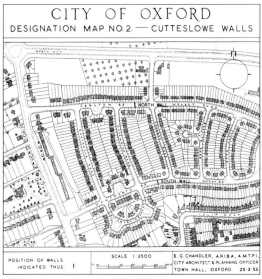

CITY OF OXFORD
DESIGNATION MAP NO. 2. — CUTTESLOWE WALLS

NORTH WALL

SOUTH WALL

POSITION OF WALLS
INDICATED THUS : I

SCALE 1:2500

E. G. CHANDLER, A.R.I.B.A., A.M.T.P.I.
CITY ARCHITECT & PLANNING OFFICER
TOWN HALL, OXFORD.   25·3·53.

The Cutteslowe walls were only fully dismantled in 1959 after Oxford City Council fought a long legal campaign to have them removed. By this time the walls, topped with spikes and broken glass, had divided the two estates for a quarter of a century.

Power, influence and money photographed on an English lawn, July 1935.
Prime Minister Stanley Baldwin and his wife (front row, centre) are flanked by
Sydney Butler (left) and Mrs Malcolm Sargent (right). Standing (from left to
right) are the well-known conductor Malcolm Sargent, Samuel Courtauld,
Lord de la Warr, Rab Butler and Sir Geoffrey Fry.

Portrait of Stephen and Ginny Courtauld by Campbell Taylor.
Stephen and Ginny were one of the most glamorous couples
in inter-war London.

An upper middle-class childhood: Rab Butler, aged six, with his bearer at Lahore in British India.

August Courtauld eschewed the family firm for the life of the gentleman adventurer. His self-sacrificing courage during the British Arctic Expedition of 1930 hit the headlines and captured the public imagination.

Above: A house divided against itself: middle-class radicals have been the butt of jokes, and often rancour, from within the middle classes themselves since at least the time of Dickens. Here the satirical magazine *Private Eye* lends its voice to the tradition.

Left: The Aldermaston marches comprised a wide grouping of people with diverse political agendas. Their social profile, however, was overwhelmingly middle-class and educated, and many of the campaigners were young.

Opposite page: Middle-class rebels: campaigners for nuclear disarmament gather at Turnham Green in London on the first day of the first Aldermaston march at Easter 1958.

Above: A female version of the bracing public-school ethos: Roedean girls practising their cricket.

Below: In the 1960s, comprehensive education such as that offered by Woodberry Down School in north London seemed to many to offer genuine equality of access to opportunity.

Opposite page: Pupils at Beckenham and Penge Grammar School working to secure their place in society in the 1950s.

The new hedonism: racegoers at Royal Ascot. The entrepreneurial revolution of the 1980s fostered new attitudes to money among the middle classes as the deferred gratification of saving was overtaken by conspicuous consumption and the flaunting of wealth.

The shape of things to come: the notorious Conservative election poster of 1979 reflected the return of mass unemployment to Britain for the first time since the 1930s.

Margaret Thatcher supervises a fund-raising drive at the Tory party conference in Blackpool in 1983.

The middle classes past and present.
Above: Yuppies at play in the 1980s.
Below: 'A gentle, balanced life' (Ray Pahl, *see* p.195). *Andrew and Hugh in the Garden at Lainston House* by Gerald Kelly (1879–1972).

Guardian as the trumpet which sounded the pure note.'[20] Martin and his sisters grew up surrounded by the nitty-gritty of constituency politics: bazaars, loud-hailers to play with, 'a lot of sitting at polling stations taking numbers', and entertaining visiting speakers: 'The first thing you did was go to the sherry cupboard and offer them a sherry.'[21]

The Wainwrights chose to live in Cookridge, an area of Leeds which had 'one street of middle-class houses like ours, detached houses, but they were surrounded by working-class estates …, so it was a very socially mixed area'.[22] Hilary, Martin's sister, recalls the books they were encouraged to read, or had read to them, as important influences. They were children's books which would have been found in most affluent homes of the time, but which she felt encouraged 'a kind of free-spirited independence, and also had really good role models for women. I remember the Louisa Alcott books, *Jo's Boys* and *Little Women* – they were always about tomboys and girls that were naughty – and then there would be *Uncle Tom's Cabin* by Harriet Beecher Stowe about slavery, [and] Oscar Wilde's children's books *The Happy Prince* and *The Selfish Giant* which still make me cry when I think about them. They were about equality and poverty, but they were also witty and beautifully written.' For Hilary Wainwright they were both engaging and inspiring.[23]

Hilary was sent to a Quaker boarding school at York, The Mount, and here too there were lessons to be learnt about individual conscience: 'All the religious lessons we had were not about scriptures but were about people who … stood up for their values, their morality, their religion, often against the law of the day.'[24] Both at home and at school the Wainwright children grew up with a strong sense of the need to be socially useful and to support those who were fighting oppression. One influence the whole family shared was that of Methodism. The hymns in particular seem to have struck home. A family favourite was 'The Ninety and Nine':

> There were ninety and nine that safely lay
> In the shelter of the fold;

> But one was out on the hills away,
> Far off from the gates of gold.

Although the Wainwright children were brought up in the 1950s to see themselves as part of a small band of pilgrims marching onwards for a better world, politics around them were about to change dramatically. It is perhaps not surprising that Hilary and Martin Wainwright both became strongly political in the widest sense; the extraordinary thing is that they were to be far from isolated in their own generation, that for a decade or two the small group of pilgrims became a mass movement of protest.

By the time Hilary and Martin Wainwright were in their teens, no one of their generation could have been oblivious to the notion of protest. The Aldermaston marches were the visible emblem of radicalism and dissent in mid-twentieth century Britain, focused on the issue of nuclear weapons. The first Aldermaston march was organised in the spring of 1958 by the Direct Action Committee, a group determined to use direct non-violent action on a large scale to draw attention to their campaign. Five thousand people marched from London to the Atomic Weapons Research Establishment at Aldermaston, even though it was the coldest and wettest Easter for forty years. The following year the march (now organised by the Campaign for Nuclear Disarmament) went the other way, from Aldermaston to London. It stretched for four miles as it wound its way towards Trafalgar Square and culminated in a gathering of some twenty-five thousand people. The Aldermaston marches became an annual event during the next decade and the most dramatic symbol of public protest in the years before the student uprisings of 1968.

The march of 1960 was perhaps the apogee of this phase of the anti-nuclear movement. Over the course of the Easter weekend that year thousands upon thousands of people marched behind a CND banner, with a bunch of daffodils tied to the top, from Aldermaston into the heart of London. Along the way they had slept in schools and meeting houses, in tents and railway stations, supported by a supply train of Elsans, food and baggage pantechnicons. Once again the march culminated in Trafalgar Square, where somewhere between thirty and one hundred thousand people were estimated to have gathered. Veteran campaigner and CND activist Peggy Duff's lyrical description captures the image of the marchers:

> They were always anonymous. Though they carried their banners – Twickenham CND, Harrow Society of Friends, Gorbals Young Socialists or North London AEU – they had no names. They were just the sort of people who marched, most of them young, wearing anoraks and sandals, a few with bare feet, a few with funny hats, and, with them, mothers and fathers and prams and babies and toddlers and all the rest of the marchers, clergymen, scientists, trade unionists, members of parliament, professors and students, teachers and schoolchildren, librarians and nurses, actors and printers, entomologists and engineers, philosophers and plumbers, doctors and draughtsmen, firemen and farmers, every possible trade and profession.[25]

But while the image of the Aldermaston marchers promoted by the activists was that of a wide range of people drawn from 'every possible trade and profession', the reality was that the majority of them were from the ranks of the middle classes. At the time the most significant thing seemed to be how young most of the protestors were; it was left to slightly later commentators to draw attention to their largely middle-class backgrounds.[26] As the sociologist Frank Parkin put it in 1968, CND 'presented Marxists with the puzzling and somewhat disturbing spectacle of a radical movement with an absentee proletariat'.[27] Parkin did a thorough survey of the movement's supporters at the 1965 Aldermaston march. Over four-fifths of them were drawn from professional, managerial or white-collar workers – there were more clergymen and university lecturers alone in its membership than

there were unskilled manual workers.[28] While later analysts have
challenged some of the conclusions Parkin drew from his survey,
there is little dispute that the movement was largely composed of
people, many of them young, from the educated middle class.[29]
For some of the protestors, though, it continues to be important
that the movement is not dismissed as solely middle-class, with
the overtones of privilege which that conveys. The historian and
feminist Sheila Rowbotham insists that the movement crossed
the class spectrum, albeit in terms which imply how exceptional
non-middle-class people were on the marches: 'CND was a real
mixture of people of different classes. I mean a friend of mine
was a docker from Hull who walked all the way with his
winklepicker shoes. I said to him, you know you are going
to have real trouble with those shoes, Dave, but he wouldn't
have it because he said he wasn't one of those people who eat
carrot sandwiches. He had terrible trouble with his winkle-
pickers.'[30]

While at its peak the movement attracted numerous young
people from families with no tradition of protest, many of the first
wave of protestors came from families with a history of dissent. By
the time of the Aldermaston march of 1960 the anti-nuclear
movement had been in existence for only ten years. One of the
movement's early leaders was Michael Randle. Born in 1933, he
was the son of a Catholic clothing manufacturer who had been a
conscientious objector during the First World War. When the time
came for Randle to do National Service he too refused, not
because he was against all war, but because he felt that once
nuclear weapons were a possibility no war could be justified. His
views soon hardened into conviction, partly through reading the
magazine *Peace News*: 'One of the things that swung me away from
being just purely against nuclear weapons to taking a pacifist position was reading about Gandhi and the method of non-violent
action. This came like a revelation that it was possible to resist evil
and oppression without recourse to arms.'[31]

In 1951 Randle joined a small group who were trying to use

non-violent action to protest against nuclear weapons. Over the next few years they staged peaceful demonstrations of about thirty or forty people outside nuclear establishments like Alder-maston and Harwell. In 1956 Randle set out to walk on his own from Vienna to the Hungarian border, handing out leaflets advocating non-violent forms of resistance to the Russian invasion of Hungary. He was detained at the border and given two days to leave Austria. 'I think what gave me the confidence [to do it] was a tremendous feeling of certainty in the possibilities of non-violent action, and a certain sense of mission. It may have been something to do with my upbringing and background ... it was encouraged that you could change things, you didn't have to accept them.'[32]

Religious belief and conscience clearly played a part in pushing people into protest in the 1950s, just as they had in the nineteenth century. Not surprisingly, many Quakers were involved in the peace movement from the outset. In December 1958 a group including the cleric Michael Scott and Michael Randle marched to an obscure American rocket base at Swaffham in East Anglia. After a lengthy stand-off, the protestors finally attempted to invade the base and were arrested. A significant number of those arrested came from Quaker backgrounds. In prison after the Swaffham protest, the prisoners were put to work sewing mail bags. Michael Randle recalls that 'on one occasion one of the prison officers ... came round and started telling us what to do with these mail bags, but there was quite a heavy Quaker concentration there and they were having a silent meeting. They asked him to be quiet and he didn't know how to respond.'[33]

Michael Randle was at the first rally organised by the Campaign for Nuclear Disarmament, in 1958 in Central Hall, Westminster. The events of that rally challenged his belief in non-violent protest. After the meeting a small crowd of people went to Downing Street: 'We were able to get right outside Downing Street and the police came. I think they panicked and they were very heavy-handed. One incident that I saw was some-body took a photograph and the police chased after him and beat him, took the camera and took the film out of it.' Randle told the policeman that he thought this action unreasonable and that he had been brought up to think the best of the police. 'He said, "shut up or I'll smash your face in". That was the beginning of my disillusion.'[34] For the first time since the suffrage movement, a generation of middle-class people began to experience the police and the law as repressive, leading some to question the status quo more widely.

The Aldermaston marches organised by CND pulled together a wide grouping of people with diverse political agendas. There were pacifists and Christians, anarchists and rationalists, and plenty of quiet, concerned young parents pushing prams or carry-ing children. They joined together in singing 'Ban, ban, ban the bloody H-bomb' to the tune of 'John Brown's Body'; another favourite was 'When the Saints Go Marching in'. Although Elvis Presley was king of the pop charts, the protestors tended to be jazz fans; musical taste was an important cultural marker for the youth of the 1950s. 'Jazz was the suburbs' escape from their lot. The audience was middle-class and suburban, with a strong element of students, particularly from art schools. Trad was the music of the Aldermaston marches', recalled George Melly, one of the best-known British jazzmen of the day.[35] Kingsley Amis' Lucky Jim adored revivalist jazz and so did John Osborne's Jimmy Porter, the original fictional Angry Young Man. Trad jazz 'appealed to the antiquarian enthusiasm of the middle-class young in Britain, the grammar school and provincial university student generation, often scientific, spectacled and sweatered'.[36]

One of the myths of the 1950s was that Britain was becoming increasingly classless, although it was in fact a time of enormous sensitivity about class. The visible distinctions of class continued to flourish well into the 1960s. As Peter Jenner, then an econom-ics lecturer at the London School of Economics, put it: 'If you lived in England then you knew that class was very important.

You knew who people were from the way they spoke, you knew where they came from, the way they dressed, you knew what sort of jobs they did … The idea that you could distinguish people between the cloth cap and the bowler hat was something which would be absolutely indescribable now, but that sort of thing did exist.'[37] Movements like CND seemed to offer the possibility of an escape from the constrictions and rigidity of the 'class system' and to bring people together in a way that was democratic, daring and fun. The uniform of the male protestors – duffel-coats and rollneck sweaters – was a way of dressing that symbolised a set of opinions rather than one's position in society, in contrast to the class-bound hierarchy of cloth caps and bowler hats. It was not just the politics but the whole cultural ensemble that appealed and it drew in young people from families with little previous experience of radicalism or dissent.

One such young man was Max Farrar: 'I came from the sort of family where a boy of thirteen would wear cavalry twills … Your hair would be measured to see how close to your collar it was becoming and if it was getting [too long] you would be forcibly barbered.'[38] Farrar came from a service family and because of his father's job as an officer in the RAF, they moved around a lot. He describes them 'as coming from that section of the middle classes which was blighted by philistinism … There would be no pictures on the wall, nothing that you collected or took some pleasure in displaying, where all the signs and symbols of your class had to be in place all the time. So for instance I was trained, and I don't regret this actually because I think politeness has got its place, to shake hands and say "how do you do, sir" from the age of four onwards.'[39]

It was at boarding school in Liverpool that Max Farrar first came into contact with 'beat poetry and Jack Kerouac novels and jazz'. The young people of CND appealed to him immensely:

When the CND period was most dramatic I would see photographs in the newspapers of men in polo-necked jumpers and duffel-coats with a Penguin book stuffed into their pockets and hair that was kind of out of place, and these groovy women who I could see were probably beatniks ... All these things inspired in me a sense of cultural breakage ..., of people expressing themselves symbolically and culturally in a different way... I thought these people were very sexy. I imagined myself to be part of this kind of bohemian/radical/jazz/poetry/expressive/protesting action. The pictures that you saw of people being carried off by a policeman were terribly inspiring to me as a teenager.[40]

Suddenly, protest and radicalism had become 'groovy'. They had enjoyed brief periods of fashionability before, in limited circles, but the 1950s and 1960s marked the first time that protest had a really large-scale appeal. This, in turn, was possible only because of the kind of social changes that had led to a youth movement in the first place.

THE INVENTION OF YOUTH: PROSPERITY, PROTEST AND THE POST-WAR YEARS

The late 1950s and the 1960s were a period of considerable optimism and material prosperity. After the difficulties of the 1930s and the privations of war and post-war austerity, many people – and their children – were far better off than they had ever been. It was a long economic boom, the golden summer, as the historian Eric Hobsbawm called it.[41] There was a sense that full employment was not only desirable but achievable and that there would be no return to the slum conditions which had blighted so many lives in the 1930s. Part of this boom was fuelled by a new idea of consumerism, which in turn created a new set of potential consumers – the teenagers. Being young became a specific consumer identity and helped create among those who were young at the time a sense of being part of a particular and distinct generation, one which resented the assumptions and conventions of their parents' generation. The bestseller *Catcher in the Rye* by the

American novelist J. D. Salinger was first published in 1951: for Max Farrar, and many others, it was a formative book. Its hero, Holden Caulfield, spoke an international language of youthful disaffection. In his red hunting cap with the peak pulled round to the back, he weighed up the adult world and found it 'phoney'.

But the newly invented youth market was not homogeneous. It was cut across by class and other forms of distinction, as evidenced in the divisions between those who loved jazz and the adherents of rock and roll. Furthermore, although for the postwar generation education and the grammar school system offered a more effective vehicle for class mobility than any which had previously existed, their immediate effect was less to dissolve class divisions than to create what the headmaster of one of the leading grammar schools described at the time as 'a new middle class'.[42] The expansion of secondary education is dealt with in Chapter Six, but it is of significance for an understanding of the youthful protestors of the late 1950s and 1960s.

The changes in the state education system brought about by the Education Act of 1944 had led to more children than ever before being exposed to the world of books and ideas. CND was itself disproportionately composed of the minority of the country's youth who had been to grammar school.[43] They were comfortable with ideas and abstract argument and confident of their own ability to make a stand, whether they came from middle-class or working-class backgrounds. Indeed, the grammar school graduate had often experienced first-hand the continuing realities of class distinction and inequality. The playwright Dennis Potter was the son of a miner from the Forest of Dean. In 1958, at the age of eighteen, he won a scholarship to Oxford and was forced to confront directly the painful realities of class difference:

For example if you take the first week of coming-up in the new term, and the first week of the Vac, leaving Oxford, I think then the tensions became most obvious to myself. And when I

first came up to Oxford, I wanted to enter into this new way of
life and leave my old background … I looked around my
college room, very big and comfortable and happy, and there
was the inevitable knock on the door and the college scout –
that's the college servant – came in and he called me 'sir'. Not
like the shopkeepers call you 'sir', but [with] more deference
than that. And I felt for the first time what it was like to be
called 'sir' from a class position.[44]

For many this education and the disjunction it created between
themselves and their parents was a radicalising experience. Sheila
Rowbotham came from a lower middle-class, Methodist background and was the first in her family to go to university. Her
father was very proud when his daughter got a place at Oxford,
but many of his acquaintances were concerned: 'His friends said
it was a big mistake to let me go to university because they said
she'll get funny ideas and won't want to get married.'[45] They were
right. She enjoyed Oxford precisely because of its unregenerate
intellectual culture. As a child her father 'used to come upstairs
and try and get me to watch television because he thought it was
very unnatural to sit in your room and read books'.[46] At Oxford
she was regarded as working-class because of her northern
accent. 'What I really liked about the upper middle-class Oxford
thing was the interest in culture and books and the fact that
people took ideas seriously and that was considered to be perfectly normal.'[47] Sheila Rowbotham was conscious that by
attending university she had changed the way she might live her
life:

There were questions being raised about what to do and how
to behave as a girl in our generation because we didn't want to
be like our mothers. On the other hand, there weren't really
any rules about how you behaved. I think those of us who
were young in the early sixties did feel that we had to make
our own rules of how to be and how to live. The idea that it

was normal to go to university was not really there for my generation, so when we had this chance to go we thought we're just going to do everything completely new.[48]

Many commentators at the time put the radicalism and activism of the new generation down to the political upheavals of these years. Certainly events piled on one another in the 1950s and early 1960s: the British decision to produce an H-bomb, the uprisings in Poland and Hungary, the debacle of Suez followed by the Cuban missile crisis. But this is not a sufficient explanation – the great majority of people, including the young, seem to have remained largely unconcerned by the major international events of the period. Contemporary surveys show that the overwhelming majority of 'young people' ranked the independent nuclear deterrent near the bottom of the list of issues felt to be of political importance, well below items like the cost of living, housing and even pensions.[49] Rather, the events fed into an established mood of intransigence among a specific section of the population. Education, affluence, history and current events all combined to create a particular cultural and political milieu.

John Osborne's 1956 play *Look Back in Anger* was celebrated then and now as capturing the spirit of the 1950s. Its hero, Jimmy Porter, was the archetypal grammar school boy who found the conventions of British life stifling and hankered after the kind of 'good, brave causes' embraced by earlier generations.[50] As Sheila Rowbotham put it: 'There was a kind of defiance around in the late fifties which was to do with personal behaviour and sexuality and rebelling against marriage. We had all these discussions about how we could live a different kind of life, an existential existence.'[51] 'The Bomb' provided a focus for this anti-authoritarian, anti-establishment spirit. It was a symbol of the older generation's moral and political bankruptcy and in demonstrating against it the young could show their own high moral purpose. In the words of Peggy Duff, the Aldermaston marches represented a 'community for which no vows were required. All you had to do to belong was to step off the pavement and join it. While the bomb was the main occasion and theme it was much more than that. It was a mass protest against the sort of society which had created the bomb, which permitted it to exist, which threatened to use it. This is why so many of them were young – still free enough to reject it.'[52]

Crucially, though, the section of the population amongst whom the protest movement took deepest root was, by education, income and background, overwhelmingly middle-class. As we have seen, many of the protestors, like Michael Randle, came from families with a tradition of radicalism. In his survey in 1965, Frank Parkin found that the majority of protestors felt their political actions to be supported by their parents. A hundred or so years earlier a segment of the middle classes had felt itself pressed into political protest by reasons of religion. Now it was a segment that felt it had a moral mission to combat authority by virtue of its youth. The established church was now an irrelevance; the new target was the establishment itself. According to Parkin, most CND members were opposed not only to nuclear weapons but also to capital punishment, apartheid, immigration laws and the monarchy.[53] Their main preoccupation was not with economic or party political issues but with broad moral concerns. This was the politics of principle, not expediency, and in this the anti-nuclear protestors showed all the characteristics of the more high-minded of the Victorian protest movements.[54]

THE ALDERMASTON LEGACY: PERSONAL POLITICS AND THE SYMBOLS OF CLASS

Despite the high public profile of the thousands of Aldermaston protestors, radical elements were nonetheless a minority within the middle classes and often felt themselves to be so. One CND-supporting schoolteacher recounted to Frank Parkin in 1965 her experiences of ostracism, living in the commuter belt: 'We moved into this house about a year or so ago. To begin with the neighbours couldn't have been more friendly and helpful. One day I put a Ban-the-Bomb poster in the window and from then on things changed. They couldn't have avoided me more if I had caught the plague.'[55]

In small yet significant ways, though, middle-class radicals were often keen to signal their difference from their more conventional neighbours or family, just as they had in their rejection of the distinctions of bowler hats and cloth caps. In the 1960s hair-length was a potent symbol by which the rebellious young could show their alienation and annoy their parents. Sheila Rowbotham recalls how when she was a teenager 'my poor parents had to live with this creature who became more and more peculiar-looking because I was constantly trying to grow my hair and have it long and straight'.[56] It was a simplistic association between haircuts and political views that was later to embarrass her:

> When I was first involved with CND, a guy came to the door. I thought he must be a policeman because he had short back and sides and I was not very forthcoming about how to get hold of this document ... He was actually a trade unionist from the Cowley car plant who was coming to get them to give out at work. I was very ashamed when I discovered I had been keeping things away from this genuine worker.[57]

Beards were also significant, and were far more common among CND supporters than among men in general. They were a handy symbol for those men who did not wish to be seen as conformist, whatever their profession or background.[58] During the mid- and later 1960s, the concern with personal politics and the desire to distinguish oneself from the bourgeois herd became more marked. Peter Jenner was the grandson of a Labour MP and the son of a pacifist Church of England clergyman. He graduated from Cambridge in 1965: 'To this day I don't have a suit, and to me that's very important. I've never worn a dinner jacket ...

because to my generation these sorts of symbols were very important symbols of class.'[59]

This rejection of the symbols of class reflected an acute aware-ness of its continuing importance. When Jenner took up his lecturer's job at the London School of Economics he went, like many of his friends, to live in Notting Hill: 'The young middle classes moved in because it was a culturally rich area, reasonably central and reasonably cheap, but for working-class people it was ruinous, especially for the West Indians. We would sit around… and talk about how we were going to change the world.'[60] Jenner and his friends launched a short-lived free school movement, teaching classes open to all:

> The idea for the free schools was to provide an alternative education for the people of the area. [We felt] that we who were the beneficiaries of an education system for the chosen few had some social obligations to try and bring our information to the ordinary people. We had an awareness that we had a very rich life in comparison with the working people but it was always that slightly sort of patronising thing, we can improve your life for you, come and smoke dope and listen to weird music, and a lot of the ordinary working-class people would bugger off. Leave me with my pint and singing 'My Old Man's a Dustman', you know.[61]

For Jenner and his friends the free school movement was all part of a libertarian politics not aligned to party: 'The issues that were important to us were the issues of personal freedom, of sexual freedom, the freedom to smoke dope.'[62] Many others in Jenner's generation took personal politics a step further and found in the women's movement their next great campaign. At the end of 1968, after the May events in Paris and the barricades and demonstrations, Sheila Rowbotham began to express in writing her developing feminist consciousness and her growing frustration with existing forms of radical organisation. She addressed her fellow radicals, men and women:

> Okay, so what are we complaining about? Okay so you're bored, but meanwhile we still get less pay for the same work as you, we're less likely to be educated, less likely to be unionised … so what are we complaining about? All this and something else besides, a much less tangible something, a smouldering bewildered consciousness with no shape, a muttered dissatisfaction which suddenly shoots to the surface and explodes. We want to drive buses, play football, use beer mugs, not glasses, we want men to take the pill … But these are only little things, revolutions are made of little things.[63]

Rowbotham wrote these words in 1969 for an issue of the radical magazine *Black Dwarf* which was dedicated to the year of the Militant Woman: 'Normally people on the left make prophecies that things are going to happen and they don't. Well, 1969 did become the year of the Militant Woman.'[64]

Over the following decades feminism, anti-apartheid, gay rights, animal rights and environmentalism were all to result in movements with widespread support. The anti-nuclear movement of the 1950s and 1960s had a profound influence on the style of many of these campaigns: the use of direct action, the sheer scale of the marches, the acceptance by so many people of the notion that individuals should stand up and be counted. For those who took part, and for those who were too young to do more than watch and admire, CND and the Aldermaston marches were formative experiences. Many have continued to be involved with radical politics and protest groups. Just as the Nonconformist protestors of the mid-nineteenth century turned to John Bunyan and Oliver Cromwell for a sense of their own place in history, so the traditions of middle-class protest still resonate for protestors today. As one anti-nuclear campaigner, Angie Zelter, puts it: 'I see myself in a long, long tradition of women struggling for a fairer and more just world.'[65] In the words which Zelter uses to describe her own motivations one can hear a clear echo of the great crusades of the nineteenth century:'I can't just sit down and enjoy myself or cut off from all these people's stories. I hear so many stories … and I don't actually feel happy unless I am trying to do something about all these issues, so you could say it is actually quite a self-centred process that I am going through. I'm doing all these things in order to feel more at ease with myself and happier with myself.'[66] For all the difference of cause and idiom, it is a sentiment Josephine Butler would surely have recognised.

CHAPTER 6

LESSONS IN CLASS

Secondary education in England

Education is absolutely central to the English middle classes: they are the people who pass exams. The idea of professionalisation which developed in the nineteenth century and became so crucial a part of middle-class identity depended upon a system of education which led to recognised qualifications. By the 1880s, for an individual to be a professional, with its concomitant status and career structure, he had to have a piece of paper which proved his fluency and ability in a particular field. Education, and its verification in the form of qualifications, became a form of capital which could be turned into lifelong prosperity and security. Passing the examination became the key turning-point for an individual's future and getting their children an education which would lead them to exam success became one of the main ambitions of middle-class parents, however much it cost. For generations of parents investment in education became a priority, what one commentator has called 'the inalienable right of the middle class to educate their children beyond their means'.[1]

But while the middle classes have generally been extremely successful at passing on their own position in life to their children through schooling, education has also increasingly operated as one of the main channels of social mobility for individuals. This is a process that has often been recognised and encouraged by schools, to the extent that, along with their studies, children have been taught ways of speaking and behaving that are permeated with notions of class identification. For children of working-class parents the effect was often to make them feel that they were changing their class as well as their academic prospects. One such person is Dorothy Thomson. She was the illegitimate child of a barmaid, born in Yorkshire in the late 1930s, and one of the many beneficiaries of the Butler Education Act of 1944, which for the first time made secondary education compulsory and free for all children. Her grammar school education took her away from life in the mining village where she grew up: 'It opened up a whole new area for us. We went on school trips, we went swimming, we went on field studies in the sixth form. It was about preparing us for jobs that we wouldn't normally get if we'd stayed in our own culture. The grammar school made good.'[2]

Through the twentieth century education became progressively more important and available, while it also continued to play a distinctive role in the formation of middle-class identities. Indeed, at some points in the twentieth century, education – and in particular secondary education – became a kind of litmus test by which parents and children identified what sort of middle-class person they were. The confusing battleground of education has seen a variety of opposing forces – state versus private, grammar school versus comprehensive – drawn up in a conflict about the nature of being middle-class. It is a battle that still rages today. As the journalist Melissa Benn, the daughter of distinguished left-wing parents Tony and Caroline Benn, puts it: 'Education has come to resemble a minefield where the aim seems chiefly to negotiate your child's safe passage through the system.'[3]

As we shall argue in Chapter Seven, class in its inherited forms has become of diminishing relevance in English society in the early twenty-first century. The education system, however, is one of the arenas where its influence continues to be strongly felt. This is true for all levels of education – primary, secondary, further and higher. But it is secondary education, involving children between, broadly, the ages of eleven and eighteen, where the problems and anxieties can be most clearly seen, and where the historical drama of class has been most conspicuously played out. This is not to imply that universities, in particular, have not also played a vital role in middle-class life. However, until very recently, going to university has been part of the experience of a small minority, even among the middle classes, and in any case entry to university in the past hundred years has generally been dependent upon the type of secondary school attended. This chapter will therefore attempt to unpick the ways in which secondary education has continued to both form and reflect middle-class identities from the nineteenth century to the present day.

LAYING THE FOUNDATIONS: MIDDLE-CLASS EDUCATION IN VICTORIAN AND EDWARDIAN ENGLAND

The educational system that existed in England in the first part of the nineteenth century was still largely designed to cater to the needs of an aristocratic society and the demand for a different form of education was one of the key issues around which an increasingly self-conscious urban middle class convened: 'The middle class in all its sections finds no instruction which can suit their special middle-class wants', wrote the MP Thomas Wyse in 1837. 'They are fed with the dry husks of ancient learning, when they should be taking sound and substantial food from the great treasury of modern discovery.'[4] He was not alone in this complaint. Where, Frederick Hill had asked two years earlier, can the middle-class parent find for his child 'the inducement or even the opportunity, for the pursuit of mechanics, architecture, navigation, sculpture, chemistry, mineralogy, or that one among a dozen other branches of knowledge for which he may have a special aptitude?'[5] The problem identified by these nineteenth-century commentators was a simple one: it was not that there were no schools, but that the schools there were taught the wrong things – that is, not the things that many middle-class parents desired their sons to learn.

In the early nineteenth century the schools that existed comprised at the most basic level a large number of private elementary and church schools which, along with religious education, taught young children to read, write and do simple arithmetic. Above them was a network of endowed grammar schools and public schools where the curriculum was based almost entirely upon the teaching of classics and some mathematics, the traditional 'liberal education' which marked out a gentleman. The most prestigious of these were the major public schools like Winchester, Eton and Harrow. The origins of the designation 'public school' lay in their charitable foundations, endowments which were generally designed to provide education for the local poor alongside wealthier fee-paying students. Typical of these was the oldest, Winchester College, founded in the fourteenth century by William of Wykeham, then Bishop of Winchester. Its original statutes make reference to seventy poor and needy scholars from the local area who were to be educated free alongside ten fee-paying students from leading local families.[6] But by the nineteenth century Winchester, like the other public schools, had become almost exclusively the preserve of the wealthy, the quest to provide education for the poor and needy forgotten. There were local grammar schools too, many of them also of venerable foundation by charitable endowments, which provided a similarly classically based education for a much wider social spectrum than the public schools, with a body of pupils drawn from better-off local families. But this still left large areas of the country – and large sections of English society – with little in the way of schools beyond elementary level.[7]

By the 1860s the pressure to reform English schools so that their curriculum and capacity responded to the demands of Victorian society was so strong that the government was forced to take action. The Clarendon Commission in 1861 examined the curriculum of the leading public schools (of which there were recognised to be seven – Westminster, Eton, Winchester, Charterhouse, Harrow, Rugby and Shrewsbury) together with two ancient day schools, Merchant Taylor's and St Paul's, and drew up a somewhat revised version. While classics and mathematics would still have a central place, modern history, languages and science should also be taught.

A few years later the Taunton Commission (more formally known as the Schools Inquiry Commission) was set up by parliament specifically to look into the question of middle-class education. Its purpose was to secure an effective education for the middle classes as a whole and one which made due provision for class distinctions. It began by examining the endowed secondary schools (other than the handful of public schools looked at by the Clarendon Commission) of which there were nearly eight hundred. One of the key witnesses to the Taunton Commission was Lord Harrowby, who was keen to create a system of schools that reflected the nuances of social class: 'I should like to club the grammar schools with some relation to locality, and I should like to say you shall be a good lower middle-class school; you shall be a middle middle-class school; and you shall be a higher middle-class school, that which is now called a grammar school.'[8] The recommendations of the Taunton and Clarendon Commissions, and the resulting legislation, led to the reform and expansion of schools thought appropriate for the middle classes. The principal effects on middle-class education were threefold.

Firstly, there was a rapid expansion in the number of 'public schools'. The Headmasters' Conference was set up in 1869 as a body to represent the interests of the public schools and its membership had soon expanded beyond the nine schools acknowledged to have special status by the Clarendon Commission. Cheltenham, Haileybury, Wellington, Marlborough and Clifton were among the many proprietary schools of nineteenth-century foundation whose headmasters were to become members of the Headmasters' Conference and whose pupils could lay claim by the 1870s to being 'public schoolboys'. While most of the major public schools continued to cater for the sons of the aristocracy, the county gentry and the wealthiest industrialists, they were now joined by other public schools serving the upper middle and professional classes. In the words of the Taunton Commission, this class included the sons of the clergy, doctors, lawyers and the poorer gentry 'who have nothing to look to but education to keep their sons on a high social level'.[9]

Secondly, the reforms of the 1860s led to a partial codification of the status of grammar and public schools. The distinction between them was at heart a curious one. It was not a matter of endowed foundation or age. Rather, public schools were distinguished by being boarding institutions whose pupils had little connection with the immediate area and which contained pupils of a certain select social class only. The expansion of the public schools was aided by the Endowed Schools Act of 1869, which allowed schools, under the guidance of a triumvirate of commissioners, to adjust the provisions of their endowments.[10] Many schools divested themselves of the obligations of their endowments to educate local and less well-off pupils by establishing separate grammar schools. At Harrow, for instance, the headmaster Montagu Butler oversaw the creation of 'the Lower School of John Lyon', which maintained links with the original foundation while firmly excluding tradesmen's sons from 'the great school'; at Rugby, Sheriff's grammar school fulfilled the same purpose, as did Laxton's school at Oundle.[11] The distinction between these two types of school was symbolised by the continued emphasis on classics in the public school system. The majority of endowed schools remained happy to be called grammar schools, generally teaching Latin but not Greek and catering for the sons of people like larger shopkeepers and tenant farmers, who would leave school at sixteen. There was a third grade of secondary education to educate the sons of those belonging to a class 'distinctly lower in the scale', such as the sons of smaller tenant farmers, small shopkeepers and superior artisans.[12] These boys were to leave school at fourteen and were intended to learn only a smattering of Latin, along with English, history, elementary mathematics, geography and science. These schools, too, often went by the name of grammar schools.

Thirdly, the Schools Inquiry Commission also examined the condition of girls' education and found it woefully lacking. There were scarcely any schools of ancient foundation. Instead there was an assortment of 'ladies' seminaries' and other private schools, few of which offered much in the way of academic teaching, leavened by a few pioneering schools which aimed to give middle-class girls an education on a par with their brothers'. One of the earliest such schools was Queen's College in Harley Street, London, which had been founded in 1848 with the aim of educating girls to become well-qualified governesses and thus raising the status of that occupation. Other schools had followed, including North London Collegiate in 1850 and Cheltenham Ladies' College in 1853. The report of the Taunton Commission stimulated the foundation of the Girls' Public Day School Trust, which from 1873 onwards established a number of High Schools for Girls, deliberately aimed at less prosperous middle-class families.[13] The dates of foundation thereafter came thick and fast, with eight new girls' high schools in 1875 alone.[14] The great majority of the schools founded under the aegis of the Girls' Public Day School Trust still thrive today as independent girls' schools – Francis Holland, Regents Park (founded in 1878), Blackheath High (1880) and the Perse School for Girls, Cambridge (1881) among them.

The purpose of girls' education was different from that of their brothers. As we saw in Chapter Two, the suburban lifestyle of the later nineteenth century rested on female domesticity and the exclusion of middle-class women from paid work. Girls were not expected to join a profession when they grew up; they were expected to be an ornament to their home. As Maria Gray, who was instrumental in the founding of the Girls' Public Day School Trust, wrote in 1871: 'What they [women] are educated for is to come up to a certain conventional standard accepted in the class to which they belong, to adorn (if they can) the best parlour or the drawing-room, as it may be, to gratify a mother's vanity, to amuse a father's leisure hours, above all, to get married.'[15] The education of girls who were to become governesses had been taken more seriously – hence the foundation of Queen's College – precisely because these girls would be responsible for the early education of boys in the schoolroom at home before they went to public school. The founding of the girls' public day schools marked a shift in the professional classes' attitude towards their daughters. It was not that they wanted their daughters to work – few parents in straitened circumstances would have wished their daughter to become a governess – but that they wanted to prepare their daughters for 'more active and socially useful roles' than an education in needlework and deportment would fit them for.[16] As academic girls' schools became more numerous and better established towards the end of the nineteenth century, many – in particular, girls' boarding schools like St Leonard's and Roedean – also increasingly adopted a female version of the bracing public school ethos.[17] By the First World War the secondary education of girls was well on the way to becoming a mirror-image of their brothers' in all its nuances of class.[18]

The result of the educational reforms of the 1860s and early 1870s was the creation of a system of education more rigidly defined by class and status than ever before. The changes led to a hierarchy of secondary schools which was to prove remarkably resilient. Alongside these reforms at secondary level, W. E. Forster's Education Act of 1870 sought to provide universal elementary education for all. It was neither free (unless a family was so poor that the local school board considered it was impossible for them to pay the fees) nor compulsory, but locally elected school boards could now choose to levy a rate for education and enforce school attendance on children under the age of thirteen if they so wished.[19] It was not felt that working-class children required formal education beyond this age. This exclusion of working-class children from any school above elementary level was entirely deliberate. Not only was their education considered economically unnecessary and possibly politically dangerous; their mere presence was deemed 'to form an obstacle to the schools becoming attractive to others'.[20] An elaborate system of scholarships was created, however, by which a very limited number of the sons of the labouring classes might penetrate the system designed for those of a higher social class.[21]

The acute class-consciousness underlying this system of education had lasting effects and, despite the many educational reforms that have followed, its echoes can still be heard in the English educational system today. The distinction between public school and grammar school is one that continues to resonate in nomenclature, perceived social status and educational ethos, although many of what were originally boys' schools are now co-educational. The new academically selective schools founded as a result of the Butler Education Act of 1944 were known as grammar schools because their spirit and ambitions were felt to echo those of the older endowed grammar schools. Most of those state-founded grammar schools have now closed or been turned into comprehensives, but the vocabulary lingers on in the names of the older endowed grammar schools, the majority of which are now fee-paying once again. There is still a perceived social distinction between public school and grammar school, even where both are fee-paying and have entrance by competitive examination. It is a distinction kept fresh partly by the fact that most public schools (though not all) are predominantly boarding and by the disparity between the ages at which the education begins (eleven years for grammar schools, thirteen for public schools). The form that the entrance examination takes also reflects different expectations of the education the child will have had before entry. At Winchester College, one of the most prestigious and academically competitive of the public schools, the entrance exam for scholars still takes several days to complete and even for ordinary (non-scholarship) places knowledge of Latin and French is highly desirable. A former headmaster of Winchester acknowledges that it would be very difficult to gain a place unless the child has already attended a (private) preparatory school whose curriculum is specifically designed to prepare him for such an examination.[22]

The influence of the public schools on the English educational system as a whole has been enormous. In the decades after the Clarendon Report they enhanced their distinctive style. Classics remained the staple element of the curriculum, but religion, discipline, organisation and team spirit all became more important parts of the school ethos than before. Athleticism and competition for honours were also increasingly emphasised.[23] We have seen in Chapter Four how these schools deliberately set out to teach leadership and a sense of public service which helped imbue the upper middle class with a distinct ethos. In 1917 Alec Waugh described the public schools in his precocious novel *The Loom of Youth*, based on his own schooling at Lancing College, as a system designed to produce 'not great men but a satisfactory type'.[24] They formed, as one historian has put it, 'an efficient and entirely segregated system of education for the governing class'.[25]

Knowledge of the classics remained a badge of class long after the reforms of the 1860s. One boy recalled his early days at Shrewsbury public school just after the First World War. 'There was also fagging …The monitors simply shouted DOUL: at the call, all boys who had not been in the House for two years had to stop whatever they were doing and come running. My housemaster explained with some pride that doulos was the Greek for slave, as if he thought this put the system a cut above fagging.'[26] The same boy vividly recalled the class tensions between the Shrewsbury school boys and the locals, which surfaced on Sunday afternoons when the public schoolboys were encouraged to go out for walks: 'Sometimes the local oiks, as we referred to them, would hang about the right of way that provided our easiest egress to the countryside, to knock off our top hats as we went by. I was warned, though, that it was Not Done to pay any attention to them.'[27]

In the first part of the twentieth century there were considerable numbers of private schools, many desperate for the prestige of the public school. Such schools were famously satirised by Evelyn Waugh in his novel *Decline and Fall* about a young schoolmaster in the 1920s: ' "We class schools into four grades" Mr Levy, of Church and Gargoyle, Scholastic Agents, told Paul Pennyfeather: "Leading School, First Class School, Good School and School. Frankly, School is pretty bad." '[28] The imitation of public schools by others only served to emphasise the predominance of the public schools themselves. The writer Kenneth Allsop remembered his schooldays in a dilapidated private school:

> At this time, in the middle thirties, it had been in existence for twenty years or so. Upon its foundation optimistic efforts had been made to furnish it with the trappings of 'tradition'. It had a stylish name. We wore bright caps with enormous peaks. We had a motto and a school song. We, boarders and day boys, were regularly enjoined to uphold the school's honour by such measures as remaining aloof from the grammar school pupils at the bottom of the hill ... But by the time I arrived there the thin Greyfriars varnish had cracked and flaked, exposing the forlorn shanty-town structure beneath.[29]

The public school model was so strong that when state-funded secondary schools were finally established in 1902 they too furnished themselves with a simulacrum of its traditions. During the First World War the young Malcolm Muggeridge won a scholarship to his borough secondary school in Croydon which, with its four houses named Alpha, Beta, Gamma and Delta and its Latin motto *Ludum Ludite* ('Play the Game'), clearly yearned for the public school ethos. It 'limped along after the older-established grammar and public schools, cordially despised by them, but aiming at turning out a similar product'.[30] This overweening sense of institutional hierarchy, in Muggeridge's view, merely

reflected an English tradition of deference, breeding futile emulation rather than a spirit of class-conscious defiance: 'Waterloo
may have been won on the playing fields of Eton, but the class
war was assuredly lost on the playgrounds and in the classrooms
of state secondary schools.'[31] It was, as we shall see, a situation that
was in some ways reversed at the end of the twentieth century,
when the major public schools found themselves forced to adopt
a more results-driven, examination-orientated form of education, closer to the model of the grammar schools, in order to
maintain their ascendancy in the schools league tables introduced
in the 1990s.

PASSING THE TEST: THE EXAMINATION CULTURE

The demands for a different form of education in the first half of
the nineteenth century had stemmed from a desire for a more
modern and relevant curriculum, for an education that yielded
more tangible results than the gentlemanly patina endowed by a
detailed knowledge of Greek and Latin. This was fuelled by the
increasing importance of the competitive examination, a process
that went hand in hand with educational reforms. At the start of
the nineteenth century, family, influence and patronage had been
the mechanisms by which a young man had got on in the old
professions of the church, law and medicine, as well as in institutions like the army and navy. While most churchmen and doctors
had taken a degree, it was by no means compulsory and, as we
saw in Chapter Two, qualification by written exam was not
enforced in any professions until well into the nineteenth
century. It was assumed that the 'liberal education' of a gentleman
would equip him to learn what was necessary as he went on in
his profession.[32] All this changed during the course of the
century, not only in the old professions but also in the increasing
number of new occupations that came to claim the title of 'profession'. It became essential to be able to rely on the fact that
engineers would know how to build bridges and that surgeons

were aware of the latest techniques.[33] The competitive examination was fundamental to this confidence.

One of the first descriptions of a modern examination comes from the Law Society, which introduced the process in 1836: 'Fifteen questions are prepared and printed. The candidates on the day of the examination are all assembled together in the Hall of the Institution, and the questions are then submitted to them, and their answers, which are written, are carefully examined by the Examiners.'[34] The examination for entrance into high levels of the civil service was introduced in the late 1850s, that for the Indian civil service, on which the home version was modelled, in 1855.[35] By the 1860s the Oxford and Cambridge Local Examination Boards were running a system of examinations to test schoolboys' proficiency in various subjects, and therefore their suitability to enter a variety of professions.[36] By the end of the century the vast majority of students attending Oxford or Cambridge would at least have intended to take their degree – a far cry from fifty years earlier when, except for medics and clerics, actually getting a degree was at best a secondary purpose of an Oxbridge education. By then, too, the ancient English universities were finally starting to catch up with those newer foundations like University College London, and Owen's College, Manchester, as well as the old Scottish universities, in teaching vocational subjects, like engineering, to degree level.[37]

Examinations had become part and parcel of middle-class life and a familiar object of dread for the young. By the later years of the nineteenth century novels were reflecting this: the boy or girl who has a nervous collapse due to over-worrying or overworking for exams became a commonplace figure in fiction. Jessica Morgan in George Gissing's *In the Year of Jubilee* is one such character. With her 'arid little manuals and black-covered notebooks' and talk of 'matters examinational' she becomes quite overwrought.[38] The Sanatorium, founded by Thomas Holloway and built in the 1870s specifically for middle-class patients, listed among its potential clients students who had had nervous breakdowns as a result of the pressure of examinations.[39]

By the turn of the twentieth century examinations had become an indispensable component of the English concept of education. The 1902 Education Act firmly enshrined social division in education through the exam process. The mass of children would continue to go to elementary schools, with their strictly limited curriculum, and leave school by the age of fourteen at the latest, but about one in five children would have the opportunity to go on to a selective or grammar school on the basis of a scholarship exam at eleven. In 1907 the Liberal government added a further access point for a few more children by creating 'direct grant' schools. These were existing private schools (many were girls' public day schools) to which the government would now make a direct grant, without going through the local authority, to take on 25 per cent of their pupils free of charge, again on the basis of an examination at the age of eleven. This system of scholarships to direct grant schools and the establishment of local authority grammar schools was a boon for many middle-class parents who might otherwise have struggled to pay school fees. It was the abolition of this system nearly seventy years later that was to arouse such ire among the middle classes.

Until the introduction of comprehensive education in the 1960s the examination for secondary school was perhaps the most important test in a child's life, whether it was the scholarship exam to get into a state secondary or direct grant school or the 'Common Entrance' exam for those whose parents wished to send them to public school. For a working-class child like Eileen Kingsley, whose mother was a laundress and whose father was a scene painter, the scholarship examination she sat in the late 1920s was 'the only way out. If you were above average intelligence and you wanted to learn more, it was the only way to get a scholarship and go to a better school, otherwise you ended up in a factory just doing machining.'[40] Eileen Kingsley's experience was not unusual. The journalist George Scott has a similar recollection from his elementary school education in north-east England:

> The last three classrooms along the corridor were pointed out as a warning: 'that's where you'll end up if you don't work harder'. Those were the classes for the boys who had failed to win a scholarship. Although one or two might escape to a technical school, the future for a boy stranded in those classes was invariably to become an errand boy, if he was lucky enough to find work at all. He would inevitably leave school on his fourteenth birthday.[41]

The examination for secondary schooling was also all-important to children of more affluent families, like Alan Pryce-Jones who sat Common Entrance in the 1930s: 'I don't think it was ever suggested to me, either then or later at Eton, that there was any purpose in learning other than crossing the hurdle of the next exam. One was stuffed like a Strasbourg goose and it was thought rather morbid to take any interest in the stuffing. In my case my parents, belatedly alarmed, ended by getting me a tutor as well.'[42]

The rising importance of the exam represented more than just the beginning of a modern meritocracy, the idea that opportunities, including jobs, should be distributed on the basis of ability rather than connections. Making examinations the test of ability reflected the nature of the majority of middle-class occupations, based as they were on literacy and numeracy. No less important, examinations appeared to test that mixture of industriousness, ability and nerve that was at the core of the middle-class sense of self. Every time an individual passed a test they affirmed their right to their position.[43] By the twentieth century, sitting an examination had become a key rite of passage, a defining moment in the life of almost any English middle-class male and an important one for many women too. The atmosphere of the examination room is wonderfully evoked in Penelope Lively's novel *Spiderweb*. The central

character, Stella Brentwood, has an unnerving vision of the
nature of the examination system as she sits her university 'finals'
in the 1950s:

> She sees it suddenly as a ritual, entirely baffling to anyone who
> did not know what was going on. It is as though she rises and
> floats up to the top of the great room with its high windows
> and stares down at this ceremonially clad throng of initiates.
> The ranks of desks, the bent heads, the sense of portent. The
> priestly figure who walks between the rows, bestowing sheets
> of printed paper. The small defiant gestures – the men who
> wear a buttonhole, a carnation or a rose, the girls with their
> manipulations of the dress code. The scene becomes ripe for
> exegesis and deconstruction, like some inscrutable practice of
> another age. What are these people about to do? Why are there
> so many men and so few women? What is the significance of
> their apparel, their silence, their air of resignation?[44]

While passing an examination was an immediate symbol of
success, its significance lay in what it might do for an individual's
future in the longer term, either to confirm social position or to
transform it. 'If we passed then all things were possible, or, at any
rate, jobs as bank clerks, audit clerks, and draughtsmen were',
writes George Scott of the importance laid upon the scholarship
examination he and his working-class classmates were to sit.[45] No
wonder 'parents and teachers, ambitious for a white-collar job
and respectability' would impress their sons with the examination's significance.[46]

This transforming power was recognised by the schools themselves, which set out to teach their pupils lessons in class
behaviour. In the late 1920s Eileen Kingsley won a scholarship to
the Northampton High School for Girls: 'We were taught to be
ladies, and we had to wear gloves and stockings, and we had to
behave as ladies, and so you became quite a different person.'[47]
Such an education was a double-edged sword. Within the family

she was sometimes made to feel that with the cost of her uniform she had had more than her fair share of money spent on her and she was called 'grammar guts' in the street by neighbouring children. But seventy years later she was still clear that getting that scholarship was the turning-point of her life: 'It made my life totally.' She wanted to go to university, but because of the war she ended up working for the BBC as a sound engineer. After the war she married a fellow engineer and eventually in her forties did a law degree. Her younger brother Brian also won a scholarship to the boys' High School. He too revelled in it: 'It was so very important to learn to speak properly, the Wellingborough brogue was so awful. You learnt to elocute, to speak properly, and it was that education which gave me the confidence to go on to bigger things.'[48]

The sense of changing one's class along with one's school is repeated over and again in the writings of scholarship children. An account written by Mark Grossek, who gained a scholarship to his local secondary school in the years before the First World War, notes how the senior school (in his case Whitaker Foundation School) used different words to describe the same things that had existed in his elementary school: 'Whitaker Foundation School was divided, not into *standards*, but into *forms*; its wrong-doers were not *kept in* but *detained*; the year there consisted not of two nondescript periods, but of three *terms*; pupils didn't crudely go up from one class to another but were *promoted*. And plebeian *dinner* was replaced by classy *lunch* … Yes, undoubtedly by entering Whitaker Foundation School I had made a distinct advance in the social scale.'[49]

Olive Banks, who was to become a professor in the history of education, also came from a working-class background, this time in outer London. When she was at school in the early 1930s her family were very much against her education continuing beyond the age of fourteen, precisely because it would mean that she would change her class:

My mother never had any aspirations for her children to go out of the respectable working class into the middle class and she opposed all my attempts to get an education. She always said that if a son or a daughter of a working-class family got an education, they moved out of their class and out of their family, and she disapproved of this to the day she died aged eighty-two. She would never ever approve of what I had done, and if I produced another book she would just say 'I don't want to see it'.[50]

THE GREAT DIVIDE:
THE ELEVEN-PLUS EXAMINATION

The biggest and best known change to the English education system came in 1944. The Butler Education Act of that year is by general consensus 'the greatest single advance in English educational history'.[51] R. A. Butler, the Conservative politician responsible for pushing the Act through, was clear about its significance: 'I hoped to achieve what is called, in trite phrases, greater equality of opportunity which of course was achieved by creating free secondary education for all for the first time.'[52] The central achievement of the Butler Act was to make secondary schooling compulsory and free for all children, not just those who passed the examination at eleven. The Butler Act set out to create a tripartite system of secondary education whereby all children would sit an examination at eleven and then go on, according to their aptitude, to either a grammar school, a technical school or a secondary modern. Grammar schools were designed for 'the type of child who is interested in learning for its own sake, who can grasp an argument or follow a piece of connected reasoning'; technical schools were for the pupil 'whose interest and abilities lie markedly in the field of applied science or applied art'; and the secondary moderns were for the rest – those who deal 'more easily with concrete things than with ideas'.[53] Very few local authorities ever built technical schools and by default the state system became bipartite – grammar or secondary modern, with the direct grant schools effectively becoming part of the grammar school set-up. A third option remained, of course, for those who could afford it: the public school and a variety of other private schools. Although the wartime government commissioned a report on the public schools by the Fleming Committee, it was not published until after the 1944 Education Act and the status of the public schools remained untouched. As Rab Butler himself put it 'the first-class carriage had been shunted onto an immense siding'.[54] At the time, though, there was a sense that the old, élitist public school had had its day. In 1940 Churchill had told the boys of his old school, Harrow: 'After the war the advantages of the public schools must be extended on a far broader basis.' Michael Young, author of Labour's 1945 manifesto, wrote that 'it was feared the impoverishment of the middle classes would remove their capacity to pay fees, and some of the strongest supporters of the public schools looked to the state to prevent catastrophe. They were not only ready to accept a proportion of poor pupils, they pleaded with the state to pay for their places.'[55]

The Butler Act undoubtedly opened up the possibilities of education for many working–class children. However, it was also of enormous benefit to many middle-class parents, for whom it meant that, provided their children did well in the expanded scholarship examination now generally known as the eleven-plus, they would receive an academic education free at the state-funded grammar schools. The eleven-plus was only the first of many tests that these children would face. As Dorothy Thomson remarked of her grammar school education in the 1940s, 'We were tested for everything that moved, and [the results] read out in front of the class, where you were, in what position you were. It was OK when you were winning but not so easy when you didn't do too well.'[56] These new grammar schools happily took on the tradition of the direct grant and high schools which had preceded them, modelled on the public schools and with a determination to change their pupils' social behaviour along with teaching them academically demanding subjects. As we have seen, Dorothy Thomson was clear about the purpose of her grammar school in the West Riding of Yorkshire, which had an almost wholly working-class catchment area: 'the grammar school made good.' It was a process that could be divisive and cause resentment. The old taunts such as 'grammar guts' which girls like Eileen Kingsley had suffered in the 1930s were as much a part of Dorothy Thomson's experiences a decade and a world war later. The social divisiveness within working-class communities was, if anything, exacerbated as larger numbers of children went to grammar school. Dorothy's school was Heckmondwyke Grammar and the school song captures nicely its stress on tradition and 'playing the game':

> Heckmondwyke the school we honour,
> Keep its name forever bright,
> Winning, losing neither matters
> If the game be played aright.
>
> We live in dull surroundings,
> Clustered in the Vale of Spen,
> Yet a school we can be proud of
> Rears her head the smoke among.[57]

For Dorothy Thomson, as for many others, grammar school changed her social position and her outlook: 'My mother used to call the doctor "Sir" and I was brought up to defer to people in professions. Well, I became a professional and found I didn't need to defer to people.'[58] For a previous generation 'scholarship boy' was the shorthand for someone who had achieved social mobility through education. After Butler the phrase 'grammar school boy (or girl)' had the same meaning, and could be applied to many more people. Its desirability was openly acknowledged in the postwar years, when there was widespread demand to extend the benefits of education to all and to create in the process an expanded middle class. The headmaster of one of the most prestigious of the grammar schools put it succinctly in an interview he gave to the BBC in 1958: 'We have built up a new middle class. We are building it up now, a new middle class of technologists, and where is that coming from? It is coming from the grammar schools, inevitably from the grammar schools, so in a way the grammar schools are really the spearhead of the movement of social mobility.'[59]

The system was still based on the idea of different types of education for different children, although now in theory the children were differentiated by academic ability rather than by class. Yet hopes that the secondary modern would, by virtue of its more practical education, gain a prestige equal to that of the grammar school were never to be fulfilled. However much the authorities struggled to combat the perception, to have to go to a secondary modern rapidly became a label of failure. A documentary film made by the BBC in 1962 captures the kind of double-think being perpetrated by educational authorities at the time. It shows a woman and her daughter, Janet, discussing Janet's eleven-plus results with her headmaster. The mother expresses regret that Janet has 'failed' the exam, to which the headmaster replies: 'I hardly think that failed is the right word, Mrs Kitchen. You see what happened was that Janet took a test so we could find out which school suited her best. She would have failed the test if she had been selected for the wrong school and so if she has been selected for the right school, she has really passed the test.' While Janet visibly perks up at this piece of curious logic, the expression on her mother's face remains noticeably dour.[60] A converse account is given by Reefat Drabu, the daughter of immigrants from Pakistan, who sat her eleven-plus in the early 1960s. Neither she nor her parents understood the significance of the test she had sat at school until the day her headmistress came to deliver the results in person. Then 'the neighbours came over and said "congratulations, we gather your daughter has got into grammar school". My father was initially quite perplexed but realised soon after that if you wanted to get the better education you had to be in the grammar school, so it made it quite important for the rest of my brothers and sisters to try and attain grammar school.'[61] The observations of immigrant families, such as the Drabus, often shine a clear light on the many functions of the English educational system – an aspect which we explore later in this chapter.

The motivations for wanting one's child to get into a grammar school were often more complex than a simple desire that they should do well academically. Eileen Kingsley was interviewed in 1958 about why she and her husband were so keen for their children to pass the eleven-plus exam: 'We feel that by going to a grammar school they would mix with a nicer sort of child and they would get a good education so they are ready to deal with anything that comes along.'[62] It was not surprising, then, that success or failure in the eleven-plus examination soon acquired overwhelming importance for many parents and became a cause of transferred anxiety for their children. Taking the eleven-plus, and the division which resulted, was a powerful and sometimes distressing experience, even for those children who passed the exam. David Rose, who later became a professor of sociology, remembers it vividly: 'People I had been at school with one day were splitting up the next because they hadn't passed the exam.'[63] Although he was not aware of it at the time, this division often took place along class lines: 'If I think back now to the girls and boys who didn't pass the eleven-plus in my junior school, they were overwhelmingly working class children, and the ones that did were overwhelmingly middle-class.'[64] Historian Frank Mort clearly recalls the pressures put on him by his parents to succeed at the eleven-plus: 'I felt an anxiety which sometimes amounted to terror of the examination system, and I think probably this is a kind of lower middle-class emotional trope, a fear of falling into the abyss … [of] the working class.'[65] One ten-year-old child, interviewed by the BBC in 1955, was disarmingly frank with the interviewer: 'Mummy and Daddy want me to pass really. Daddy says if I don't, I'll get a thick ear.'[66]

For middle-class parents the problem was that while the success of their children at the eleven-plus was statistically probable, it was not guaranteed. The eleven-plus examination was supposed to be a test of intelligence, not of previous education. The academics who developed the tests attempted to find a way of examining children that eliminated possible class bias. Although they were hardly successful, insofar as middle-class children continued to do better overall in the tests than their working-class peers, there were nonetheless significant numbers of individual middle-class failures. Indeed, in some local education authorities approximately half the children of professional and managerial parents actually failed the eleven-plus.[67] The parents of those children were appalled. As the historian Brian Simon puts it, 'it wasn't their idea that their children should mingle with the working masses at the secondary modern'.[68] In reaction, some parents turned to the private sector to educate their children.

EQUALITY OF OPPORTUNITY? THE COMPREHENSIVE MOVEMENT AND ITS BACKLASH

By the early 1960s there was a growing movement of people – parents, educationalists and politicians – who objected to the selective system. They advocated instead a comprehensive system in which all children would be educated together, regardless of academic ability, class or ethnic background. The idea that one could create a social mix in schools and therefore contribute to breaking down barriers between working- and middle-class pupils was an appealing one for many. Furthermore, nearly three-quarters of the nation's children attended secondary moderns, schools which were generally seen to be second best, and there was a widespread sense that the country was wasting a vital natural resource by not giving these children a better chance in life. A few local education authorities in the 1950s had already set up comprehensive schools, but the process gained impetus in 1965 when the secretary of state for education, Anthony

Crosland, issued Circular 10/65, which gave encouragement and funding to all education authorities to take the comprehensive route. Crosland was confident that this was not only education- ally sound but that it would also be popular: 'The pressure on the part of parents to get rid of the eleven-plus is very, very strong … I think that this is a tidal wave and that there has been a tremen- dous shift of sentiment.'[69]

Among those who supported Crosland's initiative were an increasing number of parents who could be described as middle- class by virtue of their occupations, but who rejected the competitive system that seemed to have served the middle classes so well in the past. Two rather different motives propelled their support for 'comprehensivisation'. The first was political – many of these parents worked in the public sector as teachers, health workers, local government officials and so on. As we shall see in Chapter Seven, this group of white-collar and professional public sector workers increased significantly in the years after the Second World War and they tended to have a more communitarian, left- wing and socially inclusive ideology than the traditional middle class. Many of them were grammar school educated themselves, but this did not necessarily mean they wanted the same education for their children. Dorothy Thomson, who had gone on from her education at Heckmondwyke Grammar to become a teacher, was among them: 'I really rejoiced in the privilege and loved my grammar school, but then, as I evolved my teaching career … I began to see that [the comprehensive ideal] was right and I have a passionate belief in the ideal of the comprehensive school … We need everybody to be given the best possible education that's avail- able and to have the ability to get on with everyone across society.'[70] The second factor was the relatively high rate of failure at eleven- plus of some middle-class children, which we discussed above. One of the great attractions of the comprehensive system was that it would mean an end to the old eleven-plus – a hurdle which no child could be guaranteed to surmount. As one teacher put it, 'it meant an end to failure'.[71]

By the mid-1960s there was a sharp division within middle-class opinion between those parents who supported the idea of comprehensive education and those who remained firmly in support of the selective state system, for many ideally combined with an unchallenged private sector.[72] It was a battle bound up with the wider political protests of the 1950s and 1960s discussed in Chapter Five. One historian has represented this argument as the division between those who read the *Daily Telegraph* and those who read the *Guardian* – both middle-class groups but with very different value-systems and political outlooks.[73] Nor was it an argument that divided along party lines. By the mid-sixties the Conservative party supported comprehensives (although almost all Conservative politicians at the time educated their children at fee-paying schools).[74] Conversely, there were many within the Labour party who steadfastly supported the notion of a selective state system, seeing the grammar schools as a powerful route up for able working-class children – after all, a generation of Labour party luminaries had been the beneficiaries of the grammar school system, among them Harold Wilson, Roy Jenkins and Denis Healey. It was, in broad brush, a battle between those who emphasised the role of education in moulding society and those who were concerned with the ability of the individual to get on in that society. Yet the grammar schools had played such a central role in the lives of many individuals, and had come to represent such a powerful symbol of social mobility and meritocracy, that many were reluctant to let go of them. When the Labour prime minister, Harold Wilson, himself reportedly a reluctant supporter of 'comprehensivisation', finally backed it, it was because he was persuaded that comprehensives could offer a grammar school education to everyone and that 'we cannot afford to cut off three-quarters or more of our children from virtually any chances of higher education'.[75]

The complexity of English attitudes to education at this time is well illustrated by the decisions made by Labour politicians about their own children's schooling. Wilson himself had edu-

cated his children at fee-paying schools and did not consider that
such a decision should be an embarrassment to any Labour
politician.[76] The Labour secretary of state for education in 1967,
Patrick Gordon Walker, sent his twin sons to the public school
Wellington College. When challenged about this, he responded
that 'it is hard not to choose what you think is the best within
what is permitted to you by the law'.[77] A more blunt justification
was given by Lord Snow, a Labour peer. He had sent his own son
to Eton, he explained, because 'it seems to me that if you are
living in a fairly prosperous home it is a mistake to educate your
child differently from most of the people he knows socially'.[78]
Tony Benn (then generally known as Anthony Wedgwood Benn)
was unusual in that in 1963 he and his wife decided to remove
their children from the traditional institutions of upper middle-
class education and send them to one of the best known of the
new comprehensives, Holland Park, on the grounds that it was
hypocritical to back comprehensives for everyone else and
educate one's own children privately. His daughter, Melissa
Benn, recalled that 'in some people's eyes this made us four children a collective sacrifice, a living social experiment. We felt only
lucky. My brother Hilary remembers the strangeness of arriving
at Holland Park for the first time after attending Westminster
preparatory school where he and my eldest brother Stephen had
been usefully designated as Benn I and Benn II. He can still
remember the strange sound of so many boys – and girls – laugh-
ing and running and talking in the vast playgrounds.'[79] Given the
perception of education as vitally important to an individual's
future, the gap between what seems right for society and what
seems right for one's own child – a gap that has widened since the
introduction of comprehensive schools largely removed the possibility of education based on academic selection within the state
system – has been a recurrent concern of English middle-class
life.

The education reforms of the 1960s left the position of the
public schools unchallenged once again. This provoked little

outcry, partly because for most people the public schools appeared to be outmoded institutions whose days were numbered. The grammar schools created or enlarged by the Butler Education Act had made a significant impact on the English educational and class system. The proportion of public school-educated undergraduates at Oxford, for example, had been on a downward path since the war, from 65 per cent for male students in 1946 to 58 per cent in 1967, while the decline was clearer still among women across the same period.[80] The new comprehensives looked as if they might at last provide genuine equality of access to opportunity.

Despite the heated debates which surrounded it, it was some time before Circular 10/65 had a significant impact on the laborious and complicated administrative system for education in England. The Circular proffered only encouragement to create comprehensives, not compulsion to do so. Sheffield was among those education authorities which adopted it eagerly. They even introduced 'bussing' to ensure a social mix in the schools, rather than allow segregation by residential area. One teacher described the experience of her working-class pupils being brought from the inner city areas out to the leafy suburbs: 'They are coming from terraced houses, very little grass around them, very little greenery, and they are coming into the middle-class type area with its semi-detached and its detached houses and its greenery.'[81] In Hampshire also, home of Winchester College, the education authority adopted the comprehensive system for its state schools with enthusiasm. The old grammar schools were adapted and turned into comprehensives and new comprehensive schools were built, including the Henry Beaufort School less than half a mile up the road from the College. But Hampshire and Sheffield were unusual. In March 1975 the *Times Educational Supplement* reported that of the more than one hundred local education authorities in England and Wales only twenty were 'truly comprehensive', forty hoped to be comprehensive by the end of the year and forty-six fell into the 'sometime, possibly never or never' categories.[82] Government dissatisfaction at the rate of progress was demonstrated in 1976 by the passing of an Education Act that required local authorities to submit proper plans for comprehensive reorganisation. The direct grant system too was to be changed – schools must either come into the state fold and become comprehensive or they must go independent.

The result of the 1976 Act was a sudden upsurge of hostility. All over the country groups of parents rallied in support of their local grammar or direct grant school, with marches, petitions and campaign groups. A large part of the problem was that the comprehensive movement had become inextricably associated with notions of 'progressive' education and the idea that the comprehensives might provide a 'grammar school education for everyone' seemed to have vanished from the minds of educationalists, if not from those of parents. Lawrie Norcross was the headmaster of a comprehensive school in Islington, London, and one of those who had become increasingly disillusioned by what had happened to the comprehensive school movement: 'What I hoped would be achieved through comprehensives was that access to all the things that were taken for granted in grammar schools would be there for all pupils – I saw comprehensives as grammar schools for all. That was in 1965. I saw things rather differently by 1975.'[83] Many of the original comprehensives had begun with the idea of providing a grammar school education for all, complete with uniforms, streaming and houses. By the mid-1970s, however, attitudes in many schools had changed as they sought a more truly 'comprehensive' education without intramural divisions between pupils. Norcross and others firmly blamed the educational theorists for this change: 'It was assumed that anything that might be described as high culture was élitist. The people who were making these assertions were for the most part sending their own children to schools where they expected them to come into contact with Jane Austen, Shakespeare, Bach and all that but they didn't apply the same standards to the schools they were responsible for.'[84] 'Mixed ability teaching' – that is, no streaming – became the new mantra and as uniforms, houses, school ties and streaming disappeared, many in the middle classes began to mourn the passing of the old-fashioned grammar school with its discipline and examination culture.

The move to abolish grammar schools altogether came at a time – the mid-1970s – when many of those who saw themselves as belonging to a traditional middle class were already feeling particularly under threat from the effects of economic recession, rapid inflation and unemployment. In 1976 the journalist Patrick Hutber published a book called *The Decline of the Middle Classes and How to Stop It*, based on a series of articles he had written for the *Daily Telegraph*. The articles had unleashed a flood of letters and support from readers, lamenting their tax burdens, the increasing uncertainty of their jobs and the loss in value of their pensions. The resulting book was serialised in the *Daily Mail*, with accompanying quizzes, cartoons and headlines like 'How to be middle-class and still win.'[85] Although, as we shall see in Chapter Seven, much of what Hutber's readership was complaining about was due to large-scale economic change, the battle over 'culture' in general and education in particular loomed large in their protests. The *Daily Mail*, in sympathy with Hutber, objected particularly to the 'idea that anything that is middle-class is [now seen to be] automatically of less than general validity, and quite possibly very bad indeed … It is used to denigrate values which at most times in history have been felt to have great worth – respect for truth, the desire for objectivity, the love of scholarship … The extreme case of this is, of course, provided by those revolutionary socialist teachers who regard it as their task to indoctrinate their children in militant working-class attitudes … But in a more watered down attitude it is liable to lead to a feeling that schools should not require intellectually difficult studies since these are – or are believed to be – harder for working-class than for middle-class children.'[86] The *Daily Mail*'s coverage of the book centred on an article entitled 'How to get your child into the right school', with case studies of parents who had successfully fought to get their children into some of the few remaining state grammar schools.[87] Hutber's premise was that the middle classes were not only being squeezed out of existence by the state, but were actively colluding in their own euthanasia. He saw middle-class support for comprehensive schooling as central to this self-immolation and the book contained instructions on how readers could mount a campaign to defend their local grammar or direct grant school.

As the *Daily Mail* had recognised, the dispute over education was not simply an argument over educational theory but a battle permeated by the consciousness of class. The grammar school and its companion the direct grant school were institutions close to many middle-class hearts, even those of parents who chose to educate their children privately. They represented a notion of excellence, of competitiveness and of fairness, insofar as they were seen to give a chance to bright working-class children to progress. That section of the middle classes which used words like 'bright', 'clever' and 'hard-working' as terms of approbation firmly believed in the notion of selective education and were appalled to see it go. In their political campaigns they resorted to the familiar rhetorical accusations of privilege and exclusiveness that the nineteenth-century middle classes had levelled at the aristocracy. As Margaret Thatcher declared at the Conservative party conference in 1977, 'People from my sort of background needed the grammar schools to compete against children from privileged homes like Shirley Williams and Anthony Wedgwood Benn'. As secretary of state for education a few years previously, Margaret Thatcher had presided over the comprehensivisation of a significant number of grammar schools. But her instincts, like those of her audience, lay elsewhere and she received a resounding ovation.

After 1976 the fate of the state grammar schools rested in the hands of their local authorities, which could choose to react swiftly to the new Act or could drag their feet, as many did; nearly twenty-five years later, in 2000, there was still a handful of local authorities who maintained selective grammar schools within their boundaries. Direct grant schools were faced with a much more dramatic choice – they could close, join the state system as comprehensive schools or go 'independent'. (By the 1970s 'independent' had become the adjective of choice to describe the private sector, including the public schools.) The vast majority went independent. One grammar school which in the end opted to close rather than to go comprehensive – the lack of endowments in this case made independent status an impossibility – was the Mary Datchelor School for Girls in south London. The journalist Polly Toynbee had sent her own daughter there and was present at many of the meetings at which bewildered parents tried to work out what was best for the school and for their daughters. She herself was in favour of going comprehensive but discovered that 'these parents are among those who particularly hated comprehensives. Many would have sent their children to private schools if they could have afforded to. They are largely made up of the sort of struggling middle classes who at the moment feel more threatened than any other group of society.' She wrote sympathetically of their 'agony and jealousy at not being able to afford private education and yet having grammar schools taken away'.[88]

The 1976 Education Act consequently led to a reinvigoration of the independent school sector. Many parents who had been happy with state education when it was based on the grammar school now turned to the private sector. One such was Lawrie Norcross, still headmaster of a comprehensive. He and his wife had educated their eldest three children at grammar schools, but made a different decision for their youngest son: 'By the time he was being educated there were no grammar schools left in London so we sent him to Dulwich College. We would infinitely have preferred not to have to spend money on his education, but we felt we couldn't sacrifice our children on the altar of educational dogma.'[89] One of the minor skirmishes in the war between the different types of school was over that old class favourite, the teaching of Latin and Greek. Lawrie Norcross had fought hard to keep his own comprehensive as one of the very few at which classical languages were taught; to ensure his own son could learn them he had to send him to a private school. The pendulum had swung back – the academic results-based system beloved of the middle classes was now once again reliably available only in the fee-paying sector which was easily accessible only to those who earned enough to pay for it. By the 1980s, not only were there more independent schools than a decade earlier due to the influx of ex-direct grant schools, but while the total school roll had fallen, the number of children in private education had increased. In 1978 the proportion of school-age children in private education was 5.8 per cent; by 1997 the figure stood at over 7 per cent.[90]

The public schools, however, were not left unchanged by this reversal of fortunes. In particular, the influx of direct grant schools into the private sector gave the old public schools something of a jolt. The journalist and writer Francis Wheen attended Harrow in the late 1960s and early 1970s and remembered the ethos then as being one which discouraged over-interest in exam results:

> The thing that struck me about it was when I'd done my O-levels, GCSEs as they're now called, and we started the next term on our A-level course, I said to the form master, now – for the English A-level – what are the set books? And he said, 'I don't want anyone to ask such questions, you're not here to pass exams, I don't want anyone to mention A-levels or set books for the next two years until you do the exams. We're not here to do that, we're here just to get a good general education.' It's become much more intense now, the competition between public schools, a sort of forcing-house approach.[91]

However, by the early 1980s Harrow, like many public schools, had undergone a serious change of attitude and discovered an

appetite for examination success. This often difficult process –
one senior master at Clifton College, Bristol, described it as being
painful 'but with no sense of there being an alternative' – was
given added impetus with the introduction of school league
tables in the 1990s.[92] While independent schools dominated the
list of the 'top 200' schools judged by examination results, the
tables led to extra pressure on individual schools to do well. In
1996 the headmaster of Cheltenham College was sacked because
the school was not high enough in the tables – 'a defining
moment', as journalists Andrew Adonis and Stephen Pollard
described it in their book on the English class system, because of
its acknowledgement of the new importance of public examination results even for traditional public schools.[93]

SECURING A PLACE: THE ASIAN EXPERIENCE
OF EDUCATION IN ENGLAND

While academics and social theorists in the past few decades have
tended to concentrate more upon 'race' than class as a way of
understanding society's divisions, the experience of some parts of
the Asian community illustrates vividly that, whatever the defini-
tional problems now surrounding usages such as 'middle-class',
education still functions so efficiently as an engine of social
mobility that it can partially obviate the handicaps caused by
racism. About a quarter of students in England now studying
medicine or dentistry come from ethnic minority groups, as do
about a fifth of those going into the law. A study of the background of these students often reveals, however, a significant
persistence of expectations deriving from their families' position
in society and traditions of educational achievement. The children of Asians from East Africa, where Asians dominated the
professional and commercial sectors, make up a disproportionate
number of ethnic minority professionals in Britain. Very often
families from other ethnic minority groups are also descendants
of those who were professionals before they came to England.[94]
One such family are the Drabus, who live in Winchester and

whose families both come from Kashmir. Kurshid Drabu is a judge, his wife, Reefat, is a GP. Reefat came to England as a small child with her father, who was also a GP. He was always 'anxious to ram home the point that we people do not have roots in this country and therefore we have to nurture our future by ensuring that we take our education seriously'.[95] Kurshid Drabu's family were landowners in Kashmir, but growing up as a boy he can remember his grandfather telling him that because the family were likely to lose some of their land, he must concentrate on his education, because 'education was the way back to a position of power'.[96]

Many of these families came from a colonial background where the British middle-class emphasis on education was part of the social order. The writer Yasmin Alibhai-Brown remembers her schooling in 1960s Uganda: 'It imposed a particularly British view of the world and the liberal tradition. There was Shakespeare, many of us knew about twenty plays off by heart and we used to perform one every three months.' Consequently, when she and some of her peers came to England in the early 1970s 'there was this enormous anticipation that we were entering the heart of greatness'. Alibhai-Brown was soon disillusioned by her experiences as an undergraduate at Oxford, but she never lost the sense that education was an escape route: 'My mother drummed it into me and my teachers drummed it into me that if I wanted to escape this life that I hated [in Uganda] I would have to educate myself out of it and it's a lesson that's in my blood.'[97]

But Alibhai-Brown and others like her, including the Drabus, had also learned another lesson about English education – that it could transform your status along with your knowledge of Shakespeare. During her time at Oxford she watched the behaviour of many of her fellow students and noticed the effect that a public school education seemed to have had upon them: 'They impart an essence into the boys and the girls when they go to these posh schools, that you are better simply because of who you are, not because of what you can do – you are part of the born-to-rule brigade.' After group tutorials she would retreat to her room and wonder 'why did those people who were talking rubbish sound as if they were always right and then why was it so difficult to question them'. She put this confidence down to a public school education and, like many others from Asian families (Patel is now the most common name on the register at Dulwich College in south-east London), wanted to give her own son this perceived advantage.[98] 'I am a socialist and I hated Oxford and I hate the damn public school system but I honestly believed that the only way my people would gain any influence in this country is if our children went and learned the trick where they sound as if they were born to rule.'[99]

The Drabus made a similar decision for their four children, sending them to a nearby independent, ex-direct grant school. Reefat Drabu is entirely happy with the choice they made, feeling that their education has given them confidence, but her husband is less certain: 'I think they would have been better off in state education because I am a firm believer in articulating concerns about élitism. You tend to become a bit aloof if you have just been to a private school and you tend to mix with a certain group of people which in some ways is not healthy.'[100] Other families who have made the same kind of choice have no doubts about their decision, but do notice a change in attitudes which they also attribute to the schools. Dr Sunak is a GP and his wife, Usha, a pharmacist. They sent both their sons to Winchester College. Usha Sunak is delighted with the confidence she feels her sons have gained, but also pinpoints the differences it introduces between herself and them: 'They can stand up and talk at any time in front of a crowd – I can't do that as well as them. They come with answers and reasoning, and the only way I can reason with them is that I'm your mother.' Her eldest son, Rishi, was a school prefect at Winchester before going on to Oxford and a job in the City. His education is more important to the way he sees himself than his ethnic background: 'I am very lucky to have been at these places, it does put me in an élite in society. I always consider myself professional middle-class, I don't think being Asian is a defining feature.'[101]

VALUING EDUCATION: CLASS AND SCHOOLING IN THE LATE TWENTIETH CENTURY

Somewhere between 7 per cent and 8 per cent of British children now go to private schools of one kind or another. Not all are academically excellent of course, but such schools dominate the league tables and admissions to the more prestigious universities. In 1994 about 46 per cent of all entrants to Oxford and Cambridge were educated at private schools, compared to 38 per cent at Oxford in 1969.[102] Also in 1994, nine out of ten pupils from the private sector went on to some form of higher education – a proportion three times higher than that of pupils who attended state schools – and this at a time when a university degree has become essential for almost any career.[103]

Not all children being educated at private school come from what could traditionally be described as middle-class backgrounds and certainly not all children from such backgrounds attend them. There are no statistical studies which pull the two factors together, but the correlation between occupational background and schooling is undoubtedly close. According to the 1991 census – the most recent for which figures are available – there were 740,000 school-aged children from professional, managerial and skilled non-manual families and in that same year 610,000 children were attending private schools. The census does not ask the questions which allow one to relate the two sets of children directly, but it seems highly likely that they broadly match.[104]

The remainder of children from such homes were being educated in the state system, but this does not mean that parents were not prioritising their children's education. Moving house to get into the 'right' catchment area is a common phenomenon and has been since the early 1970s. One BBC documentary in 1975 captured a father preparing to move house to further his daughter's education:'If I live in a catchment area close to a school then I have got every good chance of getting my child in there. This particular house is right next to Silverdale school, so I came to look at it straightaway.'[105] This pattern of behaviour persists, as the *Independent on Sunday* reported in 1996:'The premiums in some towns for a top-school catchment area house are so high that families are paying up to 30 per cent more than the price for a similar property in an adjoining but non-catchment neighbourhood.'[106] As the educationalist Sally Power puts it, 'There is absolutely no doubt that middle-class parents are able to translate their advantages into giving their children an advantaged education, whether they are buying into the private sector or moving into a particular area with a good comprehensive'.[107]

The ability to pay for education, whether directly by school fees or indirectly through higher house prices, implies in most cases professional status: education is an expensive business. This of course does not automatically demonstrate that schooling is still a focus for class concerns. However, both parents and schools are acutely aware of the status dimension to choices about schools and education. A recent headmaster of Winchester College acknowledges that the parents of pupils at the school are 'predominantly professional of course. And because it is a very expensive school it has to be a profession where there are decent-sized salaries.'[108] He also recognises that the decision of parents to send their sons to Winchester 'means a certain sort of cultural attitude. It means that they are prepared to spend their money on education rather than on holidays' and cites a classical reference in support of his view:

> If you go back to the ancient Greeks, there is a play by Aristophanes called *The Clouds* which is about exactly this subject. There the message is that your class is really determined by the value you put upon education ... The fact that you are prepared to pay for a good education is an indication of your

attitude towards the culture of your own society and the determining factor of the middle classes is that they put such a value upon education.[109]

Such a perspective, however partial, echoes certain long-standing views about education and class – in particular, the Taunton Commission's notion from the 1860s of the necessity for 'first-rate' schools for the sons of the clergy, doctors, lawyers and the poorer gentry 'who have nothing to look to but education to keep their sons on a high social level'.[110]

A sense of the importance of education remains fundamental to how most well-to-do parents view their obligations to their children. A collection of interviews with parents of boys attending Winchester College in 2000 finds them repeating the same phrases over and over again. 'All the parents we have met are of similar backgrounds. They are all professional people who have made considerable sacrifices to send their sons here.'[111] 'You could say we have made sacrifices to send our sons here. We could have lived a different lifestyle but we have spent most of our money on the boys' education.' 'I was always against private education. I think it's divisive – I went to grammar school myself. But my eldest son was in a class of thirty-six so we had to make a choice for him. It's been a struggle but we wanted to do the best for him.' The same emphasis on education, but with a different political slant, is revealed by parents interviewed at the Henry Beaufort comprehensive school up the road. One mother, herself a primary school headmistress who had moved to Winchester from London to gain access to 'good' comprehensives for her children, put the argument of the pro-comprehensive professional classes succinctly: 'We are politically committed to the state system and we wouldn't like to consider a public school partly because we believe that they cream off some of our best children. We feel that by people like us committing to the state system we help to keep it a good system.'[112]

The demise of the state grammar schools and the dilemmas of

the comprehensives have if anything exacerbated the social divisions in education in the last thirty years. The choice for parents at the beginning of the twenty-first century often feels starker than it did for parents in the 1960s. Melissa Benn gives this account of children's tea parties in north London: 'For those of us who still want to live the comprehensive dream for our children it is getting much harder. Anxiety about education has reached almost fever-pitch. I have been at three-year-olds' birthday parties where the parents sit, chomping crisps and swapping information about the local secondary schools with all the intensity of Pokémon obsessives.'[113] Beyond the worries about the curriculum and exam results she identifies a further fear: 'What remains, as ever, is anxiety about social mixing. This is partly an age-old middle-class fear of the underclass, partly a wish to educate one's children with other children of the same background and partly a pretty simple kind of snobbery that uses education as a way of keeping one's children separate from most ordinary children. But for that, there are always private schools.' A significant élite still choose private education for their children. 'Prime ministers may send their children eight miles across London', the sociologist David Rose comments in a pointed reference to the choices made by Tony and Cherie Blair, 'but most managerial and professional people with that kind of salary are sending their children to private schools. They know why. They know it buys them a position in the next generation – that's what it's all about.'[114]

As this chapter has shown, the relationship between the middle classes and forms of education has been a complex one. It has not always been private good, state bad; but the essence is that education is always important and says something about the parents as well as the child. As the old notion of middle-classness recedes, this sense of the importance of education has if anything been taken on by a wider section of the population. But for the current generation of parents, many of whom experienced first-hand as pupils the arguments over the eleven-plus, grammar schools and comprehensives, it remains an issue permeated with the anxieties about class which they learnt in their own childhoods. A sketch entitled 'The proud middle classes' from the satirical television series *The Fast Show* in 1997 put it in a more entertaining form.

Three men in their thirties are sitting around a table, having an after-dinner argument about which of them is the most middle-class. One proffers his public school education as proof of status, but one of the others scoffs – and delivers the punchline: 'My parents could easily have afforded to send me to a public school but they were liberals – they chose to educate me at a comprehensive. That makes me much more middle-class than you.'[115]

CHAPTER 7

FIN DE SIÈCLE

*Work and money in the late
twentieth century*

M ike Emens is a surgeon at the Queen Elizabeth hospital in Birmingham. Having undergone a long training,
he has been at the peak of his profession for many
years and is now nearing retirement. He continues to draw great
satisfaction from practising his skills: 'I think the main thing about
medicine and particularly surgery is that you get a great kick out
of it going right. You actually do something positive. You see your
patient after surgery and they say, "thank you, I'm better". You
never lose that buzz – it's something very, very satisfying. You are
privileged to be able to do a job that you actually enjoy doing.'
Vocation, dedication, 'duty of care'; these are the watchwords in
Mike Emens' description of his work. They contrast markedly
with the terms in which his son, Tim, describes his own life as a
chartered accountant with a company in the Midlands. Insecurity, pressure and performance are the recurrent themes in Tim's
account of his professional existence: 'It's a perpetual quest these
days to secure your job, trying constantly to prove yourself and
knowing that there are people ready to fill your position. I feel
that I've been constantly measured, constantly tested and if I
don't measure up then I'll be out. At the end of the day they
measure you on your revenue or your gross profits.' Money is
what he is measured by and money, not a sense of vocation, is
what motivates him: 'If I'm brutally honest about why I'm at
work I wouldn't say it's for pleasure. I'm trying to earn money to

guarantee a sense of security for myself and for my family. Money is what drives me to be at work.'[1]

The differences between Mike and Tim Emens' attitudes to work are not simply a function of their different occupations or the particular sectors of the economy in which they operate. They reflect the dramatic changes in middle-class work over the last thirty years, identified with the decline of the traditional career and the growth of a new economy of short-term contracts, long hours and performance-related pay. In the 1950s and 1960s solicitors, bank managers and civil servants were typically viewed as engaging in careers that were dull, predictable but stable – a job for life. Today, work in many areas of management and the professions is seen as subject to rapid change and inherently insecure. In this sense, as father and son, Mike and Tim Emens are placed on either side of a great divide. Mike's expectations of work are rooted in an older idea of the professional career as vocation, while Tim has grown up in an economic world that is at once more entrepreneurial and more precarious.

The character and meaning of these large-scale changes are the subject of this chapter. They are of great significance because, historically, work has played a central part in the self-definition of the English middle classes. As we have seen, in the early nineteenth century the engagement in the productive economy of manufacturers, merchants and members of the professions was essential to their identity as the 'middle classes' and integral to their critique of an idle, non-productive aristocracy. 'Industry' was a prime Victorian virtue; conversely, the ability of the male household head to maintain female dependants without the need for them to engage in paid work was an essential criterion of middle-class respectability. Furthermore, the distinction between mental and manual labour was a fundamental means by which middle and working classes were differentiated in English society from the Victorian period onwards. The importance of work as a guide to social position continues to be evident in the use of occupation as a standard indicator of class and status. Work, in short, has helped determine what it has meant to be 'middle-class' over the past two centuries. During the late twentieth century, however, economic changes overturned older patterns of work and unsettled the attitudes associated with them. In the process the historical identity of the middle classes has been put in question. Can the middle classes be said to exist if the ideals and values that distinguished them historically have dissolved?

ORGANISATION MAN

Writing in 1959, the sociologist Ralf Dahrendorf suggested that for the middle class, the career was the 'supreme social reality'.[2] By this he meant that it was the predominant factor affecting the lives of middle-class people. We might now wish to question this assertion by pointing out that it was so only indirectly in the case of middle-class women, since the career was largely the preserve of their fathers, brothers and husbands – of men, in short. As we have seen, married women were barred from professions like the civil service and teaching in the inter-war years and informal barriers to their engagement in paid employment remained strong after 1945. Nevertheless, Dahrendorf's statement indicates the central place that the career had come to play in middle-class life by the mid-twentieth century. In the 1950s the idea of the career was still relatively new. During the nineteenth century the characteristic middle-class figure was an employer, a manufac-turer, merchant or professional, usually in a family business. Ownership was the 'supreme social reality', not the career; sons would normally be taken into the family firm or bought partner-ships rather than having to work their way up through the ranks. Certain nineteenth-century attitudes, however, were important in contributing to the emergence of the modern career. Firstly, as we saw in Chapter Three, the volatility of the economy meant that security was a major preoccupation of the middle classes, determining strategies of investment and inheritance. Secondly, by the later Victorian period the ability to plan and predict the

future came to be seen as important, especially in families associated with the professions. Limiting family size and envisaging a
professional path through life were linked means by which a
degree of financial security could be achieved.[3]

The fundamental rationale of the career – security derived
from the ability to predict and plan the future – therefore derived
from the nineteenth century. But in its modern form the career
was the product of the large corporate organisations of the early
and mid-twentieth century. These included the burgeoning civil
service, the welfare state and large-scale business enterprises such
as banks, insurance companies and industrial firms, all with an
expanding white-collar staff. During the middle decades of the
twentieth century the career was strongly identified with those
who worked in technical, managerial and administrative posts in
these large bureaucracies. Such functions were personified by the
notion of 'organisation man', a stereotype of the upwardly
mobile corporate employee originating from the United States.
'Organisation man' worked his way up through the hierarchical
layers of the large corporation. Each step on the career path was
planned and known in advance, loyalty to the organisation being
repaid by job security and steady progress up the corporate
ladder.[4] In the mid-twentieth century more and more men were
occupying these types of roles. Between 1951 and 1971 the
numbers classified as higher professionals, administrators and
managers increased by 70 per cent to almost three and a half
million or one in five of the male working population.[5]

The model of the career was typically a product of large corporate organisations, but it pertained in wide areas of
middle-class employment: the public sector in the form of local
government, the National Health Service and education, as well
as the private sector, the professions and big business. In essence,
the middle-class notion of the career was a compact between the
organisation and the individual. The middle-class employee
promised loyalty to the organisation, personal probity, hard work
and deference to the hierarchical order. In return, the organisa-

tion repaid this commitment by assuring job security, a salary that would increase progressively with age and the opportunity of promotion over time, the peak in terms of earnings and position being reached by individuals only in their fifties. As important as the monetary rewards and security, the career promised respect from others. It was also a formative part of the identity of middle-class men and their families for much of the twentieth century. The sociologist Richard Sennett has eloquently described this situation:

> If anything characterised the old [pre-1970] middle class, it was not money but status – the respect you got from other people for the work you did and your standing within work organisations. Those organisations were stable. They offered long-term career paths for you if you worked well and were capable. You knew you would get a reward in the future and that would be a reward of respect as well as cash. To be a middle-class person was to know you could create a long-term life story.[6]

The possession of this 'longitudinal view, of developing and becoming' was something that distinguished the middle from the working classes.[7] The long-term perspective, orientated towards the future, was a product of the financial stability that the career allowed. In turn, the career depended on deferred gratification, the idea that rewards should be forgone in the present in order to be reaped in the future. Pension plans, investments and the progressive salary scale provided 'organisation man' with a sense of security deriving from the ability to guard against the unforeseen and to store up wealth that could be enjoyed in later life. All this contrasted with the endemic insecurity of the working class. Manual workers were invariably the first to be laid off in an economic downturn and had least protection from misfortune, despite the 'safety-net' of the post-war welfare state. Historians have observed that, partly as a response to economic insecurity, most sections of the working class tended to live for the present or immediate future rather than for the longer term and to choose short-term enjoyment over deferred gratification.[8] Consequently, classes in English society were divided by a specific orientation to time that was inscribed in the very language of employment – while the middle classes enjoyed a career, workers had a job.

If the career was the accepted format for middle-class work in mid-twentieth-century England, the model of the middle-class worker was a professional in law, medicine or one of the newer professions such as engineering, dentistry and academe. The number of occupations that sought recognition as professions after 1880 by forming professional bodies was striking: twenty new professions were established in this way by 1900, twenty-seven in the years to 1918, forty-six between the wars and a further forty-six between 1945 and 1970.[9] In both the public and the private sector the professional reigned supreme. Mike Emens, who was later to train in medicine himself, remembered being brushed and scrubbed before a visit to the GP in his home town, Newcastle upon Tyne: 'when I was a lad the doctor was almost a god and the surgeon one stage higher'.[10] In the National Health Service consultants wielded extraordinary power at the head of teams of junior doctors, nurses and technicians, the apex of a whole hierarchy of medical expertise. They were the 'old masters of the universe', according to the sociologist Colin Bell. When they swept past, everyone jumped to attention and obeyed.[11] The authority and prestige of professionals was based on respect for their knowledge, which was assumed to be impartial and disinterested, as well as dedication to their calling – the true profession was a vocation, not simply a means to earn money. The status of members of the higher professions, in particular, was related to their degree of autonomy from the bureaucratic hierarchy. University professors, lawyers and medical consultants appeared to be able to act more or less independently of the organisations that employed them in a way that was unthinkable for their more junior colleagues, managers or office workers.

For these reasons other middle-class occupations in inter- and post-war England sought to emulate the status and style of the professions. Bank managers and stockbrokers, teachers and accountants, all approximated in their conduct to the model of the impartial, beneficent professional. What the professions shared was the power to make decisions about the lives of others. The sociologist Richard Scase has articulated this precisely:

> If we look at the independent middle class, consisting of people like doctors, bank managers, head teachers, the clergy, a key feature of those positions – and they would regard them as positions, not as jobs – is that they are in control. The bank manager was very much in control in deciding whether to lend money to somebody, the doctor very much in control in his relations with his patients. And that created deference on the part of the person who wanted the loan or who was coming for treatment.[12]

Bank employees and insurance salesmen would undergo training to provide them not only with specialist knowledge, but also with the manner appropriate to professional status. Ken Lane, who worked for Prudential Assurance from 1930 until 1968, was among the first training officers with the company in 1951. One of the most important lessons trainee salesmen had to learn was how to comport themselves in a suitably authoritative, impartial style: 'One's clients turned to one for advice. I suppose one was slightly higher up the scale, in an advisory capacity. You had to have some authority.'[13]

Both the career and the claim to professional status gave large sections of the middle classes a sense of security in the decades between the Second World War and the early 1970s. In the aftermath of the inter-war depression, financial security and a job for life were for many a prime consideration in selecting an occupation. Leaving school in the early 1960s, Lawrie Penny sought a position with stability and prospects: 'Some jobs, I knew, had the potential to offer me a long-term career and that was important to me.' He decided to join Lloyds Bank: 'I realised that if I gained my professional exams and if I worked hard, I had a really worthwhile career ahead of me. In return for that, the bank expected loyalty from me and my colleagues, but it repaid that loyalty by the job continuity and the salary and career opportunities which were offered to us.'[14] Similarly, the stability offered by the Prudential was important to Ken Lane: 'I got married six months after joining the Pru because I then felt more secure ... The Pru were good employers. We always felt they liked their pound of flesh, with perhaps a drop of blood as well, but they looked after us if we were in trouble.'[15] Stability extended not just to the male breadwinner but to the whole family. The middle classes took advantage of the full range of financial investments aimed at securing the future: trusts to pay children's school fees, insurance against sickness, early death and loss of earnings, pensions for retirement. 'Men felt responsible in a long-term way to plan everything', the sociologist Ray Pahl observed. 'The man would be sure that his wife was properly provided for. "Provided for" was the phrase – "my wife and children are well provided for".'[16]

This sense of financial stability was underpinned by clear-cut gender roles for men and women. Masculinity was defined by career achievement. For this reason, when men engaged in socialising it was often with work colleagues; mixing business with pleasure, over dinner or on the golf course, was a characteristic of middle-class work.[17] Femininity was associated principally with the home and the upbringing of children; in the outside world the identity of a married woman was defined by her husband's position. 'You weren't really middle-class unless your wife was able to be at home', Richard Scase commented. 'In the community she would be the symbol of the husband's success. She was the bank manager's wife, the vicar's wife, the head teacher's wife. They represented their husbands in the community, reinforcing the respectability of the family units.'[18] Wives attended charitable events and company dinners with their husbands and were often vetted by heads of firms before a man was taken onto the board or into partnership – women were significant bearers of status in the middle classes. Involvement in community organisations and events – local charities, fêtes, societies – was a common means by which both men and women new to the town or to the ranks of the substantial middle classes became integrated into local society. Not everyone happily subscribed to this rigid pattern of gender roles and relationships, of course. In their study of managers in the late 1960s, the Pahls noted the feelings of boredom, loneliness and inferiority among some managers' wives and astutely predicted that the woman's role in such families was likely to become a significant source of conflict in future.[19] But for much of the period between the 1920s and the 1970s the social imperative of separate roles for middle-class men and women, especially after marriage, remained in place. As Ray Pahl pointed out, it was bound up with a larger, idealised picture of home and family which continues to be a remarkably pervasive middle-class fantasy: 'the dogs bounding round the lawn, the children with their ponies, a gentle, balanced life'.[20]

It was not just gender roles that were highly regulated in the decades before and after the Second World War. Powerful codes regarding speech, appearance and behaviour permeated the worlds of work and money-making. Money itself was taboo as a subject of discussion, even – perhaps especially – in the City of London, where money was the subject as well as the reward of most work. James Dundas Hamilton, who joined the Stock Exchange in 1946 and later became a partner in a banking firm, recalled: 'It was very bad form to talk about money and still is among my generation. One would certainly never boast about what one earned or about one's successes.'[21] Smart though sober dress at work was also *de rigueur*. At Lloyds Bank Lawrie Penny 'had to dress in the right way and that would include wearing a dark suit. I can remember that in the summer months, if we were allowed to take our jackets off, which was only on the hottest days, we were expected to have long-sleeved white shirts on and to wear those shirts with the sleeves rolled down.' The bowler hat was ubiquitous among businessmen, for insurance salesmen like Ken Lane as much as for City bankers like James Dundas Hamilton. The bowler was invented in 1850 as a democratic alternative to the top hat, but only became part of the class uniform of businessmen after the First World War. Conformity of dress was easily accepted among men who had grown used to military uniform – usually that of officers – in wartime. Beards, on the other hand, were frowned upon as raffish and as signalling untrustworthiness.[22] Forms of address at work similarly observed strict propriety. 'In my early years, the manager was always known as "sir"', Lawrie Penny recalled; colleagues 'we might know by their Christian names, but the manager would always refer to them as Mr, Mrs or Miss whoever. It was a much more formal era.'[23]

As we have seen in earlier chapters, the way one appeared to others was very important in the middle classes. It was necessary for middle-class individuals to embody a certain style. 'Class' was not something that was seen as merely innate in individuals; it had to be demonstrated to others by manners, gestures and attitudes. Overt ambition was discouraged, for example. It was essential not to appear 'pushy' or striving, not to be seen to be trying too hard. Work itself should appear effortless. In the City, according to James Dundas Hamilton, the appropriate 'attitude to work was that you could do it easily, that it didn't require too much effort or strain. Some of the best firms were absolutely brilliant at that. They were always in the first few of any new venture without appearing to have worked very hard to get there.'[24] Codes of middle-class behaviour emphasised the 'rounded individual' as a model, as against the 'narrow' expert. These attributes of middle-class behaviour were often hard for aspirants to emulate. In the words of Richard Scase, 'the English gentleman, cool, collected, was always in charge. Nothing was a problem. This was a very strong theme within the traditional middle class and if you were a self-made man it was almost impossible for you to take on that form of behaviour. It was difficult to acquire that way of walking down the street, that form of body language. These qualities could only really be acquired in the traditional middle class, through family upbringing and through being sent to certain kinds of school.'[25]

The effect of such codes was to endow the established middle classes with a sense of poise and self-assurance. Among professionals like medical consultants, lawyers and academics it could also be combined with an element of moral superiority, which tended to grate with other elements of the middle classes, such as corporate managers and self-employed businessmen. However, the preference for relaxed geniality over active and assertive intelligence was a persistent motif in middle-class life. As Ray Pahl has pointed out, it is reflected in the well-known children's story *The House at Pooh Corner* by the unfavourable contrast of pushy, intelligent Rabbit with amiable, stolid Winnie-the-Pooh:

> 'Rabbit's clever', said Pooh thoughtfully.
> 'Yes', said Piglet, 'Rabbit's clever.'
> 'And he has Brain.'
> 'Yes', said Piglet. 'Rabbit has Brain.'
> There was a long silence.
> 'I suppose', said Pooh, 'that's why he never understands anything.'[26]

The characteristic, unhurried affability of the professional middle class gave the impression of a deep and enduring stability. Despite signs of change – the welfare state, post-war 'affluence', sixties 'permissiveness' – to many the middle-class world seemed outwardly resilient, absorbing shifts affecting English society without itself being transformed in any significant way. One higher civil servant interviewed by the Pahls in the late 1960s saw the essentials of middle-class life in the London suburbs as having altered little over his working life: 'The style of life now is remarkably similar to what it was thirty years ago. I simply see the 1960s as the 1930s writ large.'[27] Far from being immutable, however, this middle-class world stood on the verge of disintegration by the late 1960s. In Chapter Four we saw that the foundations of the English upper middle class were quietly eroded in the post-war decades; but in the 1970s the foundations of the middle classes as a whole were to be visibly and radically shaken. When change came, it was felt first and most profoundly in the world of work. The effect was to challenge most of the assumptions of middle-class life of the previous hundred years.

'LUNCH IS FOR WIMPS': THE TRANSFORMATION OF MIDDLE-CLASS WORK

In retrospect, it is possible to see the seeds of change in the 1950s and 1960s. The rise in working-class standards of living and of forms of consumerism directed, for the first time, specifically at the young tended to diminish class distinctions based on taste and lifestyle. Harold Wilson's Labour government of the 1960s attacked the 'grouse moor' mentality of the old landed classes. 'They cling to privilege and power for the few, shutting the gates on the many', Wilson asserted. 'Tory society is a closed society in which birth and wealth have priority, in which the master-and-servant, landlord-and-tenant mentality is predominant.'[28] A culture of patronage based on family background and the old boy network was seen as stifling meritocracy and innovation. Meanwhile, mergers and buy-outs threatened the remains of an older family-based capitalism. But as we saw in Chapter Four, such developments tended to affect, first and foremost, rich upper middle-class families, like the Courtaulds, and to undermine the grand lifestyle and the ethos of *noblesse oblige* identified with them before the Second World War. The material wellbeing of the bulk of the middle classes was perpetuated into the post-war period by the long economic boom that lasted from the late 1940s to the early 1970s. In reality, Britain's economic performance was among the most sluggish in the Western world during this period. Between 1953 and 1973 the annual increase in economic growth was over 5 per cent in France, Germany, Italy and Austria, 4 per cent in the United States, but only 3 per cent in the United Kingdom. Moreover, the British share of world exports halved between 1951 and 1971.[29] But the economy continued to grow at a sufficient rate in the 1950s and 1960s to sustain the middle-class career, the job for life and the secure, family-centred world of bank managers, solicitors, teachers and others. On average, real incomes grew steadily, increasing at a rate of roughly 2 per cent a year between 1950 and 1970.[30]

If economic boom underwrote the stability of middle-class work, economic depression destroyed it. In 1973 the West entered a severe recession, triggered by a sudden rise in oil prices in the Middle East. In Britain the crisis was deepened by the fundamental weakness of the economy, stemming from a long-term failure to restructure and renew the country's aged industrial base. Between 1973 and 1980 overall economic growth rates slowed to 0.6 per cent. Manufacturing industry suffered particularly acutely; between 1973 and 1983 Britain was unique among developed economies in suffering a sustained absolute fall in manufacturing output. By the early 1980s manufactured imports exceeded exports for the first time since the industrial revolution.[31] Added to this, there was persistent and virulent price inflation. In 1975 it rose to 25 per cent and remained well above the average for Western economies for most of the 1970s. Inflation, above all, was represented as draining the lifeblood of the English middle classes. 'It is not going too far to say that, until now, the middle class has been merely squeezed', a right-wing journalist warned in 1976. 'If inflation continues unchecked it will be destroyed.'[32]

The fall-out from these economic developments was rapid and serious. The three-day week, the miners' strike of 1974, a balance of payments crisis in 1976 and what was widely seen as a humiliating bail-out from the International Monetary Fund followed one another in steady succession; economic recession rapidly turned into a political and social crisis.[33] In the process, the prevailing national system of economic management, based on negotiated agreements between government, business and the trade unions, was discredited and ultimately discarded. In 1976 the leading business journal the *Economist* published a major survey entitled 'The coming entrepreneurial revolution'. Prophetically, it announced not only the end of government efforts to regulate the economy, but also the end of 'organisation man'. Big hierarchical corporations, 'with layer of management sitting upon layer' would go to the wall; they would be replaced by smaller, flatter, more flexible organisational structures, 'confederations of entrepreneurs' backed by high technology rather than armies of office workers. Citing the conservative American critic Irving Kristol, the *Economist* argued that the 'new class of scientists, lawyers, city planners, social workers, educators, criminologists, sociologists, public health doctors', who currently preferred to work in the public sector, would see their powers diminished by the 'reprivatisation of the bureaucracy'. The world of work – and especially middle-class work – was on the brink of a revolution.[34]

In fact, other developments were simultaneously reshaping the face of middle-class work. Firstly, middle-class women, including married women, began to enter the paid workforce in rising numbers as the unofficial 'marriage bar' began at last to crumble. Between 1971 and 1999 the proportion of economically active women in the UK increased from 56 per cent to 72 per cent. Inherent in this movement was the entry of women into areas of employment that were traditionally the preserve of middle-class men, such as the professions, middle management and the higher echelons of business. A government-sponsored report underlined the historical significance of this shift: 'The increasing participation of married women has been the most outstanding factor in the changing balance between employment and non-employment – a fact which raises many questions about the

changing character of family life and the relation between marriage, kinship and economy in an advanced industrial society.'[35]
The result was that in the 1970s the conventional separation of
gender roles in the middle classes began to alter, with major
implications for the organisation of both work and home. Secondly, middle-class occupations themselves became less secure. In
the economic recession after 1973 mass unemployment returned
for the first time since the 1930s, rising from 660,000 people or 3
per cent of the working population in 1971 to 3.5 million or 13
per cent in the early 1980s. This time it was not only workers who
lost their jobs, but also managers. The effects were dramatic. 'As
soon as middle-class people found that they could get sacked,
bang went the job for life', Ray Pahl commented. 'That was a terrible shock for middle-class people who assumed that there was
some kind of progression in their career.' Richard Scase has
underscored the point by placing the onset of unemployment in
historical context:

> In the 1970s middle-class privileges are undermined in a fun-
> damental way for the first time. The major factor that
> undermines them is the end of job security, jobs for life. Sud-
> denly, because organisations are restructuring and using
> computer technology in their management systems, managers
> find that they are prone to redundancy ... In place of security
> and self-confidence comes self-doubt, anxiety and insecurity.
> From the 1970s onwards the middle classes in Britain are never
> the same again.[36]

Nor were the difficulties at work purely economic in origin. In
1979 the Conservative government of Margaret Thatcher swept
to power, determined to promote the newly advocated 'entrepreneurial revolution' as a remedy for the nation's ills. As part of this,
'restrictive practices' in all shapes and forms were to be removed.
The most notorious example of this offensive was the administration's strategic assault on the trade unions and the labour

movement, culminating in the defeat of the miners in the strike of 1984–5. But attacks on restrictive practices were not confined to the institutions of the working class. They were also aimed at the professions and the public sector, including the so-called 'immune targets' of the law, medicine and the church. Solicitors' monopoly of conveyancing was denounced; general managers were introduced in the National Health Service to make consultants and doctors accountable; reports by the Church of England on poverty and social conflict were derided as 'Marxist'. The government similarly confronted other powerful professional groups. The ending of a strike by civil servants for higher pay in July 1981 was celebrated as a 'victory' by the Thatcher administration in its 'war for domination'. In the universities, the system of tenure, which had underpinned academic rights to freedom of speech since the war, was abolished. On every side, so it seemed, the conventional practices of the professions were challenged and in many cases radically reformed.[37]

Why did a Conservative party traditionally considered to be the political representative of bourgeois England turn so aggressively on an important section of the middle classes? The answer lies in a mixture of prejudice and political ideology. The view of the American sociologist Richard Sennett is instructive:

> As a foreigner, one thing that struck me about the class talk of Thatcher and her acolytes was that it is about revenge. These are people who feel looked down on, who now [in the 1980s] feel that the changes in the economy mean that they can get revenge on these professional, stable, inwardly assured people, who had all the privileges. Many outside observers are struck by the contemptuousness, which was very different from the language of entrepreneurialism in the United States. Reagan was not someone who was contemptuous of the professional, he was somebody who believed that everybody should simply get rich. I don't know if that's better, but it lacked the kind of class hostility that to us foreigners seemed so pronounced in

Thatcher's attack on teachers, doctors, public service workers.[38]

More generally, as Sennett implies, the attacks represented the revenge of the private sector on the public sector, of the small businessman and the manager on the doctor and the teacher. The Conservative administration of the 1980s tapped into a deep vein of resentment against the professions, summed up in George Bernard Shaw's dictum that 'all professions are conspiracies against the laity'. The remedy was to open the professions to competition and to subject them to external regulation. Meanwhile, private sector practices such as contracting out and continuous audit were introduced into public services. All this significantly reduced the authority – and, no doubt, the moral superiority – of the professions. But with the authority also went much of the old sense of vocational worth. According to the surgeon Mike Emens, the 'hidden agenda of Thatcher was to attack the autonomy of doctors ... When I was a junior doctor it was a much more relaxed atmosphere and we were given more opportunity to actually solve the problem without interference. Now we've got governors' guidelines, time and financial constraints, which in themselves may be good, but they are not necessarily the best way of solving a problem.' In the 1980s the values of the market were imposed over and above professional pride in work and the 'duty of care'.[39]

The political and economic shifts of the 1970s and 1980s extensively reshaped middle-class attitudes to work. On the one hand, the work ethic intensified. 'Lunch is for wimps' became one of a series of slogans glorifying entrepreneurial commitment.[40] A culture of 'presenteeism', signifying the tendency for people to be continuously present in the office, began to take hold. From 1983 Britain bucked the international trend with working hours steadily rising; by 1992 almost 30 per cent of British men were working more than the European Community maximum of forty-eight hours a week, the highest proportion in

Europe. In a study of managers undertaken in 1989, over 80 per cent claimed to work in excess of fifty hours a week.[41] Work, it seemed, was becoming a way of life in itself, rather than a means to earn a living, to maintain a family or uphold status. On the other hand, the sense of company loyalty, trust and stability, which had characterised the traditional idea of the career, simultaneously dissolved. Richard Scase summed up the new mind-set of managers in the 1980s:

> We go to the culture-building away-day, we express our commitment to our organisations, our loyalty, but underneath we are very suspicious and cautious because we've seen our friends lose their jobs. We've seen this company being taken over by that company and then closed down, and we could be the next to go, so we are not going to commit ourselves. We are going to look at the world in very short-term, instrumental 'what's in it for me?' terms. That's changed the whole core of values within the middle class.[42]

Individualism supplanted corporate loyalty and short-term gain replaced the long-term view that had formerly characterised middle-class attitudes to career and financial planning. 'Ten years ago I could predict that my job would still be around in ten years' time', commented Rob Loynes, a computer software designer. 'If you can see your job lasting two years, that's probably tops now – the whole organisation seems to be reorganising itself every couple of years.'[43]

The short-term, instrumental approach to work also affected middle-class attitudes to money in the 1980s. The habit of saving for the future, of deferred gratification, which had informed much of the old outlook, was overtaken by a new hedonism. Shopping and spending became leisure activities. Wealth was to be flaunted and money itself ceased to be a taboo subject of public discussion. 'Bourgeois Britons grow rich again' the front cover of the *Economist* unabashedly proclaimed in 1988, reflecting, according to the journal, the 'new confidence' of the 'long demoralised and impoverished middle classes'.[44] In reality, however, the effects of the economic, political and entrepreneurial revolution on England's middle classes were more profound and ambiguous. Perhaps no single milieu showed this more clearly than the City of London, the exemplar and symbol of the changes overtaking the world of middle-class work in the last decades of the twentieth century.

SERIOUS MONEY: THE CITY OF LONDON

Prior to the 1970s, the City of London was one of the most traditional preserves of male, upper middle-class England. The transformation of the City in the 1980s into a byword for the new enterprise culture, characterised by exhilaration and excess, means that it serves as a striking example of the new patterns of middle-class work and money-making. The City has a long history as a centre for banking and trade, related importantly to London's role as an imperial capital and a major port.[45] The decline of the commercial and imperial functions in the course of the twentieth century led to the City's increasing concentration on banking and financial services in the aftermath of the Second World War. 'Invisible earnings' from shipping, banking, insurance and other services, much of which derived from City firms, grew dramatically from £740 million in 1965 to £12 billion by 1986. Their importance to the national economy had long been evident, but after 1973 they became even more vital, helping to compensate for the mounting deficit in 'visible' trade caused by the decline of manufacturing industry.[46] During the second half of the twentieth century the City of London loomed ever larger in Britain's economic life.

The degree of continuity in the City's role and the drawn-out nature of the functional changes that occurred, however, meant that for much of the twentieth century its organisational structures and working practices altered little over people's working lives. In the mid-twentieth century the City was a conservative place in every sense – socially, economically and politically. Those who worked there described it as a large village, a 'Square Mile' of densely clustered financial institutions whose heart was the Stock Exchange with its three and a half thousand members. The Square Mile housed the headquarters of the clearing banks and large insurance businesses such as Lloyds, but also numbers of merchant banks and broking houses, which were mainly family firms and private partnerships. James Dundas Hamilton, who became a partner in a City firm in 1948, remembered it as 'very much a gentlemen's club', where loyalty and longevity in careers was taken for granted: 'You were wedded to your firm for life. Once you took on employment, you didn't expect to move and there was no question of going and bidding somebody out of one firm because that wasn't good form – you expected loyalty and loyalty was given.'[47] Typically, recruitment into such firms occurred through family connection. David Verey entered Lazards, an established merchant bank, following an interview with the chairman, who was a friend of his father. David confessed to the chairman that his main interest was the poetry of T. S. Eliot, but the chairman invited him to join anyway with the words, 'Well, dear boy, if you want to come and be bored for a couple of years, do'. Most entrants, though, were not academic high-fliers. Evidence from oral testimony confirms that the great majority of men recruited to City firms between 1945 and the 1970s came from comfortably off middle-class homes and were public school educated.[48]

The old City was also an intensely male environment. Behaviour on the stock and commodities exchanges was often very physical, involving shouting, pushing, gesticulating and, occasionally, fighting, all of which was deemed to render them unsuitable places for women. Jane Partington was struck by the all-male atmosphere when she became one of the first women to work on the Stock Exchange in 1974: 'The men all knew each other, they had nicknames for each other, they played pranks on each other ... there wasn't a woman in sight.'[49] Much of men's social life revolved around the City. 'Of all the friends I have, the closest came from work', James Dundas Hamilton acknowledged, and many other City men interviewed about the post-war decades concurred. Long lunches, gentlemen's clubs and business camaraderie all fostered a culture of male sociability.[50] Wives were kept well away, except for the purposes of socialising with other business partners. 'My wife was obviously of vital importance to me', stated James Dundas Hamilton, 'but I don't think she actually ever came to the office except on one occasion, just to see what it looked like.' As in other areas of business and the professions, wives of new partners were normally 'vetted' as part of the appointment process. They were often regarded as intuitively good at evaluating people, but this was considered as the limit of their contribution. City men would have understood the judgement of Michael Verey, former head of Schroders, who described his wife as 'good with people – useless at business judgements, but nearly always correct as a judge of someone's character'.[51] Within the strictly demarcated boundaries of gender and class, however, much of working life was conducted in a relaxed manner. City men took time off to engage in voluntary work, charity and philanthropy: George Verey's boss in the 1940s, Albert Wagg, founded a charitable trust for the education of East End children; his son, David Verey, was chairman of trustees of the Tate Gallery. 'The great advantage of the Stock Exchange was that you were virtually your own master', James Dundas Hamilton explained. 'So if you had an interest you wanted to follow or a charity you wanted to support, the time was given you for that.' Nor was money an overriding consideration. 'It was a gentler world' according to George Verey. 'It was less grabbing. In my day no one picked up a million; five thousand a year was considered good money. The income mostly went on living – the upkeep of your family, holidays, school fees. There were virtually no "perks". If you knew someone to be greedy, you saw as little as possible of them.'[52]

The old City of the immediate post-war decades was not wholly immune from changes in the wider economic world. The 1950s saw a growing business in pension and local authority funds, the 1960s the development of a new market in 'eurobonds', enabling foreign corporations to raise dollar loans, and the introduction of computers – the first computer was installed in the Stock Exchange in 1966. Nevertheless, the City remained curiously wedded to custom and tradition even by middle-class standards, so that when changes occurred they appeared especially striking. As with other sectors of the British economy, change began to be felt in the City in the early 1970s with the onset of recession. In 1972–3 the stock market crashed as a result of banks over-lending with insufficient liquidity to compensate. As deputy chairman of the Stock Exchange James Dundas Hamilton recalled, 'We used to go to visit the governor of the Bank of England every Wednesday and listen to the appalling news of one bank after another closing its doors. The Stock Exchange had a very tough time in that period.'[53] Still more profound in the long term were the effects of the deregulation of the international money markets following the collapse in 1971 of the Bretton Woods agreement, which had underpinned and controlled the international monetary system since the Second World War. Exchange rates had previously been fixed internationally in relation to the US dollar, but from the early 1970s the system broke down and there was nothing to stop large flows of money going from one country to another. Boosted by petrodollars from the profits of the world's oil-producing countries and by the ending of exchange controls by national governments, new money flooded onto the financial markets over the next decade, largely independent of either world trade or governmental intervention.[54] These developments had major and lasting effects. London was fortuitously located in a time-zone between New York and Tokyo and thus fitted neatly into the global system of twenty-four-hour trading that evolved in line with the increased volume and mobility of international money. But while these trends augmented the importance of the City of London within both the national and the international economy, they also rapidly destroyed the old-established work practices and culture. The most powerful symbol of this was the demise of the Stock Exchange floor itself, following the introduction of on-screen dealing in 1979 and the changes introduced with 'Big Bang' in 1986. The Stock Exchange was in any case becoming an anachronism at a period when foreign banks increasingly dominated the City – traditionally only British-based institutions had access to the floor – and business was carried out between the offices of brokers and dealers.[55] Yet the phasing out of the Stock Exchange floor after 'Big Bang' symbolised in a particularly poignant way the passing of an era and a way of life. Jane Partington recalled going to the building the day the changes were announced: 'I walked through the door and the whole place was heaving with people. Anybody who had ever worked there was present. There was this extraordinary emotion as if collectively all the people knew that there was going to be a momentous change in working life. It was very, very memorable. You could touch the atmosphere, it was tangible.'[56]

Change, however, was not simply a matter of technology and economic forces. One of the most fundamental shifts after 1970 was the break-up of the City as an exclusively male, middle-class enclave. Women, of course, had worked in the City as secretaries and assistants since the nineteenth century, but not on an equal footing with men. It was only after a vote that the Stock Exchange was opened to women members in the early 1970s. Women like Jane Partington, who began work there in 1974, had to face the backlash of men who had opposed reform: 'I remember walking round the market to check the price, then going to phone the person who needed the price and the man behind me swore profanely. I turned round and said "charming" and he said "I never voted for you, I never wanted you here, you can … off as far as I'm concerned".'[57] Codes of class as well as gender were disturbed in the 1970s. The rapid expansion in the volume of business created new and lucrative openings, facilitating the influx of the so-called 'barrow boys' and 'lads from Newham', especially in the hurly-burly world of foreign exchange dealing. Valerie Thompson was the daughter of a fruit trader at Billingsgate Market, from Dagenham in Essex, who started selling for a City firm in the early 1980s: 'Trading apples and oranges isn't very different from trading securities; the principles are the same as in the City.' Through trading she found herself able to express 'all my pent-up anger against men and life that came from my childhood'.[58] Walls that had preserved the more lucrative City jobs for middle-class men were crumbling.

The 1980s were the apotheosis of the new City. The election of Mrs Thatcher's Conservative government in 1979, with its advocacy of market-led capitalism and minimal state intervention, chimed with the new, international and entrepreneurial climate of the City. Further waves of deregulation ensued, the most spectacular of which, 'Big Bang' in 1986, did away with the old divisions between banking and finance and between the roles of middle-class brokers and working-class jobbers. A further effect of 'Big Bang' was to increase the already growing presence of international banks and finance houses: between 1968 and 1986 they had risen from 125 to over 400. No other financial centre could match London for the number of foreign firms or the volume of international banking business.[59] With the opening of the City to international corporate finance, British firms found it difficult to compete. Of the old merchant banks only Hambros and Rothschilds still existed as independent entities in the mid-1990s and they were not among the leading players. 'No British house today operates in the big league', an historian reported in 1997.[60] In the changed conditions the gentlemanly ethos of trust which had characterised the old City, summed up in the phrase 'my word is my bond', was no longer recognised as an adequate safeguard against malpractice. As well as deregulating markets and working practices, 'Big Bang' also saw the institution of a new legally enforced system of business regulation intended to outlaw activities such as 'insider trading' – illegal dealing in shares by those with privileged information. James Dundas Hamilton regretted the shift, seeing in it the decline of the gentlemanly code of honour:

> Self-regulation had enormous advantages. Everybody tried to obey the code. If your client tried to cut corners and break the code, you stopped him and directed him back to the proper course of business ethics. Now, of course, the code is not a code, it's a law. People are paid to find ways round the law, so that the difference is that instead of being paid to keep a straight course, many people now are being paid to avoid the penalties of keeping to the strict letter of the law. That's a big change.[61]

The City of London was given a new lease of life as a global financial centre in the 1970s and 1980s, but at the price of undermining the institutions, codes and practices that had identified it as an upper middle-class preserve. No figure in the 1980s symbolised this shift more than the 'yuppy', an acronym for 'young urban professional'. The new breed of City workers represented 'Thatcher's stormtroopers', the vanguard of the new enterprise culture against the traditional professions which remained strongly resistant to the Thatcher government's glorification of the market. The City became a byword for rocketing salaries paid to young, ambitious men and women. It has been estimated that the gross annual earnings of City workers doubled between 1981 and 1987, without counting bonuses which often represented 15 per cent or more of an individual's overall income. By this latter date men and women employed in the Square Mile accounted for half of all those earning over £100,000 p.a. in Britain.[62] Rapidly rising pay was itself related to the decline of loyalty between firm and employee; 'golden hellos' and intense competition for business made it profitable for individuals to move from job to job. 'By the time Big Bang happened the large international companies had taken over', observed Jane Partington;

'people were playing off against one other, they were working towards having contracts which they would fulfil and then move on to the next one.' For those who were successful at the game, the City in the 1980s represented a 'heady cocktail of power and money and status'.[63] The changes were epitomised by the new attitudes to money. Whereas in the past, as we have seen, it was deemed vulgar to discuss earnings openly, now wealth was there to be flaunted. 'Sexy greedy' was the epithet that Carol Churchill invented to define the new *Zeitgeist* in her play *Serious Money: A City Comedy* in 1987.[64] The 1980s, according to Richard Sennett, saw a significant shift in favour of values 'which privilege the entrepreneur, short-term work at the expense of long-term careers and the making of money as a sign of self-worth'. The new hedonism signified the end of the old ethic of moderation and deferred gratification; the new message was 'that there are no rewards for delay, there are rewards for doing things right now'.[65] The yuppy of the 1980s was, in effect, the antithesis of the old merchant banker. In less than a generation the City had witnessed a revolution of values, transforming it from a bastion of gentlemanly capitalism to the cutting-edge of the new entrepreneurial economy.

THE END OF MIDDLE-CLASS WORK?

The history of the City exemplifies many of the changes that overtook the middle classes at work in the last third of the twentieth century. A hard-edged, individualist work culture gradually encompassed more occupations and more sectors: financial services, advertising, high-tech manufacturing, management in the private and public sectors, the legal and other professions. Few if any areas in which middle-class people worked were left untouched by this new work culture. But by the 1990s the heady excitement that had marked the City in the previous decade had gone, replaced by recognition of the insecurity as well as the freedom that the world of work now offered. Following the world stock market crash of 1987, which pricked the City bubble, financial services went into crisis. Between 1990 and 1992 it was calculated that 75,000 jobs were lost in the banking sector, the big four clearing banks – Barclays, Lloyds, National Westminster and Midland – accounting for 20,000. Other sectors and companies formerly considered 'safe' likewise suffered the shock of mass redundancies. The privatised telecommunications giant British Telecom reduced its managers and staff by 80,000 between 1989 and 1993, while the management of over 44,000 civil service jobs was put out to private tender.[66] A series of scandals overtook long-standing financial institutions. Barings bank collapsed in 1995 as a result of rogue trading; the Prudential, formerly a byword for financial probity, was found guilty of misselling personal pensions. In public services, such as health and education, subcontracting and 'flexibilisation' (a euphemism for a host of changes to conventional working practices) were introduced no less enthusiastically than in cutting-edge industries. Meanwhile, a series of new words related to work insecurity entered the *Oxford English Dictionary* in the 1990s: 'downsizing', 'presenteeism' and 'karoshi' (a Japanese term meaning killing yourself by overwork).

Whereas the late 1970s and early 1980s saw the working class suffer the brunt of mass unemployment with the savage contraction in manufacturing industry, the 1990s appeared to witness a similar phenomenon occurring among the middle classes. 'Nobody is safe' ran an article in the *Independent on Sunday* in 1993; the 'casualisation' of the middle classes was in full swing.[67] In some ways, perception and reality did not appear to match. Research on the labour market consistently showed that blue-collar workers were more likely to be made redundant than managers or white-collar workers, while historically speaking there was nothing new about job insecurity – it had been an endemic feature of large swathes of the nineteenth-century economy.[68] However, such observations missed the point. Unemployment on the scale of the 1990s *was* a new phenomenon for many professions, unlike manual or clerical occupations, and perception rather than reality tended to shape the collective outlook of the middle classes. For example, in a Mori survey in the *Sunday Times* in 1994 over a third of the managerial, professional, administrative and clerical workers interviewed said that they feared redundancy in the next twelve months. A report in the *Guardian* reached a similar conclusion: 'Britain's middle classes have found that the market economy intended for the working classes has come to their own door with a vengeance … The freedom promised by markets has created huge swathes of anxiety.'[69] For the first time since the 1930s, job insecurity had come to haunt the middle classes. This time, though, insecurity was not the product of temporary recession; it appeared to be an endemic feature of the new enterprise economy.

At work, insecurity meant that individuals felt under intense pressure to perform. Tim Emens, the chartered accountant, graphically illustrated this point in describing his own work-life and that of his friends: 'The pressure to deliver results has been non-stop. I could lose my job reasonably quickly if I don't deliver. We're all very insecure. I don't think any of my friends or colleagues in similar positions feel they can rest easy in their jobs. They expect to be moved within two or three years.' This perception that the situation could rapidly change, that unemployment and moving jobs were ever-present realities, affected Tim's decisions in other areas of his life: 'In my case I will take out short-term mortgages, rather than a long-term, twenty-five-year fixed rate. I won't join an expensive club with high subscription fees because I may have to move in a couple of years.' Anxiety did not diminish with age; on the contrary, getting older only increased the risk of redundancy: 'I have fears about where I am going to be when I reach the age of forty, let alone fifty. I feel that if I haven't reached a certain level in my company by the time I'm forty, then I'm in trouble and I don't know what I'm going to do about it.'[70] Pressure at work produced various responses in stressed managers and professionals.

One was to undertake a middle-class form of 'work to rule', following the routine but withholding commitment from the employer and refusing to engage in any work activity beyond the immediately defined role. Another response was to 'go on the sick'. While the average length of working hours increased between 1984 and 1991, most markedly among managers and professionals, so too did the proportion of employees absent from work owing to sickness or injury, among all age groups, male and female.[71]

More generally, the intensification of competition bred a rapacious individualism. In the City, the old camaraderie dissolved with 'Big Bang'. According to Jane Partington, 'the difference was that it became much more the cult of the individual. The stress levels were higher because you couldn't off-load to anyone, you didn't automatically go out to the pub together, you didn't all automatically cover for each other. I've watched people forget to pass on messages which normally they would have done. That breeds its own kind of edge.'[72] New extreme forms of individualism became a strategy for getting on. Ray Pahl, the sociologist of work, argued that in the middle classes the CV (curriculum vitae) replaced the institution, corporation or firm as the focus for individual careers. Rather than working their way up the corporate ladder as in the past, people worked for their CV, which could then be traded in for a new job. The career had been taken out of corporate hands and privatised or individualised.[73] More radically still, executives and professionals were urged to engage in personal 'branding', to market themselves as employable commodities. 'Hardly anyone can expect to relax and enjoy twenty years of secure tenure in a job any longer', one corporate guru advised, so individuals needed constantly to reinvent themselves in order to survive professionally. 'We even have to brand ourselves within organisations, because overlaying the corporate ideal today everyone needs to be entrepreneurial, in charge of their own career and destiny. The challenge is to create a personal brand that is unique yet synergistic with the corporate one we are working for at the moment.' The logic of this strategy was that 'Me plc' became the only company to which individuals owed loyalty.[74]

The extensive changes in the character of middle-class work in the late twentieth century had positive aspects. Average real earnings progressively rose, mobility between jobs increased and for many people the decline of the old career structure with its hierarchies and rigidities was liberating. For middle-class women, in particular, who were previously denied access to the professions and the higher reaches of business, the working world was opened up, though not without considerable struggle. Arguably, the new 'flexibilisation' of work, which was often seen as augmenting job insecurity and pressure, was advantageous to women, for whom work often needed to be fitted with the demands of childcare.[75] Furthermore, the old arrogance of the professions dissipated – medical consultants, academics and civil servants were rendered accountable to managers and public regulators by the 1990s. The old 'masters of the universe' were no more.

But many aspects of change were experienced by the middle classes – or at least sections of them – as negative. The persistent political attacks on the professions and their increasing regulation by outside agencies sapped the sense of vocational pride. For Ray Pahl, 'to be a professional means that you've got a sense of autonomy, you've got independence. You've got a specialist training that is in your head. Now if that is taken away from you, if your independence is taken away, you just become an employee and a lot of the satisfaction of being a professional goes.' The gratification of monetary reward could not replace the work satisfaction enjoyed by the old-style family doctor or university professor: 'You can never get enough gratification; someone else has always got more. Satisfaction lasts.'[76] The decline of the middle-class presence in community life has also been significant. In Leamington Spa, Tim Emens and his wife invested little time in local associations or getting to know people: 'I don't really participate

in the community at all. I'm aware that it exists and fortunately
we have a good relationship with our neighbours, so we have a
little community where we live. But outside of that I guess we're
pretty insular. My wife loves the cinema but we don't go. So far as
culture is concerned, it's not very high on the agenda.' Philanthropy, once a talisman of middle-class community involvement,
has waned. Between 1974 and 1994 the proportion of British
households giving to charity fell by 5 per cent – an apparently
small figure, but significant when seen as part of what experts
have termed a 'persistent decline'. While the middle-aged and
elderly maintained their contribution, the greatest falls were
recorded among households headed by adults in their twenties
and thirties, trends which, as a report put it, 'do not bode well for
levels of voluntary income in the future'. Meanwhile, middle-
class activity in local organisations such as Rotary clubs and
parent-teacher associations visibly weakened, threatening their
continued viability in many towns and villages.[77] The old link
between the middle classes and voluntary activity, for so long a
feature of English community life, was broken in the late twentieth century.

The demise of the bank manager is symptomatic of many of
these changes. Once a pivotal figure in local business and social
life, especially in small towns, the traditional bank manager
became an endangered species in the 1990s. The automation of
many financial transactions, the growth of call centres and corporate centralisation in banking as in other sectors all undermined
the importance and, in many cases, the viability of the old-style
local bank. As a branch manager at Lloyds, now retired, Lawrie
Penny lived through the years of upheaval in banking, which
began with the introduction of large-scale redundancies in the
1980s: 'In a way, the bank was having to tear up its social contract
with its employees and that was a painful process.' Segmentation
and specialisation became key terms in the brave new world of
finance: 'The ordinary high street bank provides a whole mixture
of businesses within it. As a consequence, you have fewer bank

managers, in the accepted sense, but what you do have is a lot of
business managers who are running the business in a very different sort of way.' In the process, the relationship of the bank
manager to the community altered, as Richard Scase has suggested: 'With the rationalisation of banking, the bank manager is
moved from one community to the next. The bank manager has
performance targets to achieve. The bank manager is no longer
encouraged, except in a minimal way, to be involved with local
charities. And so that pillar in the local community has been
removed.'[78] Bit by bit, the bonds that linked the middle classes to
neighbourhood, locality and community dissolved during the
1980s and 1990s.

Changes at work inevitably affected the middle-class family.
For Rob Loynes, the computer software designer, the impact of
working longer hours on home life only dawned gradually: 'It
puts an enormous strain on your family. My wife would be
expecting me to come home early, having promised, something
happens in the office and suddenly it's six o'clock. It becomes part
of your life so you don't even start looking at your watch till six
o'clock. It only strikes you when somebody reminds you of your
normal hours. It brings it home when somebody in the family
actually tells you that.'[79] The entry of women into the labour
market and high-pressure jobs has created fresh demands, both on
women themselves and on families where both parents are
working. For many women, having a career and having children
appear to have become mutually exclusive: in the 1991 census, half
of all female senior managers lived in households without children. An alternative for those who could afford it was to have
household help, a factor that did much to account for the unex-
pected revival of domestic service in the 1990s. Nicola Horlick, a
fund manager who considered herself 'an ordinary woman doing
an ordinary job', employed a nanny and servants. For her, as for
many other professional men and women, servants were there to
allow not for increased leisure, but for longer hours in the office.[80]

The cumulative significance of these changes was that they

served to undermine the historical centrality of the family in English middle-class life. The fact of both partners working, in the view of Ray Pahl, meant that 'the other complexity of life, whether to do with children or to do with running one's home, and so on, has to be squeezed in the evenings and weekends. That adds a greater degree of insecurity and pressure on to middle-class life, which in the past wasn't there.' This, in turn, threatened the family as the bedrock of middle-class life, the institution that generated, historically, those patterns of behaviour and attitudes that defined middle-class identity: 'It was in the home that the whole middle-class style of values was maintained and perpetuated. If you take away the factory for middle-class values, how can you expect the same middle-class values to be continued?'[81]

The 1970s and 1980s witnessed the crumbling of the historic institutions of the English working class. The trade unions, the Labour party, the council estate, the co-op, together with manufacturing industry and the commitment to full employment, were severely weakened or transformed out of recognition. A decade or so later the institutions and ideals of the English middle classes were similarly overturned. The burden of the career passed from the corporation to the individual; personal ambition supplanted vocation in professional life. The place of the family as the principal site for the reproduction of middle-class values disintegrated, along with the model of gender relations, of distinct roles for men and women, which had underpinned the middle-class family for over two hundred years. Simultaneously, the middle classes ceased to take the leading part in the community, in voluntary associations, charities and governing bodies, that had long been a characteristic feature of English villages and towns. Local life atrophied as a result. Most fundamentally of all perhaps, the orientation of the middle classes to time altered. In the past, the existence of job security, a progressively rising salary, respect in the community and a stable context for family life meant that it was reasonable to plan ahead, to take the long view, to defer gratification now for a reward in the future. In the 1980s and

1950s the imperatives were different: spend today for next week you may be out of a job; enjoy now for who knows what tomorrow will bring. 'The great thing in the past was that you could predict the future', the sociologist Colin Bell has observed. 'The problem now is that you can't.'[82]

Many of the widespread social changes that affected the middle classes from the 1970s have their origins in the economy and work. While the impact of these changes has been substantial, their meaning in the longer term is less clear. Richard Sennett, who has researched and written on the future of work, is gloomy about the prospects:

> My own view is that the crisis of the middle class is just beginning. When people don't have the prospect of endless new work, when there isn't a lot of money around, working in short-term, disloyal institutions is truly going to become a massive social problem. People have always been able to think in the last fifteen years, 'well, somebody is making it, so why not me?' But when you have an economic downturn, coupled with the wrecking of the institutions of middle-class life, you have the ingredients of a real social disaster.[83]

Sennett, like other sociologists and commentators, foresees the end of middle-class work – the end, that is to say, of the structures and patterns that have distinguished the working lives of professionals, managers and businessmen over the past century. But this leaves further questions unanswered. Given the centrality of work to the historical identity of the middle classes, do the changes at the workplace have wider implications for English society? Rather than marking the end of middle-class work, do they spell the end of the middle classes themselves? And if so, what might the 'end' of the middle classes mean?

CONCLUSION

The end of the middle classes?

We hear the term 'middle class' used every day, in conversation, the media and political debate. It usually refers, in a vague way, to people with money, who enjoy a particular lifestyle or who are seen as exclusive and snobbish. But over the past thirty years 'middle class' has become an increasingly shadowy and elusive term of description. It is no longer clear precisely who the middle classes are or what the concept stands for. Many sociologists, of course, would disagree. For them, as we saw in Chapter One, the middle classes are defined less by appearances, such as lifestyle and attitudes, than by their structural position in social and economic life. The structural position of the middle classes is based on factors such as occupation, market situation, property ownership and education – factors that can be objectively measured and analysed. Sociologists see class as an objective social structure, not as a matter of individual choices or outlook. Consequently, from their perspective the middle class remains as much a feature of English society in the twenty-first century as it did a hundred years ago.

This book has proposed a different way of understanding the English middle classes. It has argued that, above all, 'middle class' is a concept that requires to be understood historically. Studying the middle classes over time is helpful in several ways. It indicates, firstly, that 'middle class' is a term with a traceable history. The concept of the 'middle classes' has been identified with specific institutions, meanings and values in English society over the past two centuries. However, and secondly, the history of the middle classes is less the story of a fixed social group than of a changing set of ideas about what constituted the 'middle' in English society. It concerned those groups between, on the one hand, the established aristocracy and gentry and, on the other, the working class which accounted for the majority of the population. These 'middling' groups did not automatically cohere into anything resembling a modern class. In Chapter One we saw that the 'middle classes' only emerged as such under the pressure of political circumstances in the late eighteenth and early nineteenth centuries. Nor was there a single, unchanging set of meanings attached to the middle classes. What it meant to be 'middle-class' depended on when you were born, as well as which part of them you were born into. In short, the English middle classes are better understood as an historical than as a sociological formation. They were the product of arguments about what the 'middle' or the centre of English society was. It is partly for this reason that the middle classes have tended to be identified with a particular set of ideas or attitudes rather than with a definite economic or social position. As Richard Scase succinctly put it, 'What defined the middle classes was not their material conditions, not how much money they had to spend, but their attitudes and values'.[1]

The meanings of 'middle class', and the values associated with it, have changed over historical time; the concept has accreted new meanings while some older emphases have dropped away. As we saw in Chapter One, in the early nineteenth century the term came into usage to delineate a political middle between, on the one hand, radicals linked with support for the principles of the French Revolution, and, on the other, conservatives like Edmund Burke who wished to preserve the status quo. The 'middle classes' represented that section of political opinion in favour of moderate constitutional reform. Allied to this was an emerging conception of the middle classes as the moral arbiters of the nation, itself rooted in a new emphasis on the importance of domesticity and the family. By the mid-nineteenth century the middle classes were identified with political Liberalism and religious Nonconformity, especially in the industrial towns of the north of England (though, as we saw, not all sections of the middle classes were Liberal, dissenting or industrial). All these elements combined to construct a middle-class identity hostile to the social and political predominance of the landed aristocracy and gentry. To these characteristics was added the development of a home-centred, suburban civilisation during the later Victorian and Edwardian periods. A recognisable 'middle-class' way of life began to develop, balancing privacy and smaller family size with conspicuous consumption and urban display. But it was notable that at no stage were the middle classes a stable or fixed social group. Those occupational elements described as 'middle-class' in the first half of the century, like merchants and manufacturers, were joined by new professions, such as engineers and architects, teachers and clerks, in the second half, all of whom laid claim to middle-class status.

Many of these features were carried over into the twentieth century. The identification of the middle classes with 'mental' as opposed to 'manual' labour became, if anything, a stronger line of demarcation between middle and working classes than in Victorian society, enabling new, salaried groups such as managers, administrators and technicians to be assimilated into the ranks of the expanding 'middle'. Patterns of education reinforced this division, as we saw in Chapter Six; middle and working classes were differentiated by types of schooling, expectations of academic achievement and the importance attached to passing exams. Similarly, more people were drawn into a suburban way of life between the wars, when home ownership became a further dividing line between classes, symbolised in the creation of the select private estate and the council estate. But the twentieth century witnessed significant changes in the middle classes as well as continuities. Both political Liberalism and religious Nonconformity suffered a spectacular eclipse between 1914 and 1930. Although, as Chapter Five demonstrated, their inheritance infused the politics of conscience evident in protest movements from the 1950s onwards, after the First World War the interests of business and large sections of the middle classes were yoked to the Conservative party, with Labour playing an equivalent role for the trade unions and manual workers. Instead of being seen as the scourge of the aristocracy and the establishment, as in the nineteenth century, the middle classes were portrayed by Conservative leaders from the 1920s as 'middle England', the unchanging soul of the nation, home owning, patriotic, unassuming yet fiercely proud when roused. This shift was itself related to changes in the world of work, especially the rise of the career for men, on which a whole set of assumptions about gender roles, family and home life and community involvement was seen ultimately to rest. By the 1980s, with the long-term decline of the aristocracy and the 'forward march of labour halted', the middle classes appeared to be the ascendant force in English society, even the victors in the long class war.[2]

In fact, we argued in Chapter Seven, such pretensions turned out to be illusory; much of what had defined the world of the English middle classes from the later nineteenth century collapsed in the last three decades of the twentieth. By the 1990s it became possible to speak of the end of the middle classes as a recognisable entity. This statement is prone to misunderstanding, to be confused with simplistic assertions that 'we are all equal' or, indeed, 'we are all middle-class' now. It therefore needs careful explanation. It is important to recognise that the idea that the middle classes are somehow imperilled, or even on the verge of extinction, has a long pedigree in England. We find it in the 1970s, with dire warnings that the middle classes were being taxed to death, and around the First World War, when bodies like the 'Middle-class Defence Organisation' and the 'Middle-class Union' loudly protested that the middle classes were being squeezed out of existence by the big battalions of capital and labour.[3] Indeed, the theme can be traced back to the mid-Victorian period, with the complaints of Liberals such as Richard

Cobden, John Bright and John Morley, as well as the criticisms of socialists like Marx and Engels, that the wealthiest and most powerful sections of the urban middle classes were being seduced by the influence of the landed gentry and aristocracy.[4] For varying reasons, and from all parts of the political spectrum, the middle classes, it seems, have repeatedly been portrayed as an endangered species.

While acknowledging this ideological tendency, it is nonetheless clear that substantive changes occurred after 1970 that fundamentally destabilised the historical identity of the middle classes. The institutions and attitudes traditionally associated with the concept of the middle class disintegrated, so that it was no longer the bearer of a recognisable set of meanings. Put bluntly, it became more and more difficult to know what 'middle class' meant. Some of the factors that contributed to this unravelling were long-term. Perhaps the most fundamental was the changing balance of social forces in society as a whole. In 1911 over three-quarters of the population of Britain were manual workers; by 1991, this had shrunk to just over a third, with office-based occupations representing a growing majority of the working population.[5] Not only did the steady expansion of white-collar jobs invert the relative importance of middle and working classes, but in a world where knowledge itself became a prime commodity and manufacturing was carried out by computerised processes, the distinction between 'mental and 'manual' labour no longer had as much resonance. At the same time, the long-term rise in real income of the majority of the population after the Second World War weakened differences of lifestyle and class culture. In the 1960s sociologists rejected the idea of *embourgeoisement* associated with the 'affluent worker', arguing that despite relatively high pay, skilled manual workers, like car workers, did not possess aspirations to 'middle-class' status.[6] This ignored, however, the long-term tendency for the patterns of consumption of *all* social classes to converge over time. As the social historian Harold Perkin put it, reviewing changes in leisure and

lifestyle since the 1950s: 'Although there were differences in taste
… there was an astonishing similarity between the way of life of
all classes, which would only become more similar with time.'
This process was evident in that most sensitive indicator of social
change in Britain, home-ownership. Between the wars approximately a third of homes were owner-occupied in England and
Wales; owner-occupation became an important emblem of
middle-class status. By 1990, however, the figure had risen to
two-thirds, including three-quarters of trade unionists; home-
ownership had long ceased to be a reliable indicator of the
division between middle and working classes.[7]

Changes that were long-term in origin therefore became
acute in the late twentieth century, loosening the hold of the old
class divisions on English society. Other more immediate factors
also affected the middle classes. The most important was the
series of economic eruptions from the mid-1970s that shook the
ideal of the stable professional career, helping to create an environment of job insecurity, work pressure and intense
competition. This was disruptive in two ways. Firstly, it dislodged
work and career from the central place they had historically
occupied in the construction of male middle-class identity. Secondly, and ultimately more important, it weakened the sense of
stability, of control over the future, that had characterised the
middle-class world since the later nineteenth century. This
affected not just the workplace, but marriage, the family and
community – in short, some of the key sources from which
middle-class identity and values had historically been generated
and replenished.

The eroding of many of the institutions of middle-class life in
the 1970s and 1980s was obscured at the time partly because
commentators were fixated on the simultaneous and spectacular
decline of the historical institutions of the working class, in the
form of the labour movement. Between 1979 and 1992 the trade
unions lost between a third and a half of their members, while the
Labour party ceased to be the natural political home of trade

union voters – in 1987 58 per cent of trade unionists voted for parties other than Labour, 30 per cent for the Conservatives.[8] In effect, 'class' ceased to be a reliable predictor of social and political behaviour in the later twentieth century. The corollary of this was that 'class' ceased to be an effective vehicle for the mobilisation of large numbers of people. For most of the century, the labour movement had rallied support by identifying the trade unions and the Labour party with manual workers; these institutions were important in sustaining an idea of working men and women as an historical collectivity – the 'working class'. Equally, from the 1920s Conservatism relied on its capacity to mobilise the middle classes as a social and political force in the guise of 'middle England' – the responsible, respectable backbone of the nation. For much of the twentieth century Conservatives sought to identify the middle classes with 'public opinion', or even with the nation itself, against Labour and the trade unions, viewed as the unpatriotic representatives of a sectional interest, endlessly seeking a bigger share of a dwindling national cake.[9] But by the 1980s appeals to these old, class-based identities and allegiances could no longer be relied on to muster support for parties and institutions. They no longer seemed to reflect the realities of contemporary England. At worst, they appeared to be cynical and self-interested rhetorical interventions, at best a nostalgic harking back to a vanishing industrial society.[10]

Do these changes signify the 'death of class'? Was the dislocation of the middle classes in the late twentieth century part of a larger crisis of 'class' itself?[11] Such questions are complex, not least because, as we have seen, there are very different definitions of what class is and how it should be understood.[12] For instance, it is possible to speak of the 'end of class' in an historical sense, of the declining salience of the customary divisions between upper, middle and working classes in English society, without suggesting that class in a Marxist sense, as the struggle between contending social forces based on capital and labour, has in any way diminished. Such a viewpoint might seem difficult to sustain, ignoring as it does the primary historical manifestations of class in English society. But it would equally be naïve to assume that the declining salience of the old forms of middle and working classes means the end of social conflict. Nor does the passing of the old class order imply the end of inequality and the emergence of a more just, meritocratic or free society. Quite the reverse: almost all the relevant indicators suggest that British society became more unequal and less open in the later twentieth century. For example, the poorest 10 per cent of Britons were 13 per cent worse off in 1997 than in 1979; by the 1990s the gap between the highest and lowest paid was the widest since records began; and there is clear evidence of declining social mobility among the poorest third of society.[13] As we saw in Chapter Six, private education has increased in desirability since the late 1960s and early 1970s, when it appeared to have diminishing appeal even to those who could afford it. For the wealthy in the 1990s, it became more not less essential to educate their children in isolation from the rest of the population. Private schooling has been one of the principal means by which social divisions are produced and perpetuated in England and it continues to flourish. A respected economic journalist could thus plausibly argue in 1997 that 'inequality is perhaps the single most salient fact in contemporary British society'.[14]

All this, however, does not mean that Britain is still a class-ridden society in the old historical sense. It simply, if depressingly, means that it is an increasingly unequal society. The traditional configuration of middle and working classes appears of diminished validity partly because it fails to reflect the changed nature of this escalating inequality. To call the poorest third of British society 'working-class', for example, is to miss the point, when what defines this group is precisely the absence – or perhaps more accurately the intermittence – of paid work in the conventional sense. Equally, the concept of the middle classes becomes meaningless when the institutions, way of life and values which defined the group no longer pertain. 'Middle classes' is now little more than a loose social description, lacking a substantive social, political or cultural referent. As a term, it has lost its significant historical meanings. In this specific historical sense, it is possible to speak of the 'end of the middle classes'. More than this, it becomes politically necessary to do so, since not only are the old categories increasingly irrelevant, but a continuing reliance upon them actually prevents us from understanding our present social condition. References to class have become tired and formulaic, obscuring rather than revealing. As a recent study puts it, 'the concept of class drags on, wearily seeking to cloak new formations in its ancient and tattered garments'.[15]

The end of the middle classes in this sense is neither an occasion to be lamented, nor a moment of liberation. It represents a moment of transformation. It opens up a space for developing new ways of combating exclusion and inequality that are attuned to the changing pattern of society in the twenty-first century. It offers the opportunity, not to discard an important part of our history, associated with the old class order, but to use our expanded understanding of that history constructively as the basis of a critical engagement with English society in the present. The challenge today is not simply to comprehend class, but to begin to think outside and beyond it.

ENDNOTES

PREFACE

1 In *Aristocracy* we had covered Great Britain and Ireland. Both series
began in the nineteenth century before Irish independence, but
while the experience of the Anglo-Irish had seemed central to the
story of the upper classes, the parallel did not work comfortably for
the middle classes. It reflects a significant historical difference
between the aristocracy as a national, territorial class and the middle
classes as a pre-eminently English and locally based formation.

CHAPTER 1

1 C. F. G. Masterman, *The Condition of England* (London, Methuen,
1960 [1909]), p. 14.
2 George Orwell, 'The lion and the unicorn' in *Collected Essays, Journalism and Letters, Volume 2: 1940–1943* (Harmondsworth, Penguin,
1970), pp. 87–8.
3 For scholarly comparisons see Jurgen Kocka and Allan Mitchell, eds,
Bourgeois Society in Nineteenth-century Europe (Oxford, Berg, 1993);
Arthur Marwick, *Class: Image and Reality in Britain, France and the
USA since 1930* (London, Fontana, 1980).
4 Cited in Penny Junor, *The Major Enigma* (London, Michael Joseph,
1993), p. 112.
5 While any subdivision of the middle classes inevitably involves a
degree of artificiality, we follow accepted usage in dividing the group
into 'upper middle class' and 'lower middle class'.
6 For an introduction to Scotland see N. J. Morgan and R. H. Trainor,
'The dominant classes' in W. H. Fraser and R. J. Morris, eds, *People and
Society in Scotland, Vol. 2: 1830–1914* (Edinburgh, Edinburgh University Press, 1990).
7 Though studies are beginning to emerge, especially for the first half
of the twentieth century. See among others A. A. Jackson, *The Middle

Classes 1900–1950 (Nairn, David St John Thomas, 1991); Ross McKibbin, *Classes and Cultures: England 1918–1951* (Oxford, Oxford University Press, 1998) has a useful survey over a similar period; Harold Perkin, *The Rise of Professional Society: England since 1880* (London, Routledge, 1989) has the virtue of taking the story into the second half of the century within an overall argument about the direction of English society. Both these last two works, however, are overviews and are not based on substantial new research into the middle classes.

8 Roy Lewis and Angus Maude, *The English Middle Classes* (London, Penguin, 1953), p. 11; Roger King and John Raynor, *The Middle Class* (Harlow, Longman, 1981), ch. 1.

9 Cited in Marwick, *Class*, pp. 275–6.

10 The historical significance of the negative connotations of 'middle class' is discussed further in McKibbin, *Classes and Cultures*. The two- and three-class models of English society are discussed at length in David Cannadine, *Class in Britain* (New Haven, Yale University Press, 1998).

11 There are hundreds of sociological studies of class, of varying quality. Those interested in investigating this approach could usefully start with Rosemary Crompton, *Class and Stratification: An Introduction to Current Debates* (Cambridge, Polity, 1993).

12 John Seed, 'From "middling sort" to middle class in late eighteenth- and early nineteenth-century England' in M. L. Bush, ed., *Social Orders and Social Classes in Europe since 1500* (Harlow, Longman, 1992), p. 115.

13 The historian Asa Briggs attributes the first use of 'working classes' to Robert Owen in a pamphlet published in 1813; by the 1830s and 1840s it was commonplace. See Briggs, 'The language of "class" in early nineteenth-century England' in Briggs, ed., *Essays in Labour History* (London, Macmillan, 1960).

14 Stephen Fry, *Making History* (London, Hutchinson, 1996), p. 70.

15 For comments on this tendency see Peter Earle, *The Making of the English Middle Class: Business, Society and Family Life in London, 1660–1730* (London, Methuen, 1989); Cannadine, *Class in Britain*, p. 9; E. P. Thompson, 'The peculiarities of the English' in Thompson, *The Poverty of Theory* (London, Merlin Press, 1978), pp. 39–56; Jonathan Barry, 'Introduction' in Jonathan Barry and Christopher Brooks, eds,

The Middling Sort of People: Culture, Society and Politics 1550–1800 (London, Macmillan, 1994).

16 Cited in Roy Porter, *English Society in the Eighteenth Century* (Harmondsworth, Penguin, 1982), p. 243.

17 John Rule, *Albion's People: English Society 1714–1815* (Harlow, Longman, 1992), ch. 1.

18 Peter Borsay, *The English Urban Renaissance* (Oxford, Clarendon Press, 1989); Neil McKendrick, John Brewer and J. H. Plumb, eds, *The Birth of a Consumer Society: the Commercialization of Eighteenth-century England* (London, Europa, 1982).

19 *Oxford English Dictionary* (Oxford, Clarendon Press, 1989); Porter, *English Society*, p. 88.

20 The classic, though differing, analyses of social structure in eighteenth-century England are Harold Perkin, *The Origins of Modern English Society* (London, Routledge, 1969), ch. 2; E. P. Thompson, 'Patrician society, plebeian culture', *Journal of Social History*, 7 (1974), pp. 382–405 and 'Eighteenth-century English society: class struggle without class?', *Social History*, 3 (1978), pp. 133–65.

21 For further comments on this traditional view see Janet Wolff and John Seed, 'Introduction' in Seed and Wolff, eds, *The Culture of Capital: Art, Power and the Nineteenth Century Middle Class* (Manchester, Manchester University Press, 1988).

22 These arguments can be followed up variously in John Brewer, *The Pleasures of the Imagination: English Culture in the Eighteenth Century* (London, HarperCollins, 1997), esp. part VI; Borsay, *English Urban Renaissance*; Pat Hudson, *The Industrial Revolution* (London, Edward Arnold, 1992); John Smail, *The Origins of Middle-class Culture: Halifax, Yorkshire, 1660–1780* (Ithaca, Cornell University Press, 1994); Dror Wahrman, *Imagining the Middle Class: The Political Representation of Class in Britain, c.1780–1840* (Cambridge, Cambridge University Press, 1995).

23 David Ricardo, *Principles of Political Economy* (1817); James Mill, *Essay on Government* (1820).

24 Wahrman, *Imagining the Middle Class*.

25 E. P. Thompson, *The Making of the English Working Class* (Harmondsworth, Penguin, 1972 [1963]), p. 899.

26 Cited in Asa Briggs, *The Age of Improvement* (Harlow, Longman, 1979), pp. 324–5.

27 Briggs, 'The language of "class"', p. 53.

28 Thompson, *Making of the English Working Class*, p. 901.

29 Simon Gunn, *The Public Culture of the Victorian Middle Class* (Manchester, Manchester University Press, 2000), pp. 21–2 and ch. 5 for further discussion.

30 On Nonconformity see Ian Sellers, *Nineteenth-century Nonconformity* (London, Edward Arnold, 1977); Clyde Binfield, *So Down to Prayers* (London, Dent, 1977).

31 John Vincent, *The Formation of the Liberal Party 1857–1868* (London, Constable, 1966), pp. xxviii–xxix.

32 J. A. James, *Protestant Nonconformity: A Sketch of Its General History with an Account of the Rise and Present State of Its Various Denominations in the Town of Birmingham* (Birmingham, 1849), p. ix.

33 The best discussion of this remains Derek Fraser, *Urban Politics in Victorian England* (Leicester, Leicester University Press, 1976).

34 D. W. Bebbington, *Evangelicalism in Modern Britain: A History from the 1730s to the 1780s* (London, Routledge, 1995), ch. 1.

35 Thompson, *Making of the English Working Class*, p. 60.

36 Cited in Leonore Davidoff and Catherine Hall, *Family Fortunes: Men and Women of the English Middle Class 1780–1850* (London, Hutchinson, 1987), p. 151.

37 See Davidoff and Hall, *Family Fortunes*, pp. 150–5 for a perceptive analysis of the affair and its impact on the middle classes.

38 William Cowper, 'The task (Book IV: The winter evening)' in *Poetical Works* (London, Oxford University Press, 1971), p. 183.

39 Maurice Beresford, *East End, West End. The Face of Leeds during Urbanisation* (Leeds, Thoresby Society, 1989).

40 For a clear account of this process see Catherine Hall, 'Gender divisions and class formation in the Birmingham middle class, 1780–1850' in Hall, *White, Male and Middle Class: Explorations in Feminism and History* (Cambridge, Polity Press, 1992), pp. 94–107.

41 For extensive discussion of this see Davidoff and Hall, *Family Fortunes* and Hall, *White, Male and Middle Class*. See also John Tosh, *A Man's Place: Masculinity and the Middle-class Home in Victorian England* (New Haven, Yale University Press, 1999).

42 *Poor Man's Guardian*, 17 August 1833.

43 This, of course, is the period in which E. P. Thompson saw the 'making' of the English working class taking place, though his argu-

ment has subsequently been extensively challenged by historians. See Thompson, *Making of the English Working Class*.

44 For interesting further discussion of this see Geoffrey Crossick, 'From gentlemen to the residuum: languages of social description in Victorian Britain' in P. J. Corfield, ed., *Language, Class and History* (Cambridge, Cambridge University Press, 1991).

CHAPTER 2

1   For a full analysis of the 1911 census and Stevenson's categorisations see Simon Szreter, *Fertility, Class and Gender in Britain 1860–1940* (Cambridge, Cambridge University Press, 1996).

2   Figures from interview with David Rose, who devised the categories for the census in 2000, 31/3/00, transcript, p. 14.

3   Information from J.A. Banks in a private letter dated 24/04/01.

4   A. H. Halsey, *Change in British Society* (Oxford, Oxford University Press, 1978), fourth edition, p. 35.

5   Information from an unpublished history of William Simpson, one of the first inhabitants of Ashwood Villas.

6   Interview with Christopher Mackenzie-Davey, 15/4/00, transcript, p. 9.

7   William Stroud's journal in the possession of Barr & Stroud, Glasgow.

8   Information from the Royal Pharmaceutical Society of Great Britain.

9   Michael Moss and Iain Russell, *Range and Vision: The First Hundred Years of Barr & Stroud* (Edinburgh, Mainstream Publishing, 1988), p. 16.

10 For discussion of educational patterns among the Victorian middle classes see Patrick Joyce, *Work, Society and Politics: The Culture of the Factory in Later Victorian England* (Brighton, Harvester Wheatsheaf, 1980), pp. 29–34; Hartmut Berghoff, 'Public schools and the decline of the British economy 1870–1914', *Past and Present*, 129 (November 1990).

11 William Stroud, 'Apologia Pro Vita Mea', unpublished memoirs held by Barr & Stroud, Glasgow.

12 Michael Sanderson, ed., *The Universities in the Nineteenth Century* (London, Routledge and Kegan Paul, 1975), p. 19.

13 Moss and Russell, *Range and Vision*, p. 40.

14 Moss and Russell, *Range and Vision*, p. 133.

15 Most of these details of Barr & Stroud company history come from *Range and Vision*; other details from interviews with Stroud's grand-daughter, Maggie Carlow, interview 15/4/00.

16 Sanderson, *The Universities in the Nineteenth Century*, pp. 10 and 142.

17 John Burnett, *A Social History of Housing 1815–1970* (London, Methuen, 1978), p. 105.

18 Burnett, *Social History of Housing*, p. 101.

19 F. M. L. Thompson, ed., *The Rise of Suburbia* (Leicester, Leicester University Press, 1982), p. 175.

20 Information from unpublished history of the Simpson family.

21 Thompson, *Rise of Suburbia*, p. 169.

22 I. M. Beeton, *The Book of Household Management* (1861) cited in Burnett, *Social History of Housing*, p. 98.

23 J. A. Banks, *Prosperity and Parenthood: A Study of Family Planning among the Victorian Middle Classes* (London, Routledge and Kegan Paul, 1954), p. 107.

24 Thompson, *Rise of Suburbia*, p. 8.

25 Burnett, *Social History of Housing*, p. 102; Leonore Davidoff, *The Best Circles* (London, Hutchinson, 1986), pp. 41–9.

26 Burnett, *Social History of Housing*, p. 95.

27 Information on the early life of Dr Heaton drawn from Brian and Dorothy Payne, *Claremont* (Leeds, Yorkshire Archaeological Society, 1980), pp. 7–12.

28 R. W. Emerson, *English Traits* (1856) cited in Burnett, *Social History of Housing*, p. 109.

29 Details of Heaton's remodelling and extract from his journal quoted in Payne, *Claremont*, pp. 18–19.

30 Extract from Dr Heaton's journal, cited in Dorothy Payne, 'The Heatons of Claremont' in Lynne Stevenson Tate, ed., *Aspects of Leeds* (Barnsley, Wharncliffe Publishing, 1998), p. 76.

31 Extract from Dr Heaton's journal cited in Dorothy Payne, 'Clare-mont', *The Yorkshire Family Historian*, vol. 24, no. 1, p. 8.

32 Extract from Dr Heaton's journals cited in John Tosh, *A Man's Place: Masculinity and the Middle-class Home in Victorian England* (New Haven, Yale University Press, 1999), p. 56.

33 See Tosh, *A Man's Place*, p. 196 and *passim* for more on this.

34 Tosh, *A Man's Place*, p. 4.

35 Cited in Tosh, *A Man's Place*, p. 136.

36 Tosh, *A Man's Place*, p. 136.

37 Dr Heaton's journal cited in Tosh, *A Man's Place*, p. 136.

38 Cited in Asa Briggs, *Victorian Cities* (London, Pelican, 1968), p. 162.

39 Briggs, *Victorian Cities*, p. 162.

40 Cited in Briggs, *Victorian Cities*, p. 165.

41 Briggs, *Victorian Cities*, p. 182.

42 *The Times*, 4 October 1888.

43 Interview with R. J. Morris, 7/8/00, transcript, p. 25.

44 Information from Morris, transcript, pp. 24–6. On public behaviour in art institutions see Simon Gunn, 'The sublime and the vulgar: the Hallé concerts and the constitution of "high culture" in Manchester, *c*.1850–1880', *Journal of Victorian Culture*, 2, 2 (1997); Kate Hill, '"Roughs of both sexes": the working class in Victorian galleries and museums' in Simon Gunn and R. J. Morris, eds, *Identities in Space: Contested Terrains in the Western City since 1850* (Aldershot, Ashgate, 2001).

45 Nicola Humble, ed., *Mrs Beeton's Book of Household Management* (Oxford, Oxford World Classics, 2000), p. vii.

46 Humble, *Mrs Beeton*, p. 225.

47 Humble, *Mrs Beeton*, p. xxvii.

48 Benjamin Seebohm Rowntree, *Poverty: A Study of Town Life* (York, 1901).

49 Banks, *Prosperity and Parenthood*, pp. 111–12.

50 Banks, *Prosperity and Parenthood*, p. 111.

51 W. R. Greg, *Contemporary Review* (1875), quoted in Banks, *Prosperity and Parenthood*, p. 67.

52 R. S. Lambert, *The Universal Provider* (London, George Harrap, 1938), p. 91 and *passim*.

53 For details on William Whiteley see Lambert, *Universal Provider*. For department stores generally see Bill Lancaster, *The Department Store: A Social History* (Leicester, Leicester University Press, 1995); Rachel Bowlby, *Carried Away: The Invention of Modern Shopping* (London, Faber, 2000).

54 Erika Diane Rappaport, *Shopping for Pleasure: Women in the Making of London's West End* (Princeton, Princeton University Press, 2000), p. 16.

55 This and other cases cited in Rappaport, pp. 66–7.

56 Lambert, *Universal Provider*, pp. 127–8.

57 Lambert, *Universal Provider*, p. 128.

58 Simon Gunn, *The Public Culture of the Victorian Middle Class: Ritual and Authority in the English Industrial City 1840–1914* (Manchester, Manchester University Press, 2000), p. 67.

59 Gunn, *Public Culture*, p. 106.

60 The most comprehensive survey of religious attendance in the nineteenth century was the 1851 religious census. On religion generally see Hugh McLeod, *Religion and Society in England, 1850–1914* (Basingstoke, Macmillan, 1996).

61 Tate, *Aspects of Leeds,* p. 65.

62 Gunn, *Public Culture*, pp. 106–7.

63 John Vincent, *The Formation of the Liberal Party, 1857–1868* (London, Constable, 1966), introduction.

64 W. J. Reader, *Professional Men: The Rise of the Professional Classes in Nineteenth-century England* (London, Weidenfeld and Nicolson, 1966), p. 20. See also P. J. Corfield, *Power and the Professions in Britain 1780–1850* (London, Routledge, 1995).

65 Reader, *Professional Men*, p. 41.

66 Reader, *Professional Men*, p. 52.

67 Reader, *Professional Men*, p. 53.

68 Reader, *Professional Men*, p. 71.

69 Reader, *Professional Men*, pp. 164–5.

70 Appendix in Szreter, *Fertility, Class and Gender*, pp. 608–9.

71 Banks, *Prosperity and Parenthood*, p. 199.

72 Interview with J. A. Banks, 17/4/00, transcript, p. 28.

73 Cited in Banks, *Prosperity and Parenthood*, p. 191.

74 Tate, *Aspects of Leeds,* p. 65.

75 See Banks, *Prosperity and Parenthood*, p. 229 for a full list of foundation dates of girls' schools.

76 Banks, *Prosperity and Parenthood*, pp. 187–8.

77 Banks, *Prosperity and Parenthood*, pp. 176–87.

78 Banks, *Prosperity and Parenthood*, p. 193.

79 Banks, *Prosperity and Parenthood*, p. 106.

80 Cited in Banks, *Prosperity and Parenthood*, p. 193.

81 See Banks, *Prosperity and Parenthood*, ch. 3.

82 M. Vivian Hughes, *A London Family 1870–1900* (London, Oxford University Press, 1946), p. 509.

83 Banks, *Prosperity and Parenthood*, p. 5.

84 Banks, *Prosperity and Parenthood*; Szreter, *Fertility, Class and Gender*. See also J. A. Banks, *Victorian Values: Secularism and the Size of Families* (London, Routledge and Kegan Paul, 1981); Roy Porter and Lesley Hall, *The Facts of Life: The Creation of Sexual Knowledge in Britain, 1650–1950* (New Haven, Yale University Press, 1995).

85 Interview with Simon Szreter, 31/3/00, transcript, p. 30.

86 Cited in interview with Simon Szreter, p. 49.

87 Interview with Simon Szreter, p. 49.

88 For further discussion see Steven Marcus, *The Other Victorians* (London, Weidenfeld and Nicolson, 1966); Michael Mason, *The Making of Victorian Sexuality* (Oxford, Oxford University Press, 1994).

89 Lambert, *Universal Provider*, pp. 156–61.

90 Mary Charleeb, *The Seven Ages of Woman*, 1915, cited in an interview with Simon Szreter, transcript, p. 51.

91 Interview with R. J. Morris, p. 11.

92 From an account written by her husband, Arthur Rucker, held privately.

93 Cited in Tosh, *A Man's Place*, p. 101.

94 A point cogently made by R. J. Morris in his book *Class, Sect and Party. The Making of the British Middle Class: Leeds, 1820–1850* (Manchester, Manchester University Press, 1990).

95 *Bayswater Chronicle*, 2 February 1907.

96 Lambert, *Universal Provider*, p. 248.

97 Lambert, *Universal Provider*, pp. 249–52.

98 Lambert, *Universal Provider*, pp. 254–65.

99 Funeral descriptions from *Bayswater Chronicle*, 2 February 1907; details of will from copy of Whiteley's will.

CHAPTER 3

1 Interview with Irene Bacon, Hall Green, 19/5/00, transcript, pp. 1–17.

2 For example, Thomas Crosland, *The Suburbans* (London, John Lang, 1905); Charles Masterman, *The Condition of England* (London, Methuen, 1909), ch. 5.

3 Ebenezer Howard, *Garden Cities of Tomorrow* (London, Faber, 1965 [1902]), p. 145.

4 Marian Bowley, *Housing and the State, 1919–1944* (London, Allen and

Unwin, 1945), pp. 135–58, 271; Ross McKibbin, *Classes and Cultures: England 1918–1951* (Oxford, Oxford University Press, 1998), p. 75.

5   Alan A. Jackson, *The Middle Classes, 1900–1950* (Nairn, David St John Thomas, 1991), p. 15. Similar figures can be found in McKibbin, *Classes and Cultures*, pp. 45–6.

6   John H. Goldthorpe *et al.*, *Social Mobility and Class Structure in Modern Britain* (Oxford, Clarendon Press, 1980); Harold Perkin, *The Rise of Professional Society: England since 1880* (London, Routledge, 1989), pp. 270–2.

7   John Osborne, *A Better Class of Person* (London, Faber, 1981), p. 41.

8   Interview with Mavis Skeet, Stoneleigh, 12/5/00, transcript, p. 9.

9   Interview with Irene Bacon, p. 9.

10   Interview with Wilf Cross, Oxford, 17/5/00, transcript, p. 4.

11   Alan A. Jackson, *Semi-detached London* (London, Allen and Unwin, 1973), pp. 192–4.

12   Dudley Baines, 'The recovery from depression' in Paul Johnson, ed., *Twentieth-century Britain* (London, Longman, 1995), p. 196.

13   For examples of middle-class salaries and budgets see Jackson, *Middle Classes*, appendix A.

14   McKibbin, *Classes and Cultures*, p. 74.

15   Sean Glynn and John Oxborrow, *Inter-war Britain: A Social and Economic History* (London, Allen and Unwin, 1976), pp. 221–7; M. Swenarton and S. Taylor, 'The scale and nature of the growth of owner-occupation in Britain between the wars', *Economic History Review*, 38 (1985), p. 392.

16   Interview with Dermot Gleeson, Stoneleigh, 25/5/00, transcript, pp. 14–15; McKibbin, *Classes and Cultures*, p. 73.

17   Interview with Gordon Ralph, Ewell, 10/5/00, transcript, p. 13.

18   Interview with Mavis Skeet, p. 3.

19   Interview with Dermot Gleeson, pp. 26–31.

20   Interview with Mary and Allan Reed, Stoneleigh, 17/5/00, transcript, p. 16.

21   C. H. Lee, *The British Economy since 1700: A Macroeconomic Perspective* (Cambridge, Cambridge University Press, 1986).

22   Interview with Gordon Ralph, pp. 13–14; interview with Eve Mayatt, Stoneleigh, 8/5/00, transcript, p. 14.

23   Interview with Dermot Gleeson, pp. 14–15.

24   Donald Read, *The English Provinces, c. 1760–1960: A Study in Influence*

(London, Edward Arnold, 1964), p. 273.

25 For further discussion of this see Gordon Ralph interview, especially pp. 11–16. Transcripts of all interviews are in authors' possession.

26 Interview with Mary Reed, p. 4; interview with Irene Bacon, p. 10.

27 Interview with Eve Mayatt, p. 3; interview with Mavis Skeet, p. 2.

28 Sally Alexander, 'Becoming a woman in London in the 1920s and 30s' in Alexander, *Becoming a Woman and Other Essays in Nineteenth and Twentieth Century Feminist History* (London, Virago, 1994), pp. 203–7. J. B. Priestley similarly depicts the newly-built suburbs as modern and Americanised, if inevitably vulgar, in *English Journey* (London, Heinemann, 1934), esp. pp. 400–1.

29 Interview with Irene Bacon, p. 3; interview with Eve Mayatt, p. 5.

30 Cited in Jackson, *Middle Classes*, p. 84.

31 Deborah S. Ryan, *'Daily Mail': The Ideal Home through the Twentieth Century* (London, Hazar Publishing, 1997).

32 Jane Lewis, *Women in England, 1870–1950* (Brighton, Harvester Wheatsheaf, 1984), pp. 102, 199–200; Jackson, *Middle Classes*, p. 125.

33 Ryan, *'Daily Mail'*.

34 A characteristic text is Judge B. Lindsay and Wainwright Evans, *The Companionate Marriage* (London, Brentano's, 1928), with foreword by Dora Russell.

35 Interview with Suzy Harvey, Oxford, 17/5/00, transcript, p. 20.

36 Interview with Mary Reed, pp. 2–3.

37 Interview with Mary Reed, p. 16; interview with Mavis Skeet, p. 9.

38 Interview with Dermot Gleeson, pp. 15–16.

39 Interview with Dermot Gleeson, p. 15; interview with Mr and Mrs Hickson, Hall Green, 19/5/00, transcript, pp. 8, 19, 24.

40 Interview with Mary Reed, pp. 13–14; J. F. C. Harrison, *Scholarship Boy* (London, Rivers Oram Press, 1995).

41 Interview with Suzy Harvey, p. 14.

42 Alison Light, *Forever England: Femininity, Literature and Conservatism between the Wars* (London, Routledge, 1991), p. 177.

43 Interview with Suzy Harvey, p. 26.

44 Interview with Irene Bacon, p. 19; interview with Eve Mayatt, p. 15.

45 Interview with Dermot Gleeson, pp. 14–15.

46 J. M. Richards, *Castles on the Ground* (London, Architectural Press, 1946); I. Bentley, 'Individualism or community? Private enterprise housing and the council estate' in Paul Oliver, Ian Davis and Ian

Bentley, eds, *Dunroamin: The Suburban Semi and Its Enemies* (London, Pimlico, 1994).

47 Interview with Eve Mayatt, p. 12.

48 Interview with Dermot Gleeson, pp. 17–18; interview with Eve Mayatt, p. 12.

49 Interview with Eve Mayatt, p. 7; interview with Mavis Skeet, p. 20.

50 Interview with Irene Bacon, p. 3.

51 Jackson, *Semi-detached London*, pp. 279–81.

52 Interview with Mavis Skeet, pp. 5–7, 17–18.

53 Interview with Mary Reed, pp. 8–9. For operatics see John Lowerson, 'An outbreak of allodoxia? Operatic amateurs and middle-class musical taste between the wars' in Alan Kidd and David Nicholls, eds, *Gender, Civic Culture and Consumerism: Middle-class Identity in Britain, 1800–1940* (Manchester, Manchester University Press, 1999), pp. 198–211.

54 P. Oliver, 'Great expectations: suburban values and the role of the media' in Oliver, Davis and Bentley, *Dunroamin*, p. 133.

55 Jackson, *Semi-detached London*, pp. 285–6; McKibbin, *Classes and Cultures*, p. 87.

56 George Orwell, *Coming up for Air* (London, Gollancz, 1939); Clough Williams-Ellis, *England and the Octopus* (London, Jonathan Bles, 1928).

57 Interview with Eve Mayatt, pp. 3, 11.

58 Light, *Forever England*, p. 211.

59 Interview with Suzy Harvey, pp. 10–12.

60 Interview with Doris Denton, Oxford, 18/5/00, transcript, pp. 3–4.

61 Interview with Peter Collison, Oxford, 15/6/00, transcript, pp. 1–14.

62 Interview with Doris Denton, p. 6; interview with Suzy Harvey, pp. 1–2.

63 McKibbin, *Classes and Cultures*, p. 54.

64 Interview with Peter Collison, p. 12; interview with Doris Denton, p. 4.

65 Interview with Mr and Mrs Hickson, pp. 1, 20.

66 Interview with Suzy Harvey, pp. 16–17.

67 Cited in Light, *Forever England*, p. 131.

68 In academic circles the 'trickle-down' or emulation thesis is often associated with Thorstein Veblen, *The Theory of the Leisure Class* (New York, Macmillan, 1899). A similar thesis is reiterated for the British

middle classes in Martin Wiener, *English Culture and the Decline of the Industrial Spirit* (Cambridge, Cambridge University Press, 1981).

69 David Cannadine, *The Decline and Fall of the British Aristocracy* (New Haven, Yale University Press, 1990), ch. 3.

70 For further discussion of these ideas see Ross McKibbin, 'Class and conventional wisdom: the Conservative party and the "public" in inter-war Britain' in McKibbin, *The Ideologies of Class* (Oxford, Oxford University Press, 1991), pp. 259–93.

71 Stanley Baldwin, *On England, and Other Addresses* (London, P. Allan, 1926).

72 Interview with Jack Fellowes, Oxford, 17/5/00, transcript, p. 6; interview with Jerry White, London, 8/8/00, transcript, p. 8.

73 John Betjeman, 'Slough', *Continual Dew* (London, John Murray, 1937). Betjeman, of course, later turned from hardened critic to enthusiastic champion of London suburbia.

CHAPTER 4

1 J. M. Lee, *Social Leaders and Public Persons: A Study of County Government in Cheshire since 1888* (Oxford, Oxford University Press, 1963).

2 *Oxford English Dictionary*, second edition (Oxford, Clarendon Press, 1989).

3 Arnold Bennett, *Essays* (London, Chatto and Windus, 1909).

4 For Baldwin see Philip Williamson, *Stanley Baldwin: Conservative Leadership and National Values* (Cambridge, Cambridge University Press, 1999).

5 Interview with George Courtauld, 25/6/00, transcript, p. 9.

6 Interview with George Courtauld, p. 9.

7 D. C. Coleman, *Courtaulds: An Economic and Social History. Volume II: Rayon* (Oxford, Clarendon Press, 1969), p. 154. The figures here are from the same volume.

8 For a discussion of the origins and definition of the word 'rayon' see C. H. Ward-Jackson, *A History of Courtaulds* (London, Curwen Press, 1941), pp. 127–8.

9 Coleman, *Courtaulds*, p. 171.

10 Ward-Jackson, *History of Courtaulds*, p. 134.

11 *Economist*, 23 May 1936.

12 Coleman, *Courtaulds*, pp. 252, 322, 429.

13 For a standard work on this topic see Leslie Hannah, *The Rise of the*

Corporate Economy (London, Methuen, 1976).

14 David Cannadine, *The Decline and Fall of the British Aristocracy* (New Haven, Yale University Press, 1990).

15 W. D. Rubinstein, *Men of Property* (London, Routledge, 1981); W. L. Guttsman, *The British Political Elite* (London, MacGibbon and Kee, 1963).

16 Ross McKibbin, *Classes and Cultures: England 1918–1951* (Oxford, Oxford University Press, 1998), p. 21.

17 In 1856 a Limited Liability Act was passed, restricting the owner's loss in a business to the sum of the capital invested. This encouraged firms to sell shares, so allowing ownership to fragment. But the facility was taken up only gradually by English firms, beginning in the 1880s.

18 For an incisive analysis of these trends see Harold Perkin, *The Rise of Professional Society: England since 1880* (London, Routledge, 1989), esp. ch. 7.

19 Coleman, *Courtaulds*, pp. 28–31, 122, 205–8.

20 Interview with George Courtauld, p. 13.

21 On the concept of 'impersonal capitalism' see Mike Savage and Andrew Miles, *The Remaking of the British Working Class 1840–1940* (London, Routledge, 1994), pp. 48–55.

22 Interview with Lady Butler, 1/8/00, transcript, p. 11; interview with David Murdoch, 22/6/00, transcript, p. 6.

23 Perkin, *Rise of Professional Society*, pp. 258–66.

24 Roy Lewis and Angus Maude, *The English Middle Classes* (London, Penguin, 1953 [1949]), pp. 15–16.

25 Interview with Lady Butler, p. 21.

26 V. C. Buckley, *The Good Life: Between the Two World Wars with a Candid Camera* (London, Thames and Hudson, 1979), p. 44.

27 On paternalism and deference in textile communities see Patrick Joyce, *Work, Society and Politics: The Culture of the Factory in Later Victorian England* (Brighton, Harvester Wheatsheaf, 1981).

28 Interview with George Courtauld, pp. 5, 11.

29 See Chapter Six for further discussion of middle-class education.

30 Interview with Sir Adam Butler, 31/7/00, transcript, p. 6; interview with Lady Mayhew, 30/6/00, transcript, pp. 6–7.

31 Interview with Charlie Courtauld, 3/8/00, transcript, pp. 6–7.

32 Interview with Sir Adam Butler, pp. 4–5.

33 Interview with Lady Butler, pp. 8, 13.

34 Coleman, *Courtaulds*, pp. 217–18.

35 Neal Ascherson, 'The English bourgeoisie', *Games with Shadows* (London, Radius, 1988 [1976]), p. 34.

36 Lord Butler, *The Art of the Possible: The Memoirs of Lord Butler* (London, Hamish Hamilton, 1971), p. 20.

37 Interview with Sir Adam Butler, pp. 1, 5.

38 Interview with Lady Mayhew, p. 1.

39 Interview with Jonathan Charkham, 4/7/00, transcript, p. 7.

40 Interview with Lady Mayhew, p. 3.

41 Interview with Harold Perkin, 31/7/00, transcript, p. 8.

42 For details see John House, ed., *Impressionism for England: Samuel Courtauld as Patron and Collector* (New Haven, Yale University Press, 1994).

43 Butler, *Art of the Possible*, p. 19.

44 Interview with Sir Adam Butler, p. 9.

45 Coleman, *Courtaulds*, p. 217; interview with George Courtauld, p. 18; interview with Sir Adam Butler, p. 8.

46 Coleman, *Courtaulds*, vol. II, ch. 14 and vol. III, p. 305.

47 Raphael Samuel, 'The middle class between the wars: part one', *New Socialist*, Jan/Feb 1983, p. 33.

48 Interview with Lady Mayhew, p. 11; interview with George Courtauld, p. 1.

49 Angus and Maude, *The English Middle Classes*, pp. 192–3.

50 McKibbin, *Classes and Cultures*, p. 36.

51 Interview with Graham Pointon, BBC Pronunciation Unit, 6/1/00; interview with Lady Mayhew, pp. 6–7.

52 Angus and Maude, *The English Middle Classes*, p. 21. For further comment on middle-class accent at the period see Perkin, *The Rise of Professional Society*, pp. 266–8; Rick Trainor, 'Neither metropolitan nor provincial: the inter-war middle class' in Alan Kidd and David Nicholls, eds, *The Making of the British Middle Class?* (Stroud, Sutton, 1998), pp. 203–13.

53 Interview with George Courtauld, p. 16.

54 Interview with Lady Butler, p. 10.

55 Interview with George Courtauld, pp. 16–17.

56 Interview with David Murdoch, p. 3.

57 Interview with Sir Adam Butler, p. 8.

58 Butler, *The Art of the Possible*, p. 19; John Murdoch, 'The Courtauld

family and its money 1594–1947' in House, *Impressionism for England*, p. 47.

59 Andrew Stephenson, 'An anatomy of taste: Samuel Courtauld and debates about art patronage and modernism in Britain in the inter-war years' in House, *Impressionism for England*, pp. 35–46.

60 Interview with David Murdoch, p. 8.

61 Matthew Arnold, *Culture and Anarchy* (Cambridge, Cambridge University Press, 1963 [1869]).

62 Interview with George Courtauld, p. 17.

63 Interview with Lady Butler, p. 3.

64 For an account of the SOE and its workings see E. H. Cookridge, *Inside S.O.E.* (London, Barker, 1966).

65 Interview with George Courtauld, p. 2.

66 Coleman, *Courtaulds*, vol. III, pp. 23–6.

67 See Chapter Three for more on the 'marriage bar'. On attitudes to women more generally see Samuel, 'The middle class between the wars', p. 33; Angus and Maude, *English Middle Classes*, p. 198.

68 Butler, *The Art of the Possible*, p. 3.

69 Interview with Rick Trainor, 10/10/00, transcript, p. 7.

70 Arthur Marwick, *British Society since 1945* (London, Penguin, 1987), pp. 43–7.

71 Interview with David Mayhew, 6/7/00, transcript, pp. 3–4; interview with Colin Bell, 18/10/00, transcript, p. 3.

72 Lewis and Maude, *The English Middle Classes*, pp. 159–75; McKibbin, *Classes and Cultures*, p. 63; Perkin, *Rise of Professional Society*, p. 315.

73 The literature on these topics is voluminous but see for example Corelli Barnett, *The Audit of War* (London, Macmillan, 1986); P. J. Cain and A. G. Hopkins, *British Imperialism: Crisis and Deconstruction, 1914–1990* (Harlow, Longman, 1994); Michael Dintenfass, *The Decline of Industrial Britain, 1870–1980* (London, Routledge, 1992).

74 Interview with Richard Hoggart, 8/7/00, transcript, p. 12.

75 Coleman, *Courtaulds*, vol. III, p. 28.

76 Coleman, *Courtaulds*, vol. III, pp. 64–5.

77 Cited in Coleman, *Courtaulds*, vol. III, pp. 145–6.

78 Interview with George Courtauld, pp. 18–19.

79 Interview with George Courtauld, p. 6.

80 Interview with Lady Butler, p. 5.

81 Interview with Lady Butler, p. 19.

82 Interview with Charlie Courtauld, p. 3.

83 *The Leader*, 26 February 1949.

CHAPTER 5

1 Frank Parkin, *Middle-class Radicalism: The Social Bases of the British Campaign for Nuclear Disarmament* (Manchester, Manchester University Press, 1968).

2 For the early history of the *Manchester Guardian* see William Haslam Mills, *The Manchester Guardian: A Century of History* (London, Chatto and Windus, 1921); David Ayerst, *Guardian: Biography of a Newspaper* (London, Collins, 1981).

3 Interview with David Nicholls, Manchester, 18/5/00, transcript, p. 1. For more information see David Nicholls, 'The English middle class and the ideological significance of radicalism 1760–1886', *Journal of British Studies*, 24 (October 1985), pp. 415–33.

4 Interview with David Nicholls, p. 10.

5 John Vincent, *The Formation of the British Liberal Party, 1857–1868* (London, Constable, 1966), p. xliii.

6 Vincent, *Formation of the Liberal Party*, pp. xliii–iv.

7 Interview with David Nicholls, p. 10.

8 Quoted in Margaret Forster, *Significant Sisters: The Grassroots of Active Feminism 1839–1939* (London, Martin Secker and Warburg, 1984), p. 172.

9 Interview with Frank Mort, London, 21/9/00, transcript, p. 1.

10 Quoted in Forster, *Significant Sisters*, p. 181.

11 Brian Harrison, 'The act of militancy: violence and the suffragettes, 1904–1914' in Harrison, *Peaceable Kingdom. Stability and Change in Modern Britain* (Oxford, Oxford University Press, 1982), pp. 80–122.

12 Interview with Frank Mort, p. 1.

13 Information from the Joseph Rowntree Foundation homepage; www.jrf.org.uk/home.asp, 25/9/01.

14 *Dictionary of National Biography 1951–1960* (London, Oxford University Press, 1962), p. 852.

15 E. M. Forster, *Howards End* (London, Penguin, 1961 [1910]), p. 7.

16 Charles Dickens, *Bleak House* (London, Oxford University Press, 1966 [1853]), p. 34.

17 Cicely Hamilton, *William – an Englishman* (London, Persephone, 1999 [1919]), p. 1.

18 R. A. Butler, *The Art of the Possible: The Memoirs of Lord Butler* (London, Hamish Hamilton, 1971), p. 204.

19 Vincent, *Formation of the Liberal Party*, p. 69.

20 Interview with Martin Wainwright, 17/5/00, transcript, p. 8.

21 Interview with Hilary Wainwright, 17/5/00, transcript, p. 5.

22 Interview with Hilary Wainwright, p. 1.

23 Interview with Hilary Wainwright, p. 5.

24 Interview with Hilary Wainwright, p. 6.

25 Peggy Duff, *Left Left Left: A Personal Account of Six Protest Campaigns 1945–65* (London, Allison and Busby, 1971), p. 132.

26 It was estimated that 40 per cent of the crowd were under twenty-one. Peter Lewis, *The Fifties* (London, Heinemann, 1978), p. 100.

27 Parkin, *Middle-class Radicalism*, p. 92.

28 Parkin, *Middle-class Radicalism*, p. 17.

29 Paul Bagguley, 'Middle-class radicalism revisited' in Tim Butler and Mike Savage, eds, *Social Change in the Middle Classes* (London, University College Press, 1995), p. 296.

30 Interview with Sheila Rowbotham, 10/3/00, transcript, p. 1.

31 Interview with Michael Randle, 14/5/00, transcript, p. 10.

32 Interview with Michael Randle, pp. 12–13.

33 Interview with Michael Randle, pp. 17–19.

34 Interview with Michael Randle, p. 2.

35 Cited in Lewis, *The Fifties*, p. 140.

36 Lewis, *The Fifties*, p. 140.

37 Interview with Peter Jenner, 10/4/00, transcript, p. 8.

38 Interview with Max Farrar, 16/5/00, transcript p. 5.

39 Interview with Max Farrar, pp. 1–6.

40 Interview with Max Farrar, p. 12.

41 Eric Hobsbawm, *Industry and Empire* (Harmondsworth, Penguin, 1979), ch. 13.

42 Eric James, High Master of Manchester Grammar School, in BBC *Does Class Matter?: Education*, tx. 15/09/58.

43 Parkin, *Middle-class Radicalism*, p. 167.

44 Dennis Potter interviewed in BBC *Does Class Matter?: Education*, tx. 15/09/58.

45 Interview with Sheila Rowbotham, p. 9.

46 Interview with Sheila Rowbotham, p. 9.

47 Interview with Sheila Rowbotham, p. 11.

48 Interview with Sheila Rowbotham, pp. 7–8.

49 Parkin, *Middle-class Radicalism*, p. 144.

50 John Osborne, *Look Back in Anger* (London, Faber, 1957), Scene 1, Act III.

51 Interview with Sheila Rowbotham, p. 6.

52 Duff, *Left Left Left*, p. 132.

53 Parkin, *Middle-class Radicalism*, *passim*.

54 Duff, *Left Left Left*, pp. 157–62.

55 Quoted in Parkin, *Middle-class Radicalism*, p. 48.

56 Interview with Sheila Rowbotham, p. 6.

57 Interview with Sheila Rowbotham, p. 3.

58 Parkin, *Middle-class Radicalism*, p. 52.

59 Interview with Peter Jenner, p. 8.

60 Interview with Peter Jenner, p. 7.

61 Interview with Peter Jenner, p. 10.

62 Interview with Peter Jenner, pp. 8–10.

63 Sheila Rowbotham, *Black Dwarf*, January 1969.

64 Interview with Sheila Rowbotham, p. 8.

65 Interview with Angie Zelter, 11/2/00, transcript, p. 7.

66 Interview with Angie Zelter, p. 9.

CHAPTER 6

1 Alan Brien, 'The suburbs of slumdom' in Brian Inglis, ed., *John Bull's Schooldays* (London, Hutchinson, 1961), p. 29.

2 Interview with Dorothy Thomson, Winchester, 5/8/00, transcript, p. 9.

3 Melissa Benn, *Guardian Education*, 30 January 2001.

4 Quoted in Brian Simon, *The Two Nations and the Educational Structure, 1780–1870* (London, Lawrence and Wishart, 1981), p. 101.

5 Simon, *Two Nations*, p. 101.

6 Interview with former headmaster of Winchester College, James Sabben-Clare, Winchester, 1/7/00, transcript, p. 5, and Winchester College Prospectus.

7 Simon, *Two Nations*, pp. 325–35.

8 Report of the Schools Inquiry Commission quoted in Simon, *Two Nations*, p. 323.

9 Schools Inquiry Commission quoted in Simon, *Two Nations*, p. 323.

10 Simon, *Two Nations*, p. 328.

11 Simon, *Two Nations*, p. 318.

12 Schools Inquiry Commission quoted in Simon, *Two Nations*, p. 324.

13 Caroline Bingham, *The History of Royal Holloway College, 1886–1986* (London, Constable, 1987), pp. 41–2.

14 J. A. Banks, *Prosperity and Parenthood: A Study of Family Planning Among the Victorian Middle Classes* (London, Routledge and Kegan Paul, 1954), p. 230.

15 Cited in June Purvis, *A History of Women's Education in England* (Milton Keynes, Open University Press, 1991), p. 64.

16 Purvis, *History of Women's Education*, p. 76.

17 Purvis, *History of Women's Education*, p. 88.

18 These comments apply to those who were sent away to school. In many cases daughters continued to be educated at home and to study a more restricted curriculum than their male relatives.

19 Simon, *Two Nations*, pp. 364–5.

20 Schools Inquiry Commission quoted in Simon, *Two Nations*, p. 324.

21 Simon, *Two Nations*, p. 326.

22 Private conversation with James Sabben-Clare, 1/7/00.

23 J. A. Mangan, *Athleticism in the Victorian and Edwardian Public School* (Cambridge, Cambridge University Press, 1981).

24 Alec Waugh, *The Loom of Youth* (London, 1955 [1917]), p. 127.

25 Simon, *Two Nations*, p. 318.

26 Brian Inglis, 'First term' in Inglis, *John Bull's Schooldays*, p. 91.

27 Inglis, 'First term', p. 92.

28 Evelyn Waugh, *Decline and Fall* (London, Chapman and Hall, 1962 [1928]), p. 25.

29 Kenneth Allsop, 'On the way to Narkover' in Inglis, *John Bull's Schooldays*, p. 9.

30 Malcolm Muggeridge in Inglis, *John Bull's Schooldays*, p. 108.

31 Muggeridge in Inglis, *John Bull's Schooldays*, p. 108.

32 W. J. Reader, *Professional Men: The Rise of the Professional Classes in Nineteenth Century England* (London, Weidenfeld and Nicolson, 1966), pp. 10–11.

33 For more on the development of professions see Reader, *Professional Men, passim*.

34 Report of the Inns of Court Commission, 1854–1855, A1527 quoted in Reader, *Professional Men*, p. 54.

35 Reader, *Professional Men*, pp. 85–7.

36 Reader, *Professional Men*, pp. 56–7.

37 While the medical schools at both Oxford and Cambridge were of ancient foundation they had both been almost dormant for a considerable time. See Reader, *Professional Men*, pp. 130–40.

38 George Gissing, *In the Year of Jubilee* (London, Lawrence and Bullen, 1976 [1894]), p. 127.

39 Information from Anne Shepherd, who is currently writing a PhD thesis on the history of middle-class mental health.

40 Interview with Eileen and Brian Kingsley, Bath, 10/8/00, transcript, p. 5.

41 George Scott, 'Swot or bunk' in Inglis, *John Bull's Schooldays*, p. 129.

42 Alan Pryce-Jones, 'At Mr Gibbs" in Inglis, *John Bull's Schooldays*, pp. 119–20.

43 Observations drawn from interview with R. J. Morris, Leeds, 7/8/00, transcript, pp. 28–31.

44 Penelope Lively, *Spiderweb* (London, Penguin Books, 1999), p. 156.

45 George Scott in Inglis, *John Bull's Schooldays*, p. 131.

46 George Scott in Inglis, *John Bull's Schooldays*, p. 129.

47 Interview with Eileen and Brian Kingsley, p. 6.

48 Interview with Eileen and Brian Kingsley, p. 5.

49 Mark Grossek, 'First movement' (1937), pp. 89–90 quoted in Michael Hyndman, *Schools and Schooling in England and Wales: A Documentary History* (London, Harper and Row, 1978), pp. 87–8.

50 Interview with Olive Banks, 17/5/00, transcript, p. 18.

51 Keith Evans, *The Development and Structure of the English School System* (London, Hodder and Stoughton, 1985), p. 109.

52 R. A. Butler, BBC *Man Alive: The Children's Charter*, tx. 22/3/75.

53 *Norwood Report* (London, HMSO, 1943), pp. 2-3.

54 Quoted by Andrew Adonis and Stephen Pollard, *A Class Act: The Myth of Britain's Classless Society* (London, Hamish Hamilton, 1997), p. 42.

55 Adonis and Pollard, *Class Act*, pp. 41–2.

56 Interview with Dorothy Thomson, p. 5.

57 Interview with Dorothy Thomson, p. 4.

58 Interview with Dorothy Thomson, p. 10.

59 Eric James, High Master of Manchester Grammar School, in BBC *Does Class Matter?: Education*, tx. 15/09/58.

60 BBC *The Schools*, tx. 18/9/62.

61 Interview with Reefat Drabu, Winchester, 5/8/00, transcript, p. 4.

62 Eileen Kingsley interviewed in BBC *Does Class Matter?: Education*, tx. 15/9/58.

63 Interview with David Rose, 31/3/00, transcript, p. 26.

64 Interview with David Rose, p. 27.

65 Interview with Frank Mort, 21/9/00, transcript, p. 8.

66 BBC *Panorama: Eleven-plus Exam*, tx. 21/11/55.

67 Interview with Sally Power, Institute of Education, London, 2/11/00, transcript, p. 2.

68 Interview with Brian Simon, 9/8/00, transcript, p. 22.

69 Anthony Crosland, Education Secretary, ITN interview, 1965 [n.d.].

70 Interview with Dorothy Thomson, p. 18.

71 Unnamed teacher interviewed in BBC *The Schools*, tx. 18/9/62.

72 Interview with Sally Power, p. 2.

73 Interview with Sally Power, p. 13.

74 Adonis and Pollard, *Class Act*, p. 108.

75 Harold Wilson, Labour Party Conference, 1963 quoted in Hyndman, *Schools and Schooling*, p. 104.

76 Adonis and Pollard, *Class Act*, p. 104.

77 *Times Educational Supplement*, 8 September 1967.

78 *Times Educational Supplement*, 8 September 1967.

79 Melissa Benn, *Guardian Education*, 30 January 2001.

80 Adonis and Pollard, *Class Act*, pp. 43, 56.

81 BBC *Man Alive: The Children's Charter*, tx. 22/03/75.

82 Quoted in Hyndman, *Schools and Schooling*, p. 122.

83 Interview with Lawrie Norcross, 24/11/00, transcript, p. 4.

84 Interview with Lawrie Norcross, p. 2.

85 *Daily Mail*, 29 April 1976.

86 *Daily Mail*, 28 April 1976.

87 *Daily Mail*, 26 April 1976.

88 Polly Toynbee, *Observer*, undated cutting, *c.* 1976.

89 Interview with Lawrie Norcross, p. 7.

90 Adonis and Pollard, *Class Act*, p. 40.

91 Interview with Francis Wheen, 19/10/00, transcript, p. 14.

92 Adonis and Pollard, *Class Act*, p. 44.

93 Adonis and Pollard, *Class Act*, p. 44.

94 Interview with Professor Tariq Modood, Bristol, 10/8/00, transcript, p. 2.

95   Interview with Reefat and Kurshid Drabu, Winchester, 5/8/00, transcript, p. 6.

96   Information from untranscribed interview with Kurshid Drabu, 5/8/00.

97   Interview with Yasmin Alibhai-Brown, London, 2/7/00, transcript, p. 5.

98   Adonis and Pollard, *Class Act*, p. 46.

99   Interview with Yasmin Alibhai-Brown, p. 7.

100 Interview with Kurshid and Reefat Drabu, 5/8/00, transcript, p. 8.

101 Interview with the Sunak family, Winchester, 10/9/00, transcript, p. 12.

102 Adonis and Pollard, *Class Act*, pp. 50 and 56.

103 Adonis and Pollard, *Class Act*, p. 50.

104 Figures from 1991 census quoted in Adonis and Pollard, *Class Act*, p. 39.

105 BBC *Panorama Goes Comprehensive*, tx. 24/2/75.

106 *Independent on Sunday,* 8 December 1996.

107 Interview with Sally Power, p. 15.

108 Interview with James Sabben-Clare, p. 11.

109 Interview with James Sabben-Clare, p. 14.

110 Schools Inquiry Commission quoted in Simon, *Two Nations*, p. 323.

111 This and the following quotes from parents are all from interviews in BBC *Middle Classes: Their Rise and Sprawl*, tx. 23/3/01.

112 Sophy Blakeway interviewed in BBC *Middle Classes: Their Rise and Sprawl*, tx. 23/3/01.

113 Melissa Benn, *Guardian Education*, 30 January 2001.

114 Interview with David Rose, p. 42.

115 BBC *The Fast Show*, tx. 19/12/97.

CHAPTER 7

1   Interview with Mike Emens, 25/8/00, transcript, pp. 1–2; interview with Tim Emens, 16/10/00, transcript, pp. 1–2.

2   Ralf Dahrendorf, *Class and Class Conflict in Industrial Society* (London, Routledge and Kegan Paul, 1959).

3   On the importance of security see R. J. Morris, *Class, Sect and Party. The Making of the British Middle Class: Leeds, 1820–50* (Manchester, Manchester University Press, 1990); on middle-class planning see J. A. Banks, *Prosperity and Parenthood* (London, Routledge and Kegan

Paul, 1954) and also the comments in Chapter Two of this book.

4 W. H. Whyte, *The Organisation Man* (London, Jonathan Cape, 1957).

5 J. H. Goldthorpe *et al.*, *Social Mobility and Class Structure in Modern Britain* (Oxford, Clarendon Press, 1980), pp. 60–1.

6 Interview with Richard Sennett, 29/8/00, transcript, p. 19.

7 J. M. and R. E. Pahl, *Managers and Their Wives: A Study of Career and Family Relationships in the Middle Class* (London, Allen Lane, 1971), p. 259.

8 See for example P. Johnson, *Saving and Spending: The Working-class Economy in Britain, 1870–1939* (Oxford, Oxford University Press, 1985).

9 Harold Perkin, *The Rise of Professional Society: England since 1880* (London, Routledge, 1989), p. 439.

10 Interview with Mike Emens, pp. 5, 9.

11 Interview with Colin Bell, 18/10/00, transcript, p. 2. See also his study, *Middle-class Families: Social and Geographical Mobility* (London, Routledge and Kegan Paul, 1968).

12 Interview with Richard Scase, 3/9/00, transcript, pp. 16–17.

13 Interview with Ken Lane, 24/8/00, transcript, p. 16.

14 Interview with Lawrie Penny, 6/9/00, transcript, pp. 2–3.

15 Interview with Ken Lane, pp. 1, 11.

16 Interview with Ray Pahl, 25/8/00, Roll 4, transcript, p. 6.

17 M. Roper, *Masculinity and the British Organisation Man since 1945* (Oxford, Oxford University Press, 1994).

18 Interview with Richard Scase, p. 13.

19 Pahl, *Managers and their Wives*, pp. 119–20, 266–7.

20 Interview with Ray Pahl, Roll 1, p. 3.

21 Interview with James Dundas Hamilton, 5/9/00, transcript, pp. 3–4.

22 Interview with Lawrie Penny, p. 6; interview with James Dundas Hamilton, p. 2; F. Clark, *Hats* (London, Batsford, 1982), pp. 42–4, 62–6; interview with Rosemary Crompton, 18/10/00, transcript, p. 2.

23 Interview with Lawrie Penny, pp. 14–15.

24 Interview with James Dundas Hamilton, p. 5.

25 Interview with Richard Scase, p. 8.

26 A. A. Milne, *The House at Pooh Corner* (London, Methuen, 1965 [1928]), pp. 127–8; Ray Pahl, *After Success: Fin-de-Siècle Anxiety and Identity* (Cambridge, Polity, 1995), pp. 46–7.

27 Pahl, *Managers and Their Wives*, pp. 252–3.

28 Harold Wilson, *The New Britain: Labour's Plan* (Harmondsworth, Penguin, 1964), p. 9.

29 Alan Sked, *Britain's Decline: Problems and Perspectives* (Oxford, Blackwell, 1987), p. 28; Colin Leys, *Politics in Britain* (London, Verso, 1983), p. 19.

30 Sidney Pollard, *The Development of the British Economy, 1914–1990* (London, Edward Arnold, 1992), pp. 265–6.

31 Pollard, *The Development of the British Economy*, p. 294; Andrew Gamble, *Britain in Decline* (Basingstoke, Macmillan, 1991), p. 205; Michael Dintenfass, *The Decline of Industrial Britain 1870–1980* (London, Routledge, 1992), p. 10.

32 Gamble, *Britain in Decline*, p. 19; Patrick Hutber, *The Decline and Fall of the Middle Class and How It Can Fight Back* (Harmondsworth, Penguin, 1976), p. 47.

33 For a fuller account of these events see R. Coopey and N. Woodward, *Britain in the 1970s: The Troubled Economy* (London, UCL Press, 1996).

34 *Economist*, 25 December 1976, pp. 41–65.

35 A. H. Halsey, 'A hundred years of social change', *Social Trends* (London: Office for National Statistics, 2000), pp. 17–18, 65.

36 Interview with Ray Pahl, Roll 3, p. 10; interview with Richard Scase, p. 23. For a fuller study of these points see Richard Scase and Robert Goffee, *Reluctant Managers: Their Work and Lifestyles* (London, Unwin Hyman, 1989).

37 Hugo Young, *One of Us* (London, Pan Books, 1993), pp. 227–9. The terms are Young's, though the spirit of them was clearly that of the Thatcher government.

38 Interview with Richard Sennett, p. 5.

39 Interview with Mike Emens, pp. 11, 13.

40 Taken in this case from the American film, *Wall Street* (1987).

41 Scase, *Reluctant Managers*, p. 23; Richard Scase, *Britain towards 2010: The Changing Business Environment* (London, Department of Trade and Industry, 1999), p. 41.

42 Interview with Richard Scase, p. 29.

43 Interview with Rob Loynes, 30/8/00, transcript, p. 20.

44 *Economist*, 9 April 1988.

45 See David Kynaston, *The City of London, Vols I and II* (London,

Chatto and Windus, 1994 and 1995).

46 Ranald C. Michie, *The City of London: Continuity and Change 1850–1990* (Basingstoke, Macmillan, 1992), p. 25; Pollard, *Development of the British Economy*, pp. 306–7.

47 Interview with James Dundas Hamilton, p. 7.

48 Cathy Courtney and Paul Thompson, *City Lives* (London, Methuen, 1996).

49 Paul Thompson, 'The pyrrhic victory of gentlemanly capitalism: the financial elite of the City of London, 1945–90, part 1', *Journal of Contemporary History*, vol. 32, 3 (1997), p. 302; interview with Jane Partington, 6/9/00, transcript, pp. 3, 5.

50 Interview with James Dundas Hamilton, p. 15; Courtney and Thompson, *City Lives*.

51 Interview with James Dundas Hamilton, p. 13; interview with Michael, David and George Verey, 22/3/00, summary, p. 3.

52 Interview with David Verey, p. 1; interview with George Verey, p. 2; interview with James Dundas Hamilton, p. 20. For the purposes of comparison, £5,000 per year was roughly equivalent to five times the average income of a male worker in the mid-1960s. The equivalent at 2001 values would be in the region of £80,000–£100,000.

53 Interview with James Dundas Hamilton, p. 18.

54 For an overview of these processes see Andrew Leyshon and Nigel Thrift, *Money/Space: Geographies of Monetary Transformation* (London, Routledge, 1997), ch. 2.

55 See K. Durham, *The New City* (Basingstoke, Macmillan, 1992) for a basic guide to the changes brought about by Big Bang.

56 Interview with Jane Partington, p. 6.

57 Interview with Jane Partington, p. 2.

58 Courtney and Thompson, *City Lives*, pp. 31, 135.

59 Durham, *The New City*, p. 26.

60 Leyshon and Thrift, *Money/Space*, p. 137; Thompson, 'The pyrrhic victory of gentlemanly capitalism, part 2', *Journal of Contemporary History*, vol. 32, 4 (1997), pp. 436–7.

61 Interview with James Dundas Hamilton, p. 8.

62 Leyshon and Thrift, *Money/Space*, pp. 145, 171.

63 Interview with Jane Partington, pp. 8, 21.

64 Carol Churchill, *Serious Money: A City Comedy* (London, Methuen, 1987).

65 Interview with Richard Sennett, p. 6.

66 Leyshon and Thrift, *Money/Space*, p. 214; Pahl, *After Success*, pp. 42–3.

67 *Independent on Sunday*, 24 October 1993.

68 See for example Tony Fielding, 'Migration and middle-class formation in England and Wales, 1981–91' in Tim Butler and Mike Savage, eds, *Social Change and the Middle Classes* (London, UCL Press, 1995), p. 171.

69 *Sunday Times*, 26 June 1994; *Guardian*, 2 August 1994.

70 Interview with Tim Emens, pp. 5–7.

71 Halsey, 'Hundred years of social change', p. 75.

72 Interview with Jane Partington, p. 7.

73 Interview with Ray Pahl, Roll 3, p. 8.

74 Mary Spillane cited in 'Join me plc', *Livewire*, April–May 2001.

75 For comments see Rosemary Crompton, 'Women's employment and the "middle class"' in Butler and Savage, *Social Change and the Middle Classes*, pp. 58–75.

76 Interview with Ray Pahl, Roll 3, p. 1.

77 Interview with Tim Emens, p. 8; Cathy Pharoah and Sarah Tanner, 'Trends in charitable giving', *Fiscal Studies*, vol. 18, 4 (1997), pp. 427–43; interview with Colin Bell, p. 1.

78 Interview with Lawrie Penny, pp. 16, 19, 20; interview with Richard Scase, p. 30.

79 Interview with Rob Loynes, p. 11.

80 Crompton, 'Women's employment', p. 67; Andrew Adonis and Stephen Pollard, *A Class Act: The Myth of Britain's Classless Society* (London, Hamish Hamilton, 1997).

81 Interview with Ray Pahl, p. 12.

82 Interview with Colin Bell, p. 5.

83 Interview with Richard Sennett, p. 19. See Sennett's book, *The Corrosion of Character: The Personal Consequences of Work in the New Capitalism* (New York, Norton, 1998) for a fuller statement of his arguments.

CONCLUSION

1 Interview with Richard Scase, 3/9/00, transcript, p. 37.

2 David Cannadine, *The Decline and Fall of the British Aristocracy* (New Haven, Yale University Press, 1990); Eric Hobsbawm, 'The forward march of labour halted?' in Martin Jacques and Francis Mulhern, eds,

The Forward March of Labour Halted (London, New Left Books, 1981).

3 The outstanding example is Patrick Hutber, *The Decline and Fall of the Middle Class and How It Can Fight Back* (Harmondsworth, Penguin, 1977). Hutber was City editor for the *Sunday Telegraph*; newspapers like the *Telegraph* and the *Daily Mail*, as well as magazines like the *Economist*, regularly featured gloomy articles predicting the imminent demise of the middle classes during the 1970s; see also Chapter Six. For a contrary view see Ian Bradley, *The English Middle Classes Are Alive and Kicking* (London, Collins, 1982); Jilly Cooper, *Class: A View from Middle England* (London, Corgi, 1980). For the earlier period see Geoffrey Crossick, 'From gentlemen to the residuum: languages of social description in Victorian Britain' in P. J. Corfield, ed., *Language, Class and History* (Cambridge, Cambridge University Press, 1991).

4 See for example John Morley, *Life of Richard Cobden*, vol. 2 (London, 1881), pp. 481–2; Karl Marx and Friedrich Engels, *Marx and Engels on Britain* (Moscow, Foreign Languages Publishing House, 1962), especially on the 1868 election and its aftermath.

5 A. H. Halsey, 'A hundred years of social change', *Social Trends* (London, Office for National Statistics, 2000), p. 16.

6 J. H. Goldthorpe *et al.*, *The Affluent Worker in the Class Structure* (Cambridge, Cambridge University Press, 1968–9).

7 Harold Perkin, *The Rise of Professional Society: England since 1880* (London, Routledge, 1989), p. 421; Jeremy Black, *Modern British History since 1900* (London, Macmillan, 2000), p. 126.

8 Perkin, *Rise of Professional Society*, p. 515.

9 For a fuller statement of these kinds of arguments see Gareth Stedman Jones, 'Why is the Labour party in a mess?', *Languages of Class: Studies in English Working-class History* (Cambridge, Cambridge University Press, 1983), pp. 239–56; Ross McKibbin, 'Class and conventional wisdom: the Conservative party and the "public" in inter-war Britain', *Ideologies of Class* (Oxford, Oxford University Press, 1991), pp. 259–93.

10 For an early and wide-ranging reflection on – and of – these shifts see Stuart Hall and Martin Jacques, eds, *New Times: The Changing Face of Politics in the 1990s* (London, Lawrence and Wishart, 1989).

11 See for example Ulrich Beck, *The Risk Society* (London, Sage, 1992); Jan Pakulski and Malcolm Waters, *The Death of Class* (London, Sage, 1996).

12 For a fuller discussion of these issues see Rosemary Crompton, *Class and Stratification: An Introduction to Current Debates* (Cambridge, Polity, 1994); D. J. Lee and B. S. Turner, *Conflicts about Class: Debating Inequality in Late Industrialism* (London, Longman, 1996).

13 Will Hutton, *The State We're In* (London, Vintage, 1996), p. 172 and Hutton, *The State to Come* (London, Vintage, 1997), pp. 36–7.

14 Hutton, *The State to Come*, p. 6.

15 Pakulski and Waters, *The Death of Class*, p. 150. For a conspectus of recent debates about class in the context of historical writing see Patrick Joyce, *Class: A Reader* (Oxford, Oxford University Press, 1996).

SELECT BIBLIOGRAPHY

Adonis, Andrew and Pollard, Stephen, *A Class Act: The Myth of Britain's Classless Society* (London, Hamish Hamilton, 1997)

Ascherson, Neal, 'The English bourgeoisie' in Ascherson, *Games with Shadows* (London, Radius, 1988)

Banks, J. A., *Prosperity and Parenthood: A Study of Family Planning among the Victorian Middle Classes* (London, Routledge and Kegan Paul, 1954)

Bell, Colin, *Middle-class Families* (London, Routledge and Kegan Paul, 1968)

Binfield, Clyde, *So Down to Prayers: Studies in English Nonconformity* (London, Dent, 1977)

Briggs, Asa, 'The language of "class" in early nineteenth-century England' in Briggs, ed., *Essays in Labour History* (London, Macmillan, 1960)

Butler, Tim and Savage, Mike, eds, *Social Change and the Middle Classes* (London, University College Press, 1995)

Cannadine, David, *Class in Britain* (New Haven, Yale University Press, 1998)

Courtney, Cathy and Thompson, Paul, *City Lives* (London, Methuen, 1996)

Crompton, Rosemary, *Class and Stratification: An Introduction to Current Debates* (Cambridge, Polity, 1994)

Crossick, Geoffrey, ed., *The Lower Middle Class in Britain 1870–1914* (London, Croom Helm, 1977)

Davidoff, Leonore, *The Best Circles: Society Etiquette and the Season* (London, Hutchinson, 1986)

Davidoff, Leonore and Hall, Catherine, *Family Fortunes: Men and Women of the English Middle Class, 1780–1850* (London, Hutchinson, 1987)

Earle, Peter, *The Making of the English Middle Class: Business, Society and Family Life in London, 1660–1730* (London, Methuen, 1989)

Gunn, Simon, *The Public Culture of the Victorian Middle Class: Ritual and Authority in the English Industrial City, 1840–1914* (Manchester, Manchester University Press, 2000)

Hall, Catherine, *White, Male and Middle Class: Explorations in Feminism and History* (Cambridge, Polity, 1992)

Hobsbawm, Eric, 'The example of the English middle class' in Kocka, Jurgen and Mitchell, Allan, eds, *Bourgeois Society in Nineteenth-century Europe* (Oxford, Berg, 1993)

Hutton, Will, *The State We're In* (London, Vintage, 1996)

Jackson, Alan, *The Middle Classes, 1900–1950* (Nairn, David St John Thomas, 1991)

Joyce, Patrick, *Work, Society and Politics: The Culture of the Factory in Later Victorian England* (Brighton, Harvester Wheatsheaf, 1980)

Kidd, Alan and Nichols, David, eds, *Gender, Culture and Consumerism: Middle-class Identity in Britain 1800–1940* (Manchester, Manchester University Press, 1999)

Kidd, Alan and Nicholls, David, eds, *The Making of the British Middle Class? Studies of Regional and Cultural Diversity since the Eighteenth Century* (Stroud, Sutton Publishing, 1998)

Kynaston, David, *The City of London, Vols ¾–IV* (London, Chatto and Windus, 1994–2000)

Light, Alison, *Forever England: Femininity, Literature and Conservatism between the Wars* (London, Routledge, 1991)

McKibbin, Ross, *Classes and Cultures: England 1918–1951* (Oxford, Oxford University Press, 1998)

McLeod, Diane Satchko, *Art and the Victorian Middle Class: Money and the Making of Cultural Identity* (Cambridge, Cambridge University Press, 1996)

Morris, R. J., *Class, Sect and Party. The Making of the British Middle Class: Leeds, 1820–50* (Manchester, Manchester University Press, 1990)

Oliver, Paul, Davis, Ian and Bentley, Paul, *Dunroamin: The Suburban Semi and its Enemies* (London, Pimlico, 1994)

Pahl, J. M. and R. E., *Managers and their Wives: A Study of Career and Family Relationships in the Middle Class* (London, Allen Lane, 1971)

Pahl, Ray, *After Success: Fin-de-Siècle Anxiety and Identity* (Cambridge, Polity, 1995)

Parkin, Frank, *Middle-class Radicalism: The Social Bases of the Campaign for Nuclear Disarmament* (Manchester, Manchester University Press, 1968)

Perkin, Harold, *The Rise of Professional Society: England since 1880* (London, Routledge, 1989)

Reader, W. J., *Professional Men: The Rise of the Professional Classes in Nine-*

teenth-century England (London, Weidenfeld and Nicolson, 1966)

Rubinstein, W. D., *Men of Property* (London, Routledge, 1981)

Samuel, Raphael, 'The middle class between the wars', *New Socialist*, January/February 1983

Savage, Mike, Barlow, James, Dickens, Peter and Fielding, Tony, *Property, Bureaucracy and Culture: Middle-class Formation in Contemporary Britain* (London, Routledge, 1992)

Scase, Richard and Goffee, Robert, *Reluctant Managers: Their Work and Lifestyles* (London, Unwin Hyman, 1989)

Seed, John, 'From "middling sort" to middle class in late eighteenth and early nineteenth-century England' in Bush, M. L., ed., *Social Orders and Social Classes in Europe Since 1500* (Harlow, Longman, 1992)

Sennett, Richard, *The Corrosion of Character: The Personal Consequences of Work in the New Capitalism* (New York, Norton, 1998)

Simon, Brian, *The Two Nations and the Educational Structure, 1780–1870* (London, Lawrence and Wishart, 1981)

Smail, John, *The Origins of Middle-class Culture: Halifax, Yorkshire, 1660–1780* (Ithaca, Cornell University Press, 1994)

Szreter, Simon, *Fertility, Class and Gender in Britain, 1860–1940* (Cambridge, Cambridge University Press, 1996)

Thompson, E. P., 'The peculiarities of the English' in Thompson, *The Poverty of Theory* (London, Merlin Press, 1978)

Tosh, John, *A Man's Place: Masculinity and the Middle-class Home in Victorian England* (New Haven, Yale University Press, 1999)

Vincent, John, *The Formation of the Liberal Party 1857–68* (London, Constable and Co., 1966)

Wahrman, Dror, *Imagining the Middle Class: the Political Representation of Class in Britain, c. 1780–1840* (Cambridge, Cambridge University Press, 1995)

Wiener, Martin, *English Culture and the Decline of the Industrial Spirit, 1850–1980* (Cambridge, Cambridge University Press, 1981)

Wolff, Janet and Seed, John, eds, *The Culture of Capital: Art, Power and the Nineteenth-century Middle Class* (Manchester, Manchester University Press, 1988)

PICTURE CREDITS

Picture credits are in order of appearance of the pictures in the plates section.

Tea at the Women's Institute: © Martin Parr/Magnum Photos

Self-made men: courtesy of Maggie Carlow

Interior of Claremont House: courtesy of Yorkshire Archaeological Society

Boar Lane, Leeds, 1881 (oil on canvas) by John Atkinson Grimshaw (1836–93): on loan to Leeds Museums and Galleries (City Art Gallery)/Bridgeman Art Library

William Whiteley and children: *The Universal Provider*

Worcester Park Station: Hulton Archive

Middle-class housewife: Hulton Archive

Mary Reed: courtesy of Mary Reed

Metro-Land: Mary Evans Picture Library

Architect's detailed plans: Mary Evans Picture Library

Irene Bacon: courtesy of Irene Bacon

Cycling club: Hulton Archive

Cutteslowe Walls: courtesy of Oxfordshire Photographic Archive, Centre for Oxfordshire Studies

Dismantling of the Walls: courtesy of Oxfordshire Photographic Archive, Centre for Oxfordshire Studies

Stanley Baldwin and others: *The Art of the Possible, The Memoirs of Lord Butler, KG, CH* (Hamilton, 1971)

Portrait of Stephen and Ginny Courtauld by Campbell Taylor (1874–1949): © courtesy of the artist's estate/Bridgeman Art Library

Rab Butler and bearer: *The Art of the Possible, The Memoirs of Lord Butler, KG, CH* (Hamilton, 1971)

August Courtauld: Hulton Archive

Satirical cartoon: *Private Eye*

The Aldermaston marches: Hulton Archive

First Aldermaston march: Easter 1958: Mary Evans Picture Library

Roedean girls practising cricket: Hulton Archive

Woodberry Down School: Hulton Archive

Pupils at Beckenham and Penge Grammar School: Hulton Archive

Racegoers at Royal Ascot: © Ian Berry/Magnum Photos

Conservative Election poster, 1979: The Advertising Archives

Margaret Thatcher, Tory Party conference, Blackpool 1983: © Mike Abrahms/Network Photographers

Yuppies at play: © Chris Steele-Perkins/Magnum Photos

Andrew and Hugh in the Garden at Lainston House by Gerald Kelly (1879–1972): Private Collection/Bridgeman Art Library

INDEX